How to Do *Everything* with

Outl 2000

Julia Kelly

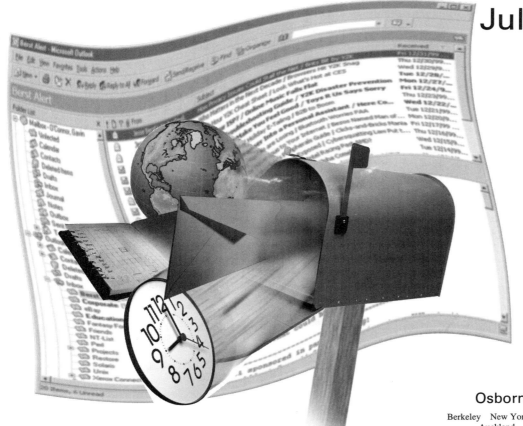

Osborne **McGraw-Hill**

Berkeley   New York   St. Louis   San Francisco
Auckland   Bogotá   Hamburg   London
Madrid   Mexico City   Milan   Montreal   New Delhi
Panama City   Paris   São Paulo
Singapore   Sydney   Tokyo   Toronto

Osborne/**McGraw-Hill**
2600 Tenth Street
Berkeley, California 94710
U.S.A.

For information on translations or book distributors outside the U.S.A., or to arrange bulk purchase discounts for sales promotions, premiums, or fund-raisers, please contact Osborne/**McGraw-Hill** at the above address.

How to Do Everything with Outlook 2000

1234567890 AGM AGM 019876543210

ISBN 0-07-212431-8

Publisher: Brandon A. Nordin
Associate Publisher and Editor-in-Chief: Scott Rogers
Acquisitions Editor: Megg Bonar
Project Editor: Betsy Manini
Acquisitions Coordinator: Stephane Thomas
Technical Editor: Will Kelly
Copy Editor: Bill McManus
Proofreader: Rhonda Holmes
Indexer: David Heiret
Computer Designer: Roberta Steele, Dick Schwartz, Jim Kussow
Series Design: Mickey Galicia
Illustrator: Brian Wells, Bob Hansen, Beth Young
Cover Design: Dodie Shoemaker

This book was composed with Corel VENTURA™ Publisher.

Dedication

To God, because You are the potter and I am only the clay.

To my family, because your love is what makes life warm and wonderful.

And to my puppies and ponies for the constant delight and laughter they provide.

About the Author

Julia Kelly, cybergirl in cowspace, ex-jet jockey, and former mad scientist, has also done time as a stable cleaner, hardware-store cashier/barrista, theme park candy girl, veterinary cat-holder, and Caribbean pilot.

She currently lives on her farm in north Idaho, where she writes books, builds databases, and shovels snow. When she's not chasing electrons in her computers, she's in her pottery studio, at Stony Keep Pottery, making clay pots and using no electrons whatsoever.

Contents

Acknowledgments

A big Thank You to everyone I've worked with on this book: Megg Bonar, acquisitions editor, who's been fun to work with from the very first; Betsy Manini, project editor, whose amiable expertise has made the process of getting this book onto paper unexpectedly painless; Stephane Thomas, acquisitions coordinator, who's been delightfully patient, even when I sent her empty Zip files; Will Kelly, technical editor, whose contributions have been illuminating and helpful; Bill McManus, copy editor, who has painstakingly cleaned up my grammatical and stylistic messes; and all the people I never meet without whom this book wouldn't get to its readers.

And last but best, thank you to my terrific agent, Margot Maley at Waterside Productions, for finding me this fun book to write and these terrific people to work with.

Introduction

Whether you work in a large corporate environment, are a self-employed sole business proprietor, or need to manage your personal information more efficiently, you have a great deal of information to keep track of. There are a lot of information-management systems available today, but few are so comprehensive, integrated, and interactive as Outlook 2000.

Outlook 2000 is a flexible information-management tool that can be adapted to any work or personal environment. You can use it by itself with no Internet or e-mail access or as part of a large corporate network with hundreds of computers around the world, or in any of many other possible scenarios. Outlook keeps your address and telephone lists, e-mail messages, to-do lists, calendar schedule, and lots of extraneous bits of information all close at hand in a single window on your computer screen. Better yet, all your information that is stored in Outlook is completely interactive with all your other information in Outlook, as well as with the other Microsoft Office programs in your computer.

Outlook's main features are folders that store particular kinds of information:

- **Inbox**   A place for sending and receiving electronic mail (e-mail)

- **Contacts**   A place for you to keep personal and business contact information, such as names, addresses, e-mail addresses, phone numbers, and personal details about contacts

- **Calendar**   A place for you to record appointments, meetings, holidays, and so forth

- **Tasks**   A well-integrated to-do list

- **Journal**   An electronic diary where you can record what you did, when you did it, how long it took, and any other details

- **Notes**   An electronic version of sticky notes, where you can keep bits of miscellaneous information

If you work alone on a single computer (no network), Outlook is a total-organization tool that makes information management and communication much more efficient.

If your computer is part of a network, Outlook can be configured to work with other computers on the network. In this environment, you can—with others on your network—share contacts assign tasks, and send e-mail without using the Internet. You can also use group-scheduling features to schedule meetings more efficiently, and share information with your co-workers in public folders on your network.

In a corporate setting, running Windows NT and the Microsoft Exchange Server, you have all of Outlook's functionality available. With the Exchange Server, you can dial in to the server from home or on the road, and have access to your e-mail, public folders on the server, and shared calendars. You can also use e-mail to send and receive voting messages, use the Out Of Office Assistant to respond automatically to incoming e-mail while you're away from the office, recall and replace messages you've sent, and make available to everyone on the network a Global Address Book of company contacts.

You'll learn how to do all of this and lots more in this book.

Who Should Read This Book

This book is written for normal computer users who have normal jobs and use computers to accomplish their work more efficiently. It's not about creating networks or establishing high-level corporate e-mail security (there are bigger, heavier books for those topics)—it's about how to get the most out of Outlook, whatever your corporate (or noncorporate) setup happens to be. Whether you work in a large company that has Outlook 2000 installed on all of its corporate workstations, or you use a single computer at home, this book will teach you how to get the most functionality and efficiency out of Outlook.

What's in Each Part of the Book

This book progresses from the most important tasks (such as e-mail) that you'll want to know how to do right away, to the more esoteric tasks (such as importing and exporting data between Outlook and other programs) that you'll want to know how to do some day. Some Outlook features are only available to those of you who use Outlook on a corporate network with Microsoft Exchange Server, and those features are covered primarily in the last few chapters.

Part I gives you a general overview of Outlook—how Outlook is organized, where to find different kinds of information, how to switch from one Outlook folder to another, and how to organize lists of items in Outlook's folders so that you can find individual items (such as a specific contact's phone number, or a particular e-mail someone sent you last month) easily and efficiently.

Part II is all about communications from Outlook—setting up your contact information and e-mail addresses; using your contacts' e-mail addresses to send them e-mail; sending, receiving, replying to, and forwarding e-mail messages; sending faxes; and using Outlook as a data source for a mail-merge operation in Microsoft Word.

Part III shows you how to use the rest of Outlook's folders to organize information, including your appointments (and reminders), your to-do list of jobs and tasks, work you've done (when and how long it took), and miscellaneous notes of information you don't want to lose. Part III also shows you how to print Outlook information, how to manage other files on your computer from within the Outlook window, and how to use Outlook to open to Web pages.

Part IV covers advanced information management in Outlook—things you'll find useful but that you don't need to learn right away. In Part IV, you'll learn how to customize your Outlook windows and folders, how to archive Outlook data for long-term storage, and how to import and export data between Outlook and other programs. Part IV also covers using Outlook in a business environment, getting e-mail when you and your computer are away from the office, and using special Outlook features that are available if you use Outlook on a network that uses Microsoft Exchange Server.

Be sure to check out Chapter 19 on troubleshooting for answers to questions other Outlook users have had (you may find a question of your own in there).

How to Read This Book

If you're learning how to use Outlook for the first time, read the book from beginning to end to learn how to do everything in Outlook, beginning with the most basic tasks and progressing to the more advanced tasks (and if you haven't installed Outlook yet, read the **Appendix** first so you get Outlook set up correctly for your situation right from the start). If you've used an earlier version of Outlook, or if you're trying to remember how to perform a particular task, look it up in the index or in the table of contents. You'll find all the information you need to perform any particular task contained in one place in the book, and cross-references to other chapters whenever information from another section of the book might be helpful.

The following conventions are used throughout this book:

- Menu commands are written like this: Tools | Options. This means: on the Tools menu, select the Options command.

- *Click* means to click an item once using the left mouse button.

- *Right-click* means to click an item once using the right mouse button.

- *Double-click* means to click an item twice, rapidly, using the left mouse button.

- Procedural steps that must be performed in a specific order are numbered.

- Optional choices that don't have to be performed in a specific order, or even performed at all, are presented as bulleted lists.

Installing Outlook

Outlook can be installed in three different configurations: Internet Mail Only, Corporate/Workgroup, or Corporate/Workgroup using the Microsoft Exchange Server. The environment in which you use Outlook determines which of the configurations is best for you.

If you use Outlook on a network that runs the Microsoft Exchange Server, you'll probably find Outlook already installed and set up for you, so you'll only need to learn how to use the Outlook features that are available under the Exchange Server (some of which are unavailable to users who don't have the Exchange Server). Your network administrator will give you any network-specific information that you need to have so you can use Outlook on the network.

If you use Outlook on a network that doesn't run the Exchange Server, you'll want to install Outlook in the Corporate/Workgroup configuration, so that you can integrate and share Outlook information with other computers on the network.

If you use Outlook on a standalone computer, either in an office or at home, you'll want to install Outlook in the Internet Mail Only configuration, because Outlook will send and receive e-mail through your Internet service provider (ISP) more quickly.

NOTE   *If you use AOL as your e-mail service, you won't be able to send and receive e-mail through Outlook (or any other software); to use Outlook for e-mail, you'll need to drop AOL and set up an account with a local ISP. If you use Outlook Express, Eudora, or Netscape for e-mail, you'll want to install Outlook in the Internet Mail Only configuration (not the No E-Mail configuration) and then transfer your account information into Outlook. Chapter 16 shows you how.*

If you haven't installed Outlook yet, see the Appendix to learn how to install Outlook in the configuration that's correct for your particular situation. If you want to switch your configuration (for example, from Internet Mail Only to Corporate/Workgroup), see the Appendix to learn how.

Part I

The Outlook Environment: Less Confusing Than It Looks

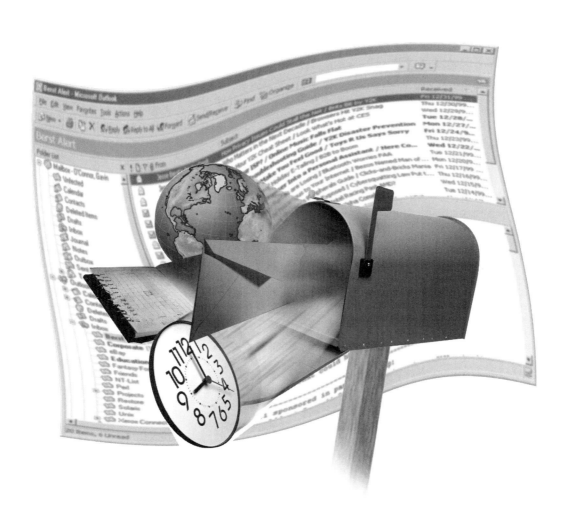

Chapter 1

Finding Your Way Around in Outlook

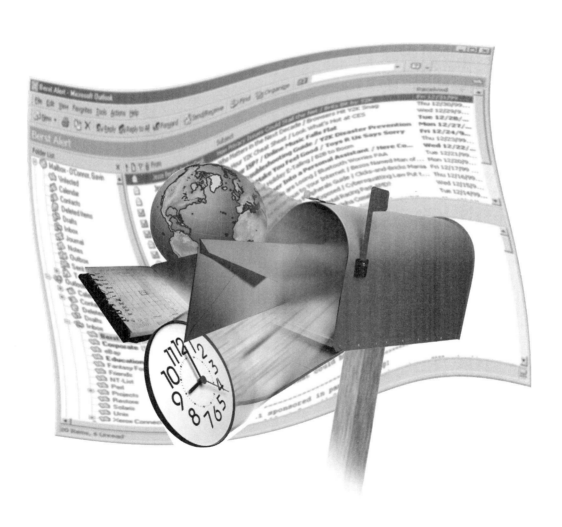

How to . . .

- Start Outlook
- Navigate in Outlook
- Get help when you're lost
- Exit Outlook

If you're new to Outlook, it looks very different from any other software program you may have used, mostly because it does so many different things in one window. Don't let that throw you, though; Outlook was designed to be easy to use as well as multifunctional. By the end of this chapter, you'll be comfortable finding your way around in Outlook.

If you've upgraded to Outlook 2000 from a previous edition of Outlook, most of this chapter will not be news. Skim through it, though, because there might be something you hadn't noticed when you were using your previous edition.

What's the Difference Between Outlook and Outlook Express?

Outlook Express is the e-mail program that comes with Internet Explorer. It only handles e-mail and newsgroups, and in that capacity, it's similar to Outlook. It even has many of the same e-mail features, such as HTML mail format, stationery for colorful messages, and hyperlinks. It doesn't have any of Outlook's management features, such as a calendar or task list, however.

Outlook Express is installed when Internet Explorer is installed, and is actually used by Outlook as the engine for some e-mail and newsreader functions.

Starting Outlook

 *If you're poking around in your computer files and come across Outlook Express, do not delete it just because you don't use it (because Outlook does use it).*

1

If you're like most people, you installed Outlook, started it up, and poked around in it before you ever bought this book, and now you want to know what to do after you start it. Patience, we'll get there soon enough. First things first, and first you have to start Outlook.

You can start Outlook by using any of several methods (try them all and pick your favorite):

■ If you have an Office Shortcut Bar displayed in the upper-right corner of your Windows desktop, click the Outlook icon. Mine is customized to show buttons for the programs I use most, and the Outlook icon is on the far-right end.

■ If you see a Microsoft Outlook icon on your Windows desktop, double-click it.

■ Click the Start button, point to Programs, and click Microsoft Outlook.

■ If your mouse dies and you want to open Outlook without waiting to get a new mouse, press CTRL-ESC, then press P, to open the Start button's Programs menu. Then, use your up-arrow or down-arrow key to highlight Microsoft Outlook, and press ENTER.

Outlook usually opens at a reduced window size. You can use it at that size or maximize the window by double-clicking the title bar.

Parts of the Outlook Window

The first time you open Outlook, you'll see the Outlook Today folder displayed. You'll learn more about Outlook Today later in this chapter; first you'll learn about the parts of the Outlook window (shown in Figure 1-1) so you'll know what's where. All the Outlook folders have the same essential elements: toolbars, menu bar, Outlook bar, data pane, and Folder banner.

The Outlook Bar

On the left side of the window is the vertical Outlook bar, with three group buttons. Each group button opens a different group of shortcut icons, and one

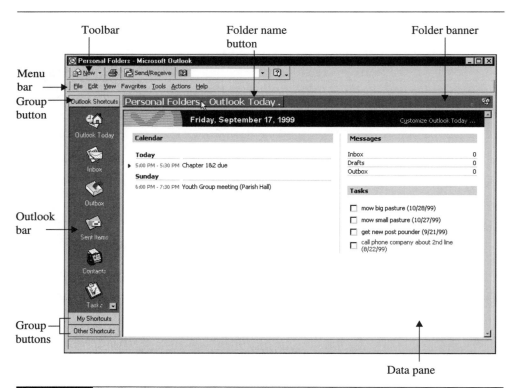

FIGURE 1-1   Parts of the Outlook window

group of shortcut icons is always in view. By clicking the Outlook Shortcuts, My Shortcuts, and Other Shortcuts group buttons, you can switch between the groups. The groups are there to organize folder icons for quick navigation between folders, and you can customize them to suit your personal work style (see Chapter 15 to learn more about customizing the Outlook bar).

The icons you see are for opening other Outlook folders, such as Inbox and Calendar. To open a folder, click its icon. You'll learn about the Outlook bar groups in more detail later in this chapter.

Right now, you'll learn how to switch the Outlook bar display from Large Icons to Small Icons. I prefer small icons, because I can see more of them at one time on my screen. Consequently, the figures in this book all show small icons. If you want to switch to small icons on the Outlook bar:

1. Right-click an empty space in the Outlook bar (anywhere in the gray background will do).

2. Click Small Icons on the shortcut menu.

The icon size changes in the group that's displayed; to change the icon size in every group, you need to open each group (by clicking its group button) and change its icon size.

Toolbars

Outlook's toolbars are similar to the toolbars in all the other Office programs, and as usual are customizable (more so in Outlook 2000 than in previous versions). There's a button for almost every menu command, and you can add, delete, and rearrange buttons to make your toolbars more efficient. The buttons on the toolbars are usually the easiest and quickest way to find the commands you need, because many perform a two- or three-step action with a single click (if you're comfortable and fast on the keyboard, however, buttons and a mouse may not be the fastest method for you).

TIP   *If you prefer key presses to mouse clicks, look up **keyboard shortcuts** in the help files' Answer Wizard to find several long lists of keyboard shortcuts.*

The buttons change according to the folder you have displayed in the data pane. If you have the Inbox open, for example, you'll have a Send/Receive button on the toolbar; but, you won't see that button when you switch to the Contacts folder. Toolbars display only the command buttons that are appropriate to the open folder.

Outlook has three toolbars, shown here from top to bottom: Standard, Advanced, and Web.

The Web toolbar doesn't change when you switch between folders, because it's for Web-related activities rather than Outlook folder activities. The Standard toolbar changes a lot, and the Advanced toolbar changes somewhat. All the commands on the toolbar buttons can be found on menus, but toolbar buttons tend to be those commands you use most often and want to perform with a single click. In Chapter 15, you'll learn how to customize your toolbars and create new ones. For now, you'll learn about the new Office 2000 way of managing toolbars to preserve precious screen space.

To show or hide any toolbar, right-click in the toolbar area and click the name of the toolbar on the shortcut menu. If there's a check mark next to a toolbar name, it means that toolbar is already displayed.

If you have two or more toolbars displayed, you can put them in the same row (all three toolbars are in the same row in the following example).

When you put two or more toolbars in the same row, there isn't enough room for all the buttons to be displayed. But at the right end of each toolbar, there's a double-right chevron (») over a small down arrow. Point your mouse at that chevron, and a ToolTip says More Buttons. Click the double-right chevron and you'll see the hidden buttons. When you click one of the hidden buttons, the command is carried out and the button moves into the displayed part of the toolbar (and a button you haven't used recently moves into the hidden part of the toolbar). If there are no hidden buttons, the double-right chevron isn't displayed.

The quickest way to put your toolbars into the same row is to drag them there. Point to the vertical bar at the left end of one toolbar, and when the pointer becomes a four-headed arrow, drag the toolbar onto the other toolbar's row.

You can shorten and lengthen a row-sharing toolbar the same way: point to the vertical bar at the left end of the toolbar and drag left or right. To separate a toolbar onto a different row, drag its vertical bar up or down until it sits above or below the other toolbar(s).

You can also drag a toolbar away from the toolbar area, into the Outlook window, and let it "float" on top of the window, or drag it to the side or bottom of the Outlook window until it "docks" in place. Wherever you leave the toolbar when you close Outlook is where it'll be the next time you open Outlook.

> **TIP** *A floating toolbar has no vertical bar at its left end. To move it, drag its title bar.*

The Menu Bar

Like the toolbars, menus on the menu bar change to fit the folder you have open. For example, Figure 1-2 shows the Actions menu for Inbox on the left, and for Contacts on the right.

> **NOTE** *Menu bars are often called "command bars" now because you can add buttons to them, and toolbars are also called "command bars" because you can add menus to them. The menu bar and toolbars no longer have completely distinct and separate functions.*

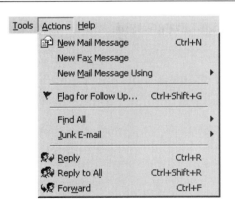
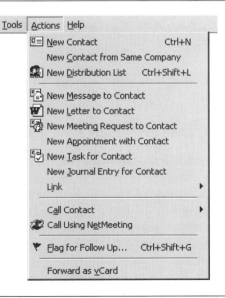

FIGURE 1-2   The Actions menus for Inbox (left) and Contacts (right)

This applicable-commands-only design is really quite clever, because you never have to search through long lists of useless commands; instead, only the commands that apply to the open folder are available.

And in that spirit of brevity, an Office 2000 feature keeps many commands hidden until you use them—at which point Outlook decides that you might want to see that command again, and displays it. The shortened-menu design ensures that only the most commonly used commands and the commands you've used recently appear when you click the menu name. It also means you might spend some frustrating moments searching menus for a command that you don't see.

Next, I'll show you how to change the menu behavior back to the traditional, all-commands-displayed mode (which is a good idea when you're first learning how to use Outlook and looking for those commands).

If you open a menu and see a double-down chevron at the bottom, click the chevron to open the menu fully and display all the commands. The light-colored commands are those you haven't used recently, and the dark-colored commands are those you have used (I'm not sure what Outlook's idea of "recently" consists of, but it doesn't matter as long as you can find a command when you need it). When you click a command, it carries out its action and joins the ranks of recently used commands for that menu.

If you really see no point in hiding the commands, you can switch to classical menu behavior and show all the commands, all the time, like this:

1. Right-click in the menu bar and click Customize.

2. Click the Options tab.

3. Clear the check box for Menus Show Recently Used Commands First.

4. Click the Close button.

Another option you have in step 3 is to leave the check box marked, and mark the check box for Show Full Menus After A Short Delay. This option keeps the menus short, but they open fully if you keep the short menu open for a few seconds or point to the double-down chevron.

NOTE *Any changes you make to the menu behavior in Outlook will apply to every Office 2000 program in your computer, so don't be surprised if you change Outlook's menus and suddenly Word's menus act the same way.*

In Chapter 15, you'll learn more about customizing the menu bar, including how to remove menus and how to get them back again.

The Data Pane

Outlook's data pane is where all the items in a folder are listed. It's where you open, create, and delete individual items, such as notes, calendar appointments, and e-mail messages, and where you can sort, group, and filter those items to organize the list. You'll see different types of data pane views later in this chapter, when you take a tour of the different Outlook folders.

The Folder Banner and Folder Name Button

At the top of the data pane is a bar called the Folder banner (in Figure 1-1, it's the bar that says Personal Folders—Outlook Today on the left side). The Folder banner always displays the name of the folder you have open. The folder name and the small down-pointing triangle are really a cleverly disguised button. If you click the folder-name button, it reveals the Folder list, which is a list of all the Outlook folders (shown in Figure 1-3).

If you find that you like to use the Folder list (it's comfortably reminiscent of every other Windows 95/98 folder list), you can display it full-time by clicking View | Folder List.

If you display the Folder list by using the View menu command, it stays open until you close it by clicking the X button in its upper-right corner.

If you display it by clicking the folder-name button (in the Folder banner), it stays open until you click a folder in the list, and then it closes. If you want it to stay open after you click a folder in the list, click the small pushpin icon in its upper-right corner (which then becomes an X button so that you can close the list when you're done with it).

The Folder list and the Outlook bar give you two different ways to do the same thing. Unlike the Outlook bar, the Folder list makes every folder and custom subfolder

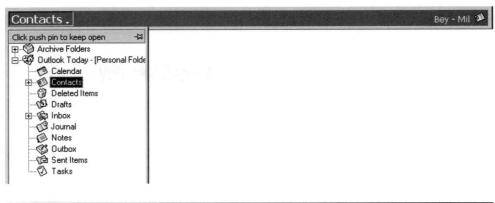

FIGURE 1-3 The Folder banner and Folder list

available in a single list. Later, when you learn how to create custom subfolders, you'll use the Folder list to create them.

If you prefer to use the Folder list rather than the Outlook bar, you can hide the Outlook bar. Either right-click in an empty space in the Outlook bar and click Hide Outlook Bar, or click View | Outlook Bar. When you want to display the Outlook bar again, click View | Outlook Bar.

Which Outlook Folder Window Do You Want to See?

Even though e-mail may turn out to be the most-often-used Outlook feature, Outlook offers a lot more than e-mail. Each Outlook activity is kept in its own folder. This section provides a quick overview of those folders; you'll learn about each one in greater detail in later chapters. You can open each folder by clicking its icon in the Outlook bar.

The Outlook Today Folder

The Outlook Today folder, which you saw in Figure 1-1 and when you opened Outlook the first time, is designed to give you an overview of what's coming up today. Do you want to customize the Outlook Today folder to show what you prefer to see first thing in the day? Point to the words Customize Outlook Today above the data pane (presto, the words are really a button) and click. In the

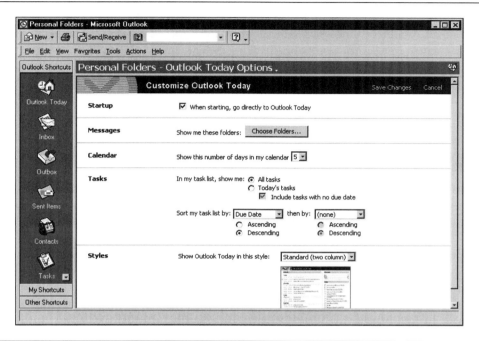

FIGURE 1-4   Customize the Outlook Today folder

Customize Outlook Today window (shown in Figure 1-4), you get to change any number of features in the Outlook Today folder. For example, you might want to see appointments for the next 2 days, or 14 days, instead of 5 days. Or you might want to see how many messages are waiting in your Inbox, but not in the Outbox or Drafts folders.

If you clear the Startup check box (the one that says When Starting, Go Directly To Outlook Today), Outlook starts with Inbox open by default; but in the section "Choose Your Startup Window," (later in this chapter) you'll learn how you can change that, too.

After you make changes, click the words Save Changes above the data pane (or click Cancel to close the Customize window without making changes).

In the Outlook Today folder, you can also open any item folder by clicking its heading. Point to all the different items in the Outlook Today window—nearly everything has an underline when you point to it, which tells you that the item or folder opens when you click it.

Inbox, Outbox, Sent Items, and Drafts Folders

The Inbox, Outbox, Sent Items, and Drafts folders are all e-mail folders. The items are displayed in a *table* view, with *fields* of specific information (such as who the message is From and the Received date) separated into columns, and each message in a separate row.

- **Inbox**   Holds messages you've received.

- **Outbox**   Holds messages you've created but haven't sent yet.

- **Sent Items**   Holds messages you've sent.

- **Drafts**   Holds messages you've created and saved, but don't want to send yet. (The Drafts icon is in the My Shortcuts group, not in the Outlook Shortcuts group—you'll see it later.)

Below the Folder banner in each of these e-mail folders is a row of column headings that double as sort buttons (Figure 1-5 shows the Inbox).

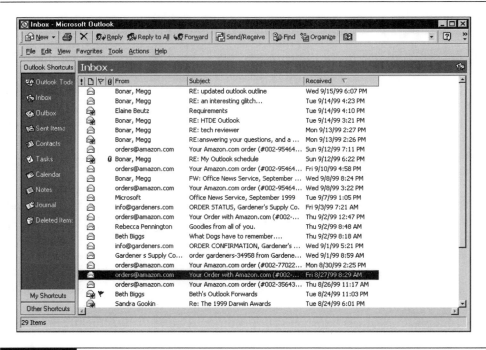

FIGURE 1-5   The Inbox, a table view

If you click a column heading once, it sorts the list in ascending order (A–Z and 1–10) by the entries in that column; if you click the same column heading a second time, it sorts the list in the opposite order. You'll learn more about sorting in Chapter 2.

Below the column headings is the list of e-mail messages stored in that folder (and if you are playing with Outlook for the first time, your lists will be short to nonexistent—but that will change soon enough). The default Inbox fields (columns) include all the tiny icons on the left, as well as who sent you the message, what it's about, and when you received it. In Chapter 2, you'll learn how you can remove existing fields that strike you as useless, or add new fields.

 *In a table view, fields are arranged in columns. Microsoft and I use both terms inconsistently, and in a table view, their meaning is the same.*

The Contacts Folder

The Contacts folder is Outlook's address book, and it can hold enough details about any given contact to make J. Edgar Hoover wannabes envious. Contacts is shown in Figure 1-6 in a *card* view, which is always sorted in alphabetical order and makes it easy to see all the details for an individual contact without scrolling around the window.

What you see in the Contacts folder is highly customizable; you can change the view to show as much or as little detail as you want to see, and you can save several different view settings for quick switches between them. You'll learn about Contacts changing the card view in Chapter 3.

The Calendar Folder

Calendar is Outlook's engagements book, in which you can record upcoming appointments and events with times and details, and set reminders that show a message or make a sound to alert you that it's time to get ready. Calendar has

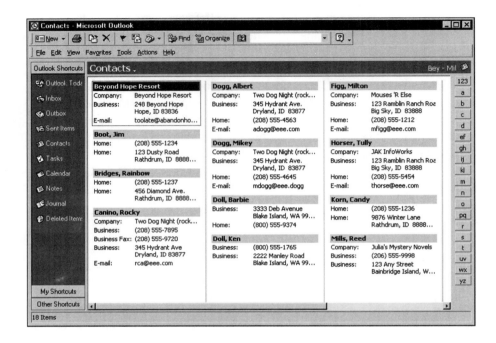

FIGURE 1-6   The Contacts folder, a card view

several views, including the day/week/month view shown in Figure 1-7. In this particular Calendar view, a TaskPad shows the tasks from your Tasks folder.

You also can print your Calendar entries in a wide variety of layouts, so that they're handy when you're away from your computer. You'll learn about Calendar in detail in Chapter 9.

The Tasks Folder

The Tasks folder, shown as a table view in the following illustration, is a to-do list that can be as quick or as detailed as you choose. You can record both the task and its due date (if there is one), and many more details, such as how far along the task

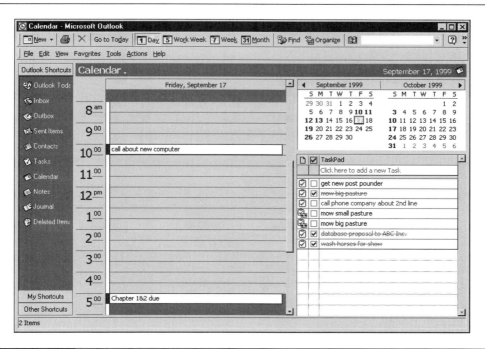

FIGURE 1-7   The Calendar, a day/week/month view

has progressed, how much time you've spent on it, the mileage you've used for it, the names of other companies involved, and more.

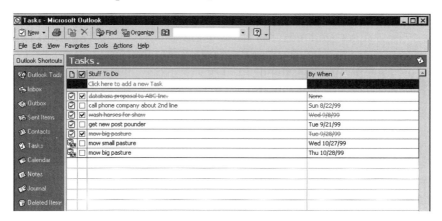

You can even set tasks to recur—to reappear on your task list automatically each time you mark the task completed. You'll learn about Tasks in Chapter 10.

The Journal Folder

Journal is an online diary in which you can record what you did, when you did it, and how long you did it for. It's easy to get a graphical sense of what you did and when by looking at Journal's timeline view.

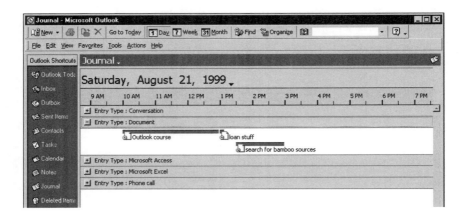

You can zoom in on the timeline and see your activities hour by hour in a single day, or zoom out to see them day by day for a week or a month at a time. Some activities can be recorded in Journal automatically, and anything can be recorded manually. You'll learn lots more about Journal in Chapter 11.

The Notes Folder

Notes are the simplest and most fun items in Outlook. They're like electronic sticky notes, shown in an icon view in the following illustration, and they are great for all those bits of information that don't really have a logical place to go but are important to save.

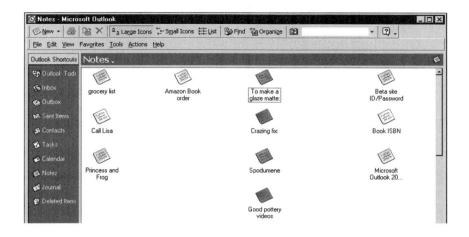

You can create a note by dragging text from another item, or even a different program file (such as Word), into the note, or you can type them. You can hold them open on the Windows desktop while you work, and you can organize them into visual groups by coloring them. You'll learn more about Notes in Chapter 8.

The Deleted Items Folder

The Deleted Items folder is Outlook's own Recycle Bin, and it functions just like the Windows Recycle Bin (but it's for Outlook only). To delete any Outlook item, you can do any of the following:

- Click the item in a list and then click the Delete button on the toolbar.

- Right-click the item in a list and then click Delete on the shortcut menu.

- Click the item in a list and then press the DELETE key.

- Drag the item from a list into the Outlook bar and drop it on the Deleted Items icon.

When you delete any Outlook item, it goes to the Deleted Items folder, shown in the following illustration, and stays there until you empty the folder. You can retrieve items at any time until you empty the folder (and then they're gone for good).

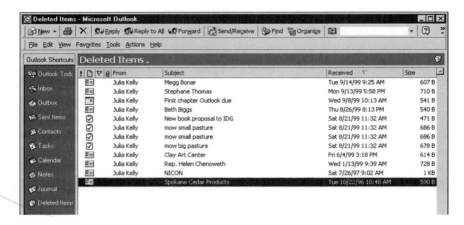

Because Deleted Items holds different kinds of Outlook items, you'll see a variety of identifying icons in the Icon field on the left side of the data pane. The icons can help you find the one item you want to retrieve: if you sort the list by clicking the Icon column heading button, you can sort the items into groups of like items and then search through a shorter list of just messages, or just notes, and so on.

To retrieve a deleted item, drag it from the list into the Outlook bar and drop it on the icon for the appropriate folder. For example, to retrieve a message you received and then deleted, locate the message in the Deleted Items list and drag it to the Inbox icon.

To empty the Deleted Items folder, right-click the Deleted Items icon in the Outlook bar and click Empty "Deleted Items" Folder. You'll see a message asking whether you're sure you want to permanently delete the items; click Yes, and they're gone forever. If you want to permanently delete specific items but not the entire folder, open the Deleted Items folder and select the items. Right-click one of the selected items and click Delete. You'll see a similar message asking whether you're sure—click Yes, and it's gone.

How to Start Outlook Automatically

If you like to start your computer in the morning and pick up your e-mail first thing while your coffee is brewing, there is an even easier way to start Outlook than by double-clicking the shortcut icon on your desktop: don't start it at all. Instead, put a shortcut to Outlook in the Windows StartUp folder, and let Windows start Outlook for you when you "boot up" (tech-speak for "turn on your computer").

Put an Outlook Shortcut in the Windows StartUp Folder

The Windows StartUp folder has shortcuts that tell Windows which programs to start automatically right after Windows starts. You can put shortcuts to any program or file you want in this folder. To put a shortcut to Outlook in Windows' StartUp folder, follow these steps:

1. Double-click the My Computer icon, which opens a window to the contents of your computer.

2. In the My Computer window, double-click your hard drive icon (you're going to navigate to where your Outlook program was installed).

3. Double-click the Windows folder.

4. Double-click the Start Menu folder.

5. Double-click the Programs folder.

6. Finally, double-click the StartUp folder. The StartUp folder contains shortcuts to items such as the Office Shortcut Bar that start automatically when you start your computer.

7. With the right mouse button, drag the Outlook icon from the desktop into the StartUp folder window and drop it (as shown in Figure 1-8).

8. On the shortcut menu, click Create Shortcut(s) Here.

9. Click the X close box to close the StartUp folder window.

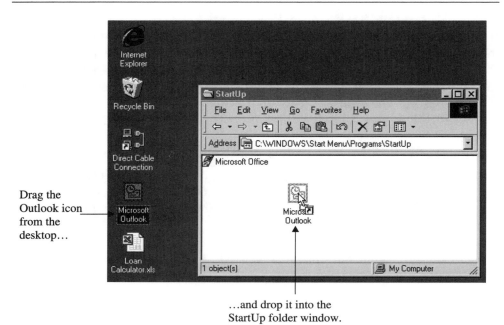

Drag the
Outlook icon
from the
desktop...

...and drop it into the
StartUp folder window.

FIGURE 1-8 Drag the Outlook icon into the StartUp folder

That's all. Outlook will start automatically and be ready to do your bidding every morning. If you want to discontinue the automatic start up, just remove the Outlook icon from the StartUp folder—either by dragging it from the StartUp folder window to the Recycle Bin, or by right-clicking the icon and clicking Delete (which also puts the shortcut icon in the Recycle Bin).

Of course, if you are one of the many who rarely turn off their computers, this won't work for you, but if you live in an area of near-constant power problems, you'll probably turn off your computer every night, and in the morning when you turn it back on, all the programs in your StartUp folder will start automatically.

NOTE *Some people argue that the constant turning off and on, and corresponding changes in internal temperature, will shorten the life of a computer, but my observation is that, these days, the accelerated obsolescence of hardware will shorten the life of a computer a lot more effectively than changes in temperature.*

Choose Your Startup Window

When you first start Outlook, it opens to the Outlook Today folder (and you learned earlier that you can customize Outlook Today so that it doesn't open at startup, but Inbox opens instead). But what if you would rather check your calendar first thing in the morning, or even your to-do list for the day? You can set Outlook to open with one of those folders displayed instead of Inbox.

To choose the folder that's displayed at startup, follow these steps:

1. In any Outlook folder, click Tools | Options.

2. Click the Other tab and then click the Advanced Options button.

3. Under General Settings, in the Startup In This Folder list box, choose the folder you want to start your day with.

4. Click OK twice to close all the dialog boxes.

Navigating in Outlook

A lot of activities are going on all in one place in Outlook, and you have many (mostly redundant) means of getting from one activity to another. You can use the Outlook bar, the View menu, the Folder list (from the toolbar button), or the same Folder list dropped from the Folder banner.

Get Around Outlook Using the Outlook Bar

Using the Outlook bar is the easiest, best, and main way to get from folder to folder in Outlook.

To open a specific folder, click the icon for that folder on the Outlook bar. If the icon you want is hidden, click the up or down button (at the top or bottom of the Outlook bar) to scroll the hidden icons into view.

The Outlook bar has three gray buttons, called Outlook Shortcuts, My Shortcuts, and Other Shortcuts. Clicking one of these buttons opens a different group of icons. In Chapter 15, you'll learn how to customize and rearrange the shortcut icons and the Outlook bar groups, so that all of your shortcuts are exactly where you want them (easy to find, no more hunting).

Outlook Shortcuts

The Outlook Shortcuts group contains most of the Outlook folder icons (except for the Drafts icon, which is in the My Shortcuts group).

My Shortcuts

The My Shortcuts group contains just the Drafts icon and a copy of the Outbox icon. Plenty of room is available here to add your own icons, which you'll learn how to do in Chapter 15.

Other Shortcuts

You can use Outlook as an entire desktop, if you want to, because the Other Shortcuts group is a gateway into your computer's file system. Even better than your regular file system, each folder you open in Outlook lists the files in that folder and displays more information about the files than you can get from your regular file system. The My Computer icon does exactly what the My Computer icon on your desktop does: it opens an Outlook window into your folders and files so that you can play (or work) with them.

The My Documents and Favorites icons are provided for your convenience and easy access. They open windows directly into your My Documents and Favorites folders so that you don't have to start at My Computer and click, click, click your way into them.

You'll learn more about working with other files from within Outlook in Chapter 12.

Get Around Outlook Using the Folder Banner and Folder List

On the left side of the Folder banner (shown in Figure 1-9) is a clever button that looks like a mere title until you point your mouse at it, whereupon it becomes a button. When you click the name button, the Folder list appears.

You also can display the Folder list either by clicking the Folder List button on the Advanced toolbar or by clicking View | Folder List on the menu bar.

Each folder in the Folder list can have custom subfolders (which you create), and you can display or hide the subfolders by clicking the tiny plus and minus symbols in the Folder list. For example, if you click the minus symbol next to Personal Folders, its subfolders (your Outlook folders) are hidden. Click the symbol again—a plus

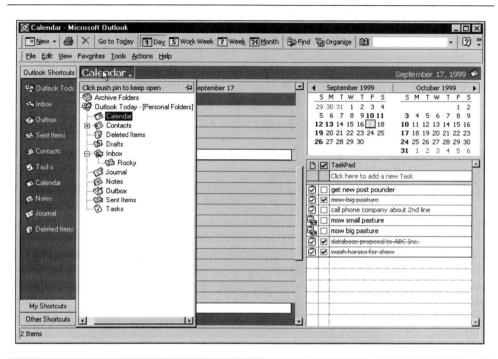

FIGURE 1-9   The Folder banner name button and Folder list

symbol now—and the subfolders are displayed. In this illustration, I have custom subfolders in my Contacts and Inbox folders.

Get Around Outlook Using the View Menu

I've saved the description of this technique for last because it's not the quickest method, but if your mouse quits on you and you've got work that's due tomorrow morning, you can use the View menu to get around, using menus and key presses. To switch folders by using menu commands, choose View | Go To and then choose the name of the folder. If you don't see the folder name on the menu, choose Folder and then choose the folder name in the Go To Folder dialog box (which looks just like the Folder list, but it's in a dialog box).

If you're mouse-addicted and you want to try keystrokes (or you're stranded without a mouse), here's how to use those key presses to get around. Press ALT-V *(V is the underlined letter in View), use your up and down arrow keys to highlight the menu command you want, and then press* ENTER *to trigger the command.*

Get Help When You're Lost

This book is designed to let you avoid using Outlook's help files, but sometimes you can't avoid doing so, such as when you're at home and you left the book at work, or your friend borrowed your book and hasn't returned it.

So, here's how to use the help files in Outlook 2000.

Get Help from the Office Assistant

The first thing you'll see when you start Outlook (or any Office 2000 program) is the Office Assistant. The Assistant is often in your way and can be really

 annoying, but it truly was designed to help. It offers tips and suggestions, and provides what's referred to as context-sensitive help, or help based on your current activities in Outlook. Fortunately, other types of help are offered, as well, so you can banish the Office Assistant if you find it intrusive.

To get help from the Office Assistant (if it's not already sitting on your desktop, waiting for a question), click the question mark button on the toolbar. If the Office Assistant doesn't have a balloon over its head, click it and a balloon appears. Then, follow these steps:

1. Type a question, phrase, or word under What Would You Like To Do.

2. Click Search. A short list of potential topics, some of which might seem useful, replaces the balloon.

3. Click a topic's option button for a likely topic.

The full Help window opens at this point, as shown in Figure 1-10. In the next section, "Get Help Without the Office Assistant," you'll learn more about using the Help window.

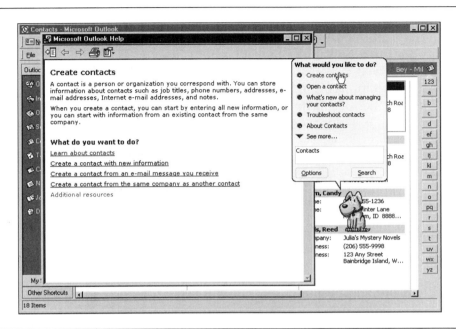

FIGURE 1-10   The Help window

Occasionally, a light bulb appears over the Office Assistant's head, which means the Assistant has a tip for you that may or may not have anything to do with your current activities. Click the light bulb icon to read the tip (you might learn the answer to a question you never thought to ask).

Customize the Office Assistant

You can change the Assistant character (Clippit, the gyrating paperclip, is widely disliked), change the kind of help you get, or just turn off the Office Assistant.

Turn Off the Office Assistant

To turn off the Office Assistant, right-click the Assistant and click Options. Then, clear the Use the Office Assistant check box and click OK.

If you miss the Office Assistant after turning it off, turn it back on by clicking Help | Show the Office Assistant.

Uninstall the Office Assistant

You can also uninstall the Office Assistant completely so that it can't be turned back on. With your Office or Outlook CD-ROM in the CD-ROM drive, click Start | Settings | Control Panel, and double-click Add/Remove Programs. In the Add/Remove Programs dialog box, on the Install/Uninstall tab, double-click Microsoft Office 2000 (or Microsoft Outlook 2000, if you installed it without Office).

In the Office 2000 Maintenance Mode dialog box, click the Add Or Remove Features button. In the Update Features dialog box, click the plus symbol next to Office Tools. Click the gray button next to Office Assistant, and click Not Available. Finally, click the Update Now button, wait a few seconds, and click OK when you see the Setup Complete message.

Close any open dialog boxes, and the Office Assistant is gone.

 When you remove the Office Assistant from any Office program, it's removed from all the Office programs.

Changing the Office Assistant Character

Eight different Office Assistant characters are available in Office 2000, and you'll like some better than others. Are you a cat person? A dog person? A back-to-nature person, or a forward-to-outer-space person? There's probably a character that's right for you. To switch characters, right-click the Office Assistant and click Choose Assistant. Use the Back and Next buttons to flip through characters, and when you find one you like, click OK.

Changing the Office Assistant Behavior

You can make the Office Assistant less annoying without banishing it completely. Right-click the Office Assistant and then click Options to see the dialog box shown in Figure 1-11.

To turn on an option, click its corresponding check box to place a check mark in it. To turn off an option, click its check box to clear it. Because the way that you can change the Office Assistant's behavior is not always intuitive, Table 1-1 describes what the options do. These options apply to Office Assistant behavior in all Office 2000 programs (not just Outlook).

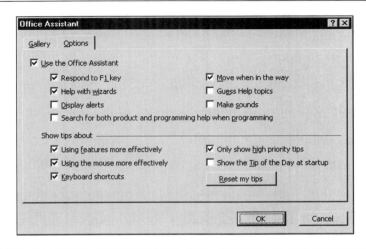

FIGURE 1-11   Office Assistant options

Option	Description
Use the Office Assistant	Turn the Office Assistant on or off—clear the check box to get rid of the Office Assistant without uninstalling it.
Respond to F1 key	If you're a keyboarder, you can wake up the Office Assistant by pressing F1.
Help with wizards	You get extra help with some of Office 2000's built-in wizards (such as Word's Letter Wizard).
Display alerts	You'll get messages that remind you to save, archive, and other stuff.
Search for both product and programming help when programming	If you're programming with Visual Basic, this option makes programming help files available (this book won't cover programming in Outlook).
Move when in the way	Whatever you're doing, the Office Assistant moves out of your way so that you don't have to keep moving it yourself.
Guess Help topics	You get help whether you ask for it or not.
Make sounds	Lets the Office Assistant make noises at you.

TABLE 1-1   Description of Office Assistant Options

Tip Option	Description
Using features more effectively	You get tips related specifically to the features of the active program (remember, these options apply to all Office 2000 programs, not just to Outlook).
Using the mouse more effectively	You get tips about using your mouse more efficiently.
Keyboard shortcuts	If you can do something without the mouse, these tips will tell you how.
Only show high priority tips	Only important, time-saving tips appear.
Show the Tip of the Day at startup	You get to see a new tip every time each program starts.
Reset my tips	Shuffles the tips around so that you get to see them all again.

TABLE 1-2   Office Assistant Tips Options

The bottom half of the Options tab of the Office Assistant dialog box has another set of options related to tips that really can help you get the most out of Outlook. Right-click the Office Assistant and click Options to see the dialog box (shown in Figure 1-11). Table 1-2 describes the Office Assistant's Tips options.

Get Help Without the Office Assistant

If the help that the Office Assistant offers isn't for you, you can turn off the Office Assistant and get other onscreen help the old-fashioned way. To get help when the assistant is gone, click Help | Microsoft Outlook Help.

Help Files

Whether you get there with the Office Assistant or without it, you'll find that the Help window is the same. The help file is shown on the right side of the Help window, and a table of contents, search engine, and index are shown on the left. If you don't see the left-side stuff, click the Show button.

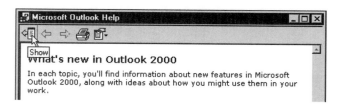

Click the tabs on the left side of the window to choose Contents (a table of contents for the help files), Answer Wizard (a search engine), or Index (an alphabetical index to Help topics).

To use the Contents tab, click the small plus symbols next to the book icons to open subtopics and files until you see a file that looks useful (the file icons look like sheets of paper with question marks). When you click a file icon, the file appears on the right.

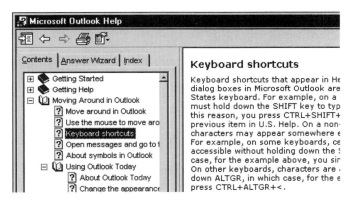

To use the Answer Wizard tab, type a word, phrase, or complete question in the upper box and click Search. A list of topics appears in the lower box; click likely topics until a useful help file appears on the right.

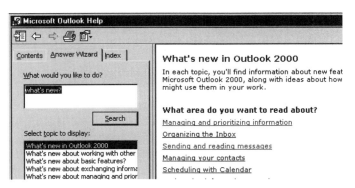

To use the Index tab, in the top box, type the first few letters of a topical word that you'd look up in a book index. As you type, the index scrolls through an alphabetical list of keywords in the middle box. When you see a likely keyword, double-click it, and a list of topics appears in the bottom box. Click a topic in the bottom box to see it on the right.

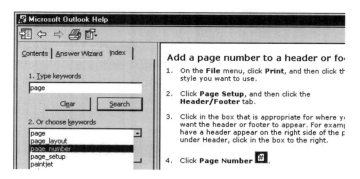

In the help files on the right, there are often *links* (blue, underlined text) that open related help files. If you open a linked help file and it doesn't help, you can return to the previous help file by clicking the Back button at the top of the Help window.

After you open and go backwards through help files, the Back and Forward buttons run back and forth through help files you've already opened; pretty soon, you can get completely lost and unable to find that one help file that was remotely useful.

If you get frustrated using the help files, you're not alone. Sometimes, switching to a different method of searching helps (for example, if you've used the Answer Wizard to no avail, try the Index), because the different search methods often turn up different help files.

> TIP
>
> *One way to keep useful help files easy to find is to drag a link (a blue, underlined hyperlink) that leads to the help file out of the help window and onto your desktop. The trick is to locate a hyperlink that leads to the file you want; once you find it, your shortcut will keep it handy.*

ToolTips

ToolTips are quick onscreen help that tell you a button's name. If you point at a toolbar button for a moment, its name appears.

Right-Click and What's This Help

Right-Click and What's This Help are two features that offer a little more in-depth help than ToolTips. The right-click option is useful in dialog boxes when you wonder what an option or check box does. Right-click the label of the mysterious option, and either a brief explanation of the option appears (shown next) or a What's This button appears—if you click the What's This button, a brief explanation of the option appears.

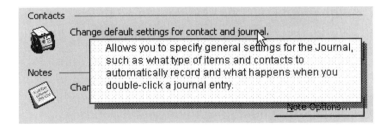

If you still can't figure out what a toolbar button does, even after you see its ToolTip, click Help | What's This. The mouse pointer becomes a What's This pointer—click the mysterious button, and you'll see a brief explanation of the button's function.

Exit Outlook

Had enough for one session? There are several ways to exit Outlook:

■ Click the X (close) button in the upper-right corner of the Outlook window.

■ Click File | Exit.

- ■ Press ALT-F4.

- ■ Double-click the Outlook icon on the left end of the title bar (an Outlook 2000 icon always looks like an L within a circle that's within a square).

- ■ Click the Outlook icon on the left end of the title bar and click Close.

That's it for getting around in Outlook—the next chapter is all about techniques for organizing lists of items in the different folders.

Chapter 2

Organizing Your Outlook Information

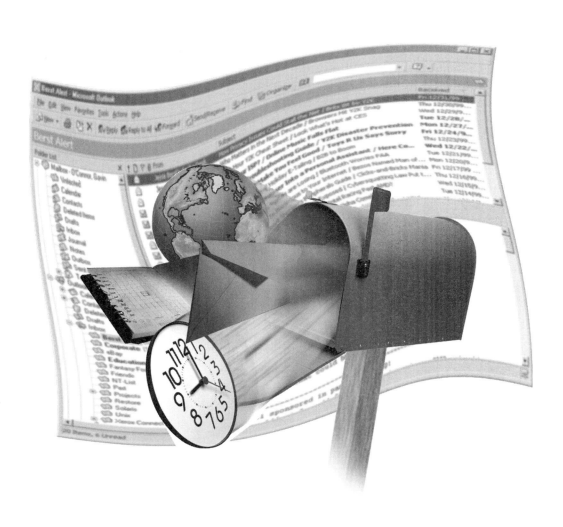

How to . . .

- Sort items
- Group items
- Filter items
- Categorize your Outlook items
- Organize your messages with colors
- Reorganize fields

It won't be long before you find yourself with lengthy lists of items, such as messages, contacts, or tasks, in at least some of your Outlook folders, and finding a specific item gets to be a tedious search.

Fortunately, Outlook provides several ways to organize all of your lists: you can sort, group, categorize, and filter any kind of Outlook item, and visually identify specific items by color. These organizational methods work pretty much the same way in all of your Outlook folders, so once you learn to organize one folder, you'll know how to organize any folder and any kind of Outlook item. You'll learn all of these organizational techniques in this chapter.

Each of your Outlook folders has a default layout and arrangement of items. These are a good starting point, and the layouts can be rearranged to suit your personal preferences. Every folder is like a miniature database that holds data arranged in *records* (each item is a record) and *fields* (each type of information, such as Subject or Start Time, is a field). Fields can be hidden, displayed, and arranged in a different order to show you just what you want to see. Knowing how to rearrange fields can help you sort, group, and filter your lists more efficiently. In this chapter, you'll learn all of these organizational techniques for use in table-type layouts (with rows and columns).

 *You'll learn about organizing other layouts (such as the Contacts card view and the Notes icon view) in the specific chapters that address those Outlook components.*

Sorting Items

Probably the most common way to organize anything, whether it's a file drawer of old tax records or a shelf of music CDs, is to sort it into categories, or fields. You pick a field (such as tax year or musical group), group together all the items that share each field, and sort the groups into some sort of logical order. Then, when you want to locate, for example, your 1993 business deductions, you can easily find the 1993 tax file and the specific form within that file.

In a list of Inbox messages, you might want to locate a message you received yesterday—you can sort the list by the Received field to find yesterday's messages quickly. Or you might need to find a message you received from a specific project partner—you can sort the list by the From field and scan the alphabetical list of senders for your partner's name.

Using the general sorting procedures you'll learn in this chapter, you'll be able to sort any set of Outlook items—messages, tasks, contacts, and other files on your hard drive. You'll also be able to sort any set of items that can be displayed in a table-type view in the Outlook window (and *all* Outlook items can be displayed in table-type views).

Sorting is an easy procedure when data is displayed in a table format. The sorted field is often called a sort *key,* and you can sort a table by a single key or by several keys at the same time, in a hierarchical sort order.

Quick Sorts in Outlook

To sort a table, click the column heading for the field you want to sort by. When you sort a table by a specific field (or sort key), all the records are sorted so that the items in the sorted field are in order.

In the Inbox table shown next, messages were sorted by clicking the From heading. The From heading button shows a faint up-pointing triangle, which indicates that the field is sorted, and that it's sorted in ascending order (A–Z or 1–10).

				From ╱	Subject	Received
				Bonar, Megg	RE: updated outlook outline	Wed 9/15/99 6:07 PM
				Bonar, Megg	RE: an interesting glitch...	Tue 9/14/99 4:23 PM
				Bonar, Megg	RE: HTDE Outlook	Tue 9/14/99 3:21 PM
				Bonar, Megg	RE: tech reviewer	Mon 9/13/99 2:27 PM
				Bonar, Megg	RE:answering your questions, a...	Mon 9/13/99 2:26 PM
				Bonar, Megg	RE: My Outlook schedule	Sun 9/12/99 6:22 PM
				Bonar, Megg	FW: Office News Service, Sept...	Wed 9/8/99 8:24 PM
				Gardener s Suppl...	order gardeners-34958 from Ga...	Wed 9/1/99 8:59 AM
				info@gardeners....	ORDER STATUS, Gardener's Su...	Fri 9/3/99 7:21 AM
				info@gardeners....	ORDER CONFIRMATION, Garde...	Wed 9/1/99 5:21 PM
				Julia Kelly	new files	Tue 8/10/99 1:14 PM
				Julia Kelly	Read: Did you get this message?	Tue 8/3/99 9:51 AM
				Julia Kelly	Read: Tea on Tuesday	Mon 8/2/99 6:57 PM
				Microsoft	Office News Service, Septembe...	Tue 9/7/99 1:05 PM
				orders@amazon....	Your Amazon.com order (#002-...	Sun 9/12/99 7:11 PM
				orders@amazon....	Your Amazon.com order (#002-...	Fri 9/10/99 4:58 PM
				orders@amazon....	Your Amazon.com order (#002-...	Wed 9/8/99 3:22 PM

To reverse the sort order, click the same heading button again. The sort order is reversed, and the faint triangle switches to point downward, which indicates a descending (Z–A or 10–1) sort order.

If you click a different column heading, the whole table is re-sorted by the new key.

 Another way to sort by a single field is to right-click the heading button for the field you want to sort, and click either Sort Ascending or Sort Descending.

Multikey Sorts

What if you want to sort by more than one field? For example, suppose you want to sort your messages so that all the messages from each sender are listed in the order in which you received them. No problem. Outlook provides two ways for you to do this.

Multikey Sorts Using the View Summary Dialog Box (the Long Way)

First, the long way to sort a list (which really is a much longer way, so you'll want to remember the short way):

1. Right-click any column heading and click Customize Current View. Or, select View | Current View | Customize Current View. The View Summary dialog box appears.

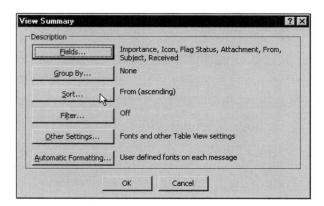

2

2. In the View Summary dialog box, click the Sort button. The Sort dialog box appears.

3. In the Sort dialog box, select the primary sort key (in the previous example, the From field) in the Sort Items By list box, and click an option for Ascending or Descending.

4. Select the second field (in the previous example, the Received field) in the Then By list box, and click an option for Ascending or Descending.

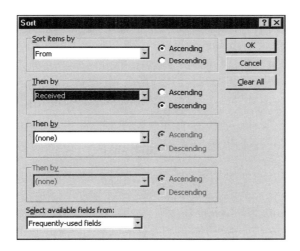

5. Select more fields in the two remaining Then By list boxes, if you want to refine your sort further.

6. Click OK twice to close the two dialog boxes.

Your table is sorted, and all the heading buttons for sort keys have faint triangles displayed.

> **TIP**
>
> *One advantage of sorting using the View Summary dialog box is that you can sort by fields that aren't currently displayed in the table. If you specify a field that isn't currently displayed, you are asked if you want to display the hidden sort key when you click OK to close the Sort dialog box. If you click Yes, the field is displayed, and if you click No, the field remains hidden even though the table is sorted by that field.*

Quick Multikey Sorts Using the Column Heading Buttons (the Short Way)

Here's the quick way to set up multikey sorts to sort a list (but it only works when all of your sort keys are displayed):

1. Click the heading button for the primary sort key (and click again, if you need to, to switch between ascending and descending order). The list is sorted by that field.

2. Hold down the SHIFT key and click the heading button for the second sort key (click again, if you need to, to switch between ascending and descending order). The list is re-sorted, by the second sort key within the first sort key. For example, if you sorted your Inbox by the From field and then by the Received field, your list would be sorted by sender, and each set of messages from a specific sender would be sorted by the dates you received their messages.

You can sort your table by up to four keys (if you try to add a fifth key, Outlook will chastise you).

 *You won't be able to sort by some fields, such as Category, because those fields can contain multiple values. You can, however, group by multiple-entry fields, such as Category (you'll learn about categories later in this chapter).*

Clear a Sort Order

To clear a sort order, regardless of which sort keys were used or how you created the sort, click a single column heading button. All previous sorts are removed and the table is re-sorted by that single key. You can also clear a sort order the long way, by opening the Sort dialog box and clicking the Clear All button, but that is, after all, the long way.

Grouping Items

Grouping is similar to sorting, but each set of items is collected into a group that shares identical entries in the grouped field, and then each group is collapsed into a single entry.

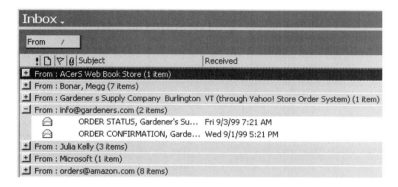

Sometimes, it's much quicker to locate a message from a specific colleague, for example, by isolating all the messages from that colleague and then looking for the message you want. After the items have been gathered into groups, you can expand a group by clicking the small plus symbol to its left; to collapse the group again, click the small minus symbol to the left of the group heading.

If you group items by Category (which you'll learn about later in this chapter), an item may have more than one category, and will appear in each of its category groups.

Group Items the Quick Way: Use the Group By Box

To group items the quick way, use the Group By box, like this:

1. Right-click any column heading button and click Group By Box. The Group By box is the dark-gray bar that appears between the Folder banner and the row of column headings.

2. Drag the column heading button for the field you want to group into the Group By box.

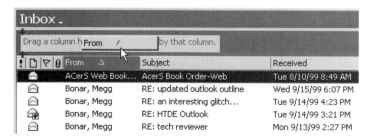

3. To group on more than one level, drag more column heading buttons into the Group By box and drop each to the right of the existing grouped fields. The grouped heading buttons assume a hierarchy in the Group By box.

 *Another quick way to group items is to right-click the heading button for the field you want to group, and click Group By This Field; the Group By box appears, and the list is grouped.*

Group Items the Long Way: Use the Group By Dialog Box

Another way you can group items is by using the Group By dialog box:

1. Right-click any column heading button and click Customize Current View. Or, select View | Current View | Customize Current View.

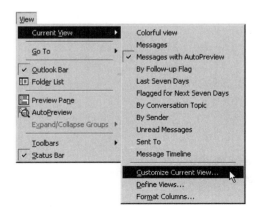

2. In the View Summary dialog box, click Group By.

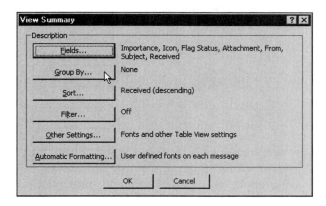

3. Under Group Items By, select the field you want to group from the list box. Select a sort order for the group while you're at it. You can group by fields that aren't currently displayed in the table view, and if you do, the Show Field In View check box will be empty (click the check box to mark it if you want to add that field to the displayed table).

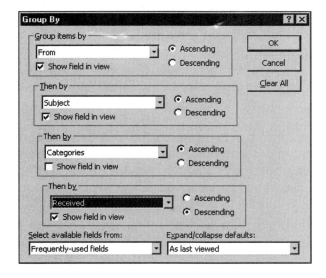

4. In the Then By list boxes, you can select more fields for a multifield grouping.

5. Click OK twice to close both dialog boxes.

If you group items with the Group By dialog box, the Group By box doesn't automatically appear above the column headings; but, if you right-click a column heading and click Group By Box, the Group By box appears and all the grouped heading buttons appear in it.

> *Grouped fields can be sorted just like normal fields: click the group heading button to sort the groups, and click it again to reverse the sort order.*

Ungroup Items

When you want to return your display to a normal list of individual items, with nothing hidden in groups, you can ungroup the list. To ungroup an entire list, or

just a single field, drag the field heading button from the Group By box back into the column heading row. When the heading button is in line over the heading row, two red arrows point out where the heading will be inserted. Drop the heading button when the red arrows point to the place you want to insert the field.

After you empty the Group By box, close it by right-clicking any column heading, and then click Group By Box. Don't close the Group By box until you've dragged all the grouped fields out of it (if you close the Group By box with grouped fields still in it, your list remains grouped).

> *You can also ungroup a list by opening the Group By dialog box and clicking the Clear All button.*

Filtering Items

Sorting and grouping are ways to organize a list while leaving all the items visible or immediately available, whereas *filtering* organizes a list by hiding all the items except those that meet specific *criteria* that you set. If your list of items is really long, filtering can make your work easier by shortening your list to show only the items you want to see.

For example, suppose your organization is proposing a new retirement policy: every retiree will receive a traditional gold pocket watch along with their pension. You've sent out a message to notify everyone in your organization and ask for feedback, and over the course of a few weeks you've received several messages with opinions about the gold watch policy. Now it's time to send a report to your supervisor about whether the employees like the idea, and you need to find all the messages you've received concerning the new retirement policy. The messages are

2

mixed in with a lot of other messages in your Inbox, and they're from several different employees.

How can you quickly locate just the messages about the gold watch policy? You can filter your entire Inbox list of messages for those that have the phrase "gold watch" anywhere in the Subject field or message body. The phrase "gold watch" is a filter *criterion.*

Criteria can be words in the Subject line, words in the text of messages, names of people who have sent you messages or to whom you've sent messages, file sizes, categories, specific field entries, and even phone numbers that have a specific number in them. Basically, almost anything can be filter criteria.

NOTE *A filter applies only to the view in which it's created; if you apply a filter and then switch views, your items won't be filtered in the new view. You'll learn about switching views in Chapter 3.*

To filter a list, you set filter criteria, like this:

1. Open the Outlook folder you want to filter (this probably seems obvious, but the Filter dialog box is specific to the folder that's displayed).

2. Right-click any column heading button and then click Customize Current View. Or, select View | Current View | Customize Current View.

3. In the View Summary dialog box, click the Filter button.

4. In the Filter dialog box, set up your filter criteria. The Filter dialog box has three tabs: one that's specific to the open Outlook folder, a More Choices tab, and an Advanced tab.

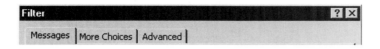

- The leftmost tab, the one that's specific to the open folder, is where you can enter words or characters that you want Outlook to search the items for. It's pretty self-explanatory; in the next illustration, I'm filtering my Inbox for messages from the Amazon bookstore about my book orders. This criterion will find messages in the Inbox that have "amazon" in the Subject field (the filter is not case-sensitive, so it makes no difference whether you type upper-case or lower-case letters).

If you want to find messages with at least one of several words or phrases, enclose each separate phrase or word in quotation marks and separate them with commas, like this: "amazon", "book", "order".

If anything in the Filter dialog box is mysterious, right-click the option's label to see a brief explanation of what the option does.

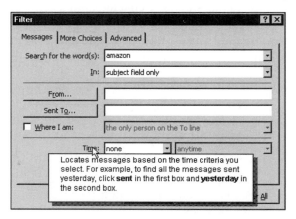

■ In the More Choices tab, you can set more general filter criteria. To choose a criterion from a grayed list box, click the check box next to it and then select an item in the list box. To set a size criterion, select an item in the left list box and then enter size limits in the Size boxes that become available on the right.

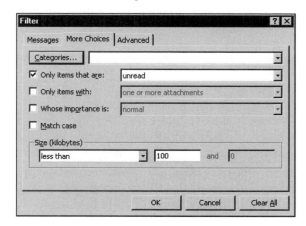

2

- In the Advanced tab, you can set field-specific criteria. For example, suppose you want to filter the Contacts folder to find contacts with a Business or Home address in the city of Spokane. If you set a criterion of "Spokane" in the address fields in the Contacts tab (the leftmost tab), you'll pull up addresses that include Spokane Street and Spokane Blvd., as well as Spokane, WA. But in the Advanced tab, you can set criteria that search for specific characters (a *text string*) in the Business City or Home City address fields. See the following section, "Build Advanced Filter Criteria," to learn how to use the Advanced tab in the Filter dialog box.

5. When you've set up your filter criteria, click OK twice to close both dialog boxes and run the filter.

Build Advanced Filter Criteria

You build advanced filter criteria one criterion at a time and add each to the Find Items That Match These Criteria list. To build the criteria in the previous example (finding contacts with addresses in Spokane), follow these steps:

1. Open the folder you want to filter, and then open the Filter dialog box and click the Advanced tab.

2. Click the Field button.

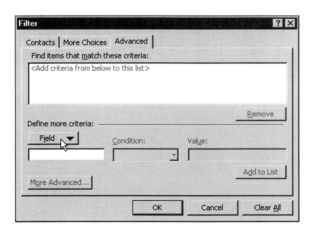

3. Point to the set of fields that contains the field you want to filter (in this case, the Address Fields), and click the specific field (in this case, Business Address City).

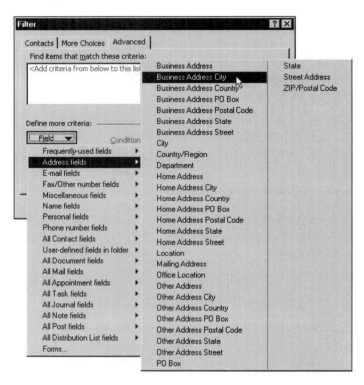

4. In the Condition list box, select a condition, such as Contains or Is Exactly (whatever's appropriate for your criterion).

5. In the Value list box, type the text string you want to filter for. The Spokane criteria is set up here:

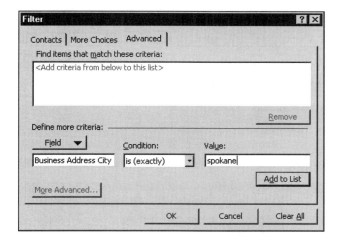

6. Click the Add To List button to add the criterion to the filter's list, and then create any other specific criteria for the filter (such as Home Address City, Is Exactly, and Spokane).

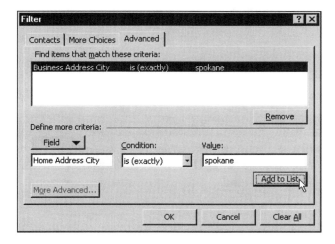

7. Click OK twice to close both dialog boxes and run the filter.

When a filter is applied, the words (Filter Applied) appear on the right end of the Folder banner and the left end of Outlook's status bar. To see all the filter criteria that are applied, or to change them, you'll need to open the Filter dialog box.

Remove a Filter

When a filter is applied, most of the items in the filtered list are hidden. This is tremendously efficient for accomplishing specific tasks, but after the task is complete, you need to see your entire list of items again. To show the entire list, you need to remove the filter, like this:

1. Right-click any column heading button and then click Customize Current View. Or, select View | Current View | Customize Current View.

2. In the View Summary dialog box, click the Filter button.

3. In the Filter dialog box, click the Clear All button and then click OK twice to close both dialog boxes.

Categorizing Your Outlook Items

A *category* identifies any Outlook item (such as a message or a contact) so that you can find it easily by grouping or filtering a list to show all the items in that category. Examples of categories are Personal, Business, Holiday, Funny Stuff, Boring Letters, and Horse Friends. (Some of these are my personal categories—you'll learn how to create your own later in this chapter.) Figure 2-1 shows an Inbox list with categories applied to several messages.

Categories are different in that you have to apply them to each item yourself, and you can apply more than one category to a single item. For example, you can categorize messages from a business contact as Business, Holiday, and Phone Calls; those messages will show up in all three categories when you filter or group your list by category.

Outlook provides a long list of ready-to-use generic categories, some of which you may find useful. You can also add your own custom categories to the list, so

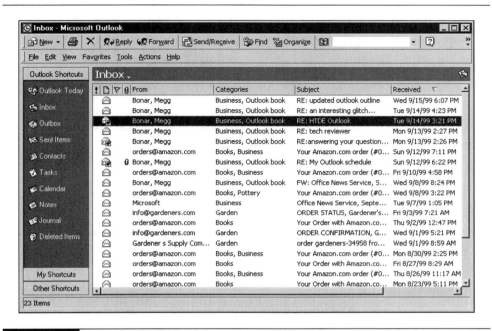

FIGURE 2-1   Messages with categories applied

that you can categorize messages, contacts, or tasks according to your hobbies, specific clients, projects, or anything you want.

Applying Categories to Your Items

You have to apply categories to items yourself, but it's a quick process. You can even apply a category to several items at one time, like this:

1. Select the item(s) you want to apply a category to. If you're applying a category to more than one item, sorting the list first can help you get all the items in one place; then, use the CTRL or SHIFT key to select multiple items.

2. Right-click any of the selected items, and click Categories.

3. In the Categories dialog box, shown in Figure 2-2, mark the check boxes of the categories you want to apply, or clear the check boxes for categories you want to remove, and then click OK.

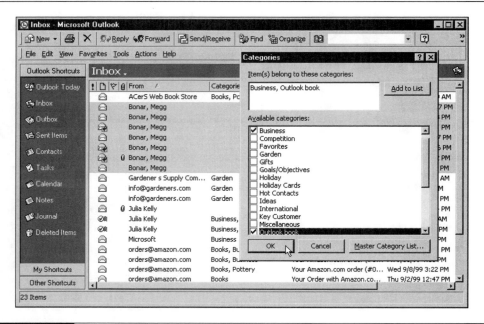

FIGURE 2-2 Apply a category to multiple items

To select adjacent items in a list, click the first item and then hold down
SHIFT *and click the last item. To select nonadjacent items, click the first*
item and then hold down CTRL *and click the remaining items.*

Creating Your Own Categories

You may find that your own categories are much more intuitive and useful than
those supplied by Microsoft. If you want to create your own categories (and of
course you do), this is how:

1. Right-click any item in any Outlook folder list, and click Categories.

2. In the Categories dialog box, click the Master Category List button.

3. In the Master Category List dialog box, type a category name in the New
Category box and then click Add.

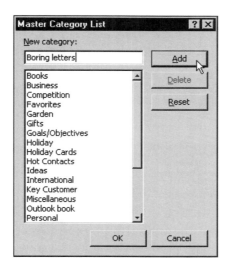

4. Repeat step 3 until you've added all the categories that you can think of.

5. Click OK twice to close both dialog boxes. All of your new categories are
available to every item in every Outlook folder.

Create Custom Categories on the Fly

Suppose you've selected several items and are ready to apply a custom category to
the lot, when you realize you haven't created the custom category yet. Aaagghh!
So inefficient! It's okay, because you can create the category you need right at the
moment you need it, like this:

1. Right-click any item in the selected list and then click Categories.

2. Type your custom category name in the Item(s) Belong To These
Categories box. If you want to create and apply more than one category to
the selected items, type all the names and separate them with commas.

3. Click the Add To List button.

Done! Your new categories are created and applied to the selected items.

Delete Custom Categories

You can delete any categories, including Microsoft's boring generic categories, like this:

1. Right-click any item in any Outlook folder list and click Categories.

2. Click the Master Category List button.

3. Select the category name you want to delete, and click the Delete button.

4. Repeat step 3 until you've deleted all the custom and generic categories you no longer want.

5. Click OK twice to close both dialog boxes.

If you delete any of Microsoft's built-in categories and then want them back again, you can open the Master Category List and click the Reset button. You'll get all the default categories back, and lose any custom categories you've created.

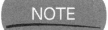 *When you delete custom categories, they remain applied to items you applied them to. Deleting them removes them only from the Master Category List, so you can't use them any more. To delete categories from items, select the items and clear the check boxes for the deleted categories.*

Organizing Your Messages with Colors

You can organize e-mail message lists by using colors, and organizing with colors doesn't rearrange or group items in any way; but, you can color-code specific items to stand out visually in your list. You can automatically apply a specific color to the message lines for all messages from or sent to a specific e-mail address. (The message itself isn't colored when you open it, but the message lines that are listed in the folder are colored.) To color the message lines in your list:

1. Open the Outlook folder that contains the messages you want to color.

2. Select Tools | Organize. A new pane, called the Organize pane, appears above your message list. It can help you organize your Inbox messages by using rules, colors, and switching views. There are other, quicker ways to use rules and to switch views, but the Organize pane is the easiest way to apply colors to messages.

3. On the left side of the Organize pane, click Using Colors. Figure 2-3 shows the Organize pane set up to apply colors.

4. In the Color Messages list boxes, leave From selected in the left list box (because this is your Inbox, and you'll only see messages from other people).

5. To set the name in the center box, click a message from that person in your message list.

6. In the right list box, select a color. There are 16 colors, so you can color-code messages from 16 different senders.

7. Click the Apply Color button. All the messages from that person are recolored, and new messages you receive from that person will also be colored.

8. To close the Organize pane, click the X in its upper-right corner.

To remove colors from messages, repeat steps 1–8, but in step 6, select Auto in the color list box.

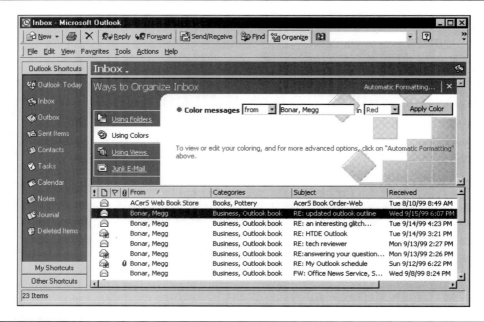

FIGURE 2-3 Color messages from a specific sender

Reorganizing Fields

Earlier in this chapter, you learned about grouping and filtering messages, contacts, and any other Outlook items that you've displayed in a table-type list. You learned to sort, group, and filter using specific fields, and you learned about creating and applying categories to individual items.

The Categories field is a terrific field for grouping and filtering a list of Outlook items, but you were probably wondering how to use the Category field if it's not displayed in the Outlook window. Now you'll learn how to display, rearrange, and remove the Category field and any other fields you want. Keep in mind that what you learn here applies to table-type layouts only—you'll learn how to rearrange the layout of other views, such as the Contacts card view, in the chapters that cover those Outlook folders.

Rearranging Fields in Your Table Views

Suppose you prefer to see your Inbox messages presented with the Received dates column on the left side of the Inbox window instead of the right side; or perhaps you want your Tasks folder to show Due Dates on the left and Subjects on the right. You can rearrange the fields in any table-type list of Outlook items to suit your working style.

NOTE   *You'll learn how to customize the view in any Outlook folder in Chapter 15.*

Rearranging fields in a table view is quick—just drag a column heading to another position in the column headings row. When you drag a heading across the headings row, a pair of red arrows point out the insertion spots; drag the heading across the row until the red arrows point to the right spot, and then release the mouse button to drop the heading.

When you drag headings, drag them left or right straight across the row. If you drag them away from the row, you'll see a big X over the heading button; the big X means "if you drop the heading now, the field will be removed from the table." If you inadvertently drop the heading out of the table, it's okay; the upcoming section "Adding New Fields to Your Table Views" explains how to get it back.

Removing Unnecessary Fields in Your Table Views

If you have a lot of fields in a table and want to reduce the clutter, even just temporarily, you can remove fields you don't need to see. The data in the field is still in Outlook, but it's removed from view. You remove a field by doing deliberately what you might have done inadvertently when rearranging the fields—drag a heading out of the headings row and drop it when you see the big X.

Adding New Fields to Your Table Views

When you want to add a new field or retrieve one you removed, here's how to do it:

1. Right-click the headings row and click Field Chooser.

2. Drag a field button from the Field Chooser and drop it on the headings row (the red arrows show you where it'll go when you drop it).

3. Close the Field Chooser by clicking the X button in its upper-right corner.

That's pretty much all there is to it. The fields in the Field Chooser are from a set of frequently used fields for the Outlook folder that's open; if you don't see the specific field you want, select a different set of fields from the list box at the top of the Field Chooser.

Now you know how to organize table-type lists of items in Outlook. You can use these sorting, grouping, filtering, and rearranging techniques in all of your message folders and in the Tasks folder right away, because the default view for messages and tasks is a table view. You can also use these organizing techniques in any other folder if you switch its view to a table-type layout. You'll learn about switching views in Chapter 3.

Next, you'll learn how to create those long lists of items so that you'll have something to organize, starting with Contacts in Chapter 3. After you create lots of contacts, you'll use them to learn how to do everything with e-mail.

Part II

Communication

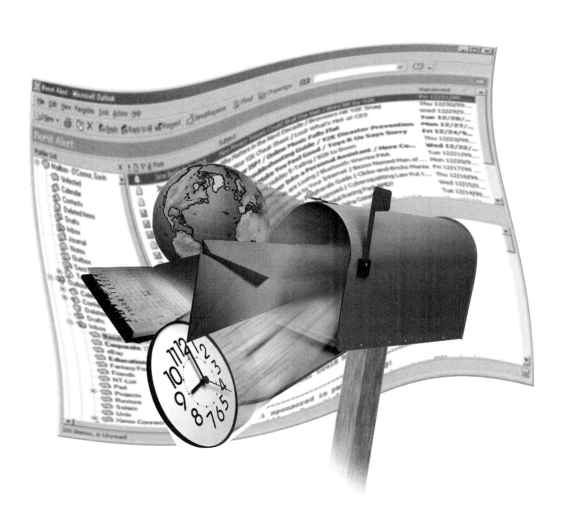

Chapter 3

Making Contacts

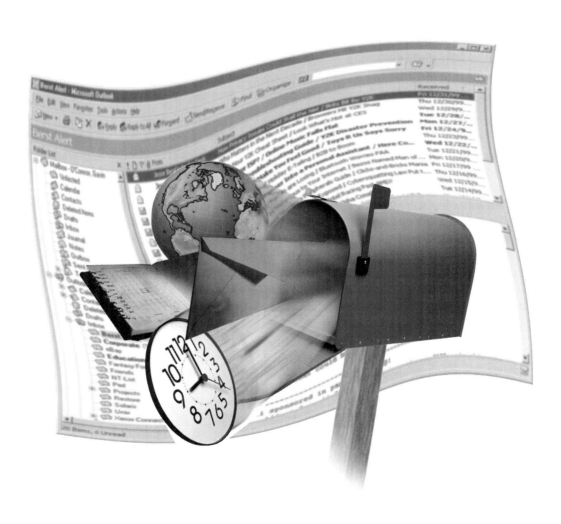

How to . . .

- Create a Contact List
- Create Distribution Lists
- Look Up Contact Information
- Organize Your Contacts List
- Create Special Contacts Subfolders
- Print a Portable Phone List
- Get the Company's Global Address Book
- Dial a Contact on Your Speakerphone

Outlook performs a lot of information management functions, but it's primarily a communications tool. Essential to communication is a list of who you're communicating with, and in Outlook, the "who" list is stored in the Contacts folder.

You can keep your contacts information as simple as names, e-mail addresses, and phone numbers, or you can keep track of details such as birthdays and names of family members. You can even create your own custom fields to track things such as Employee Number or Region (any details you want to keep track of that Microsoft didn't create a built-in field for). All of these details come in handy when you want to filter out a specific group of contacts for phone calls, meetings, or mail-merge letters.

The procedure for which you'll probably use Contacts most often is to address your e-mail messages. After you enter a contact, you simply have to look up their name in a list, and their e-mail address is entered automatically and correctly (no more looking up and typing nonsensical e-mail addresses, and getting them returned because of an inadvertent typing mistake). After you learn how to enter contacts in this chapter, you'll learn how to use them to send e-mail in the next chapter.

Create a Contact List

A *contact* is a person or an organization that you want to keep detailed information about. You can keep a record of just about any information you have about the person or organization, from the most basic facts (name and phone number) to very detailed information (multiple e-mail addresses, phone/mobile/pager numbers, hobbies, and anniversaries).

If you have a set of contacts already entered electronically in another program, such as an Excel worksheet or a contact manager like ACT, you don't have to reenter them; you can import the whole group into contacts. In Chapter 16, you'll learn how to import data from other files.

To start this chapter off right, open the Contacts folder (the quickest way is to click the Contacts icon in the Outlook bar). If contacts are already in your Contacts folder, it'll look something like Figure 3-1. If you just installed Outlook for the first time, you may have no contacts or you may have a single contact with your name in it. Either way, your folder will be full of contacts soon enough.

The *view*, or layout, of the contacts in Figure 3-1 is called a *card view*, and it's particularly efficient because you can see all the details for any contact in one place (no scrolling through a table to locate a phone number). The cards are arranged in alphabetical order, and you can scroll through them with the horizontal scroll

Open Contacts

Enter a new contact

Jump to alphabetical listing

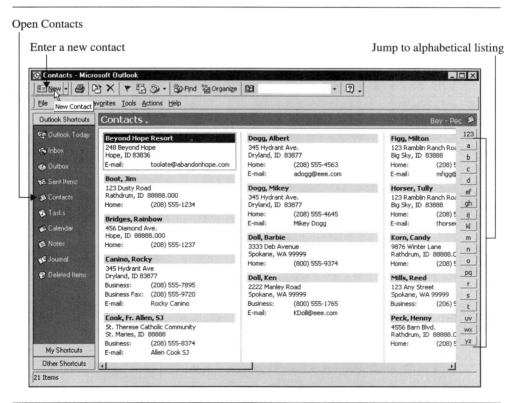

FIGURE 3-1   Contacts in Address Cards view

bar at the bottom of the Outlook window, or you can jump to a specific point in the alphabetical list by clicking an alphabet button on the right side of the window.

The card view in Figure 3-1, called the *Address Cards* view, doesn't show all the details that are entered for each contact. It shows only the most used details (addresses, phone numbers, and e-mail addresses), and it can be rearranged to show more or fewer details, or just the details you want to see. You'll learn how to change the view later in this chapter. Meanwhile, you'll learn how to create your own contacts.

Enter a New Contact

You enter a contact's information in a dialog box that's sometimes called a form and sometimes called a dialog box; in this book, it's called a dialog box, for consistency. To open a new Contact dialog box, open the Contacts folder and then do one of these things:

- Click the New button on the left end of the toolbar.
- Double-click an empty space in the main Contacts pane.
- Right-click an empty space in the main Contacts pane and click New Contact.
- Choose File | New | Contact using your mouse or keyboard.
- Press CTRL-N.

A new, untitled Contact dialog box like the one in Figure 3-2 appears.

 *Even if you're working in a different Outlook folder, you can always create a new contact by choosing File | New | Contact from the menu.*

Most of the contacts you create will only need input on the General tab in the Contact dialog box.

Names

Names, job titles, and companies are the details you use to identify a contact. Start by typing the contact's full name in the Full Name box. Most names are easy for Outlook to figure out, but it has trouble with some, in which case you can click the Full Name button to make sure Outlook understands the name. In the Check Full Name

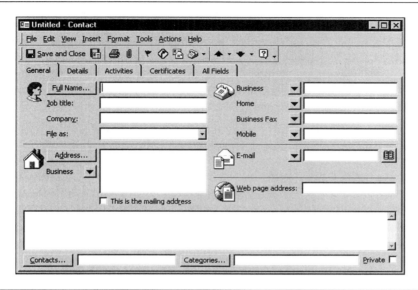

FIGURE 3-2   Create a new contact

dialog box, you can correct any misunderstandings on Outlook's part (sometimes Outlook shows you this dialog box unprompted, because it needs clarification).

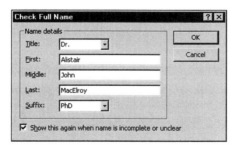

Outlook has a limited number of common titles (Mr., Miss, and so forth) and common suffixes (Jr., III, and so on) built in, but you're not limited to those. If you need to enter a title, such as Rev. or Hon., type it in the Title box; if you need to enter an uncommon suffix (such as VIII or PhD), type it in the Suffix box.

After you type the name and press ENTER or TAB (or click in another box), a potential filing name appears in the File As box. Outlook uses the File As name to find the contact a place in the list's alphabetical order, and the File As name is what you see in the gray bar at the top of each contact's card in the Contacts window.

If you don't like Outlook's File As name, you can choose an alternative from the File As list box or, better yet, type exactly what you want.

If you know the contact's job title and company name, enter them in the appropriate boxes. After you enter a company name, you'll find more File As alternatives in the File As list box.

If you can remember the company name more easily than the individual's name, use the company name, with the individual name in parentheses, in the File As box. That way, you'll be able to locate the contact quickly.

Addresses

You can store up to three addresses for a contact: a Home address, a Business address, and an Other address. Type the address in the Address box.

As with the Name entry, sometimes the addresses you type aren't clear to Outlook. To make sure that each part of the address is in the correct field, you can click the Address button and check (sometimes the Check Address dialog box opens on its own, because Outlook doesn't understand what you entered). It's important that each part of the address be in the correct field so that you can sort, group, or filter your Contacts list on a specific field, such as City or State.

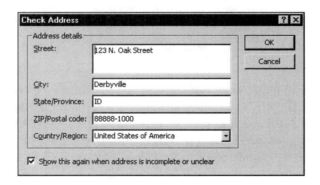

 *When you enter an address, enter the state as a two-letter abbreviation, in uppercase letters (such as WY or MN). If you open a contact and click the Display Map Of Address button on the contact toolbar, the Microsoft Expedia Web site search engine will have difficulty with states entered in any format other than two-letter, uppercase format.*

In the Check Address dialog box, you can select a different country from the Country/Region list box (which ensures that it's spelled correctly). If you don't select a country, Outlook assumes you want to use the default country that's set in your computer's Windows Regional Settings, in Control Panel, which is probably the country you live in (unless you just moved to a new country and haven't changed your Windows Regional setup yet).

 *If the words are spelled right but are in the wrong fields, you can use your mouse to select and drag the words from one field to another.*

Phone Numbers

The General tab of the Contact dialog box displays four phone number boxes in which you can enter phone numbers, as shown in Figure 3-3, but 19 phone number fields are available. For example, if your contact has no mobile phone number, but gives you a pager number, click the drop-down arrow next to Mobile and click Pager; then, enter the pager number in the box next to the label. Later, when you glance at the contact's card in your Contacts folder, that number will be labeled Pager.

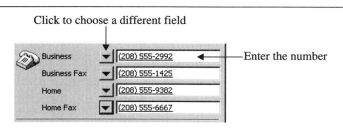

FIGURE 3-3   Four phone numbers are displayed, but 19 fields are available

You can enter phone numbers in all 19 phone number fields, but only 4 at a time will be displayed on the General tab. To enter a fifth phone number, select a new field label for any of the phone number boxes and type the corresponding number in the number box (and do the same for the sixth through nineteenth phone numbers, if your contact has that many). To display one of the many phone numbers you entered, click any drop-down arrow and select the field for the number you want to see. The following is an example of a contact who has eight phone numbers; I can select which one I want displayed in that phone number box.

When you enter a phone number, don't type the punctuation. Type only the digits.

2085552992

Outlook inserts the correct punctuation.

(208) 555-2992

If you include an area code, Outlook includes the area code correctly; if you type a local number without an area code, Outlook inserts your local area code. If you don't type the correct number of digits (either 7 or 10), you'll see a Check Phone Number dialog box, in which you can correct what you typed.

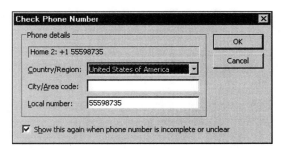

If you're entering an international phone number, double-click in the phone number box and use the Check Phone Number dialog box. In the Country/Region list box, select the country, and Outlook enters the correct country code at the beginning of the number (no more looking them up!).

If you don't get the phone number entered correctly even after using the Check Phone Number dialog box, start over: select the number in the box, press DELETE, and type it again.

 *If a contact gives you a phone number with an extension, type the number, then a space, then x, and then the extension, like this: **8005551234 x765**, which becomes (800) 555-1234 x765 after you exit the field, or press TAB or ENTER.*

3

E-Mail Addresses

You can enter up to three e-mail addresses for each contact, and they're labeled E-mail, E-mail 2, and E-mail 3. All e-mail addresses consist of three parts: a *user name* (the contact's individual identifier, such as JKelly or bossguy or whatever clever name the contact uses); the @ symbol; and the *host.domain name,* which is the address of the mail server where your contact has their mailbox. There might also be *subdomain names,* in between the host and domain name, but all you really need to know is that whatever e-mail address someone gives you, you need to enter the entire thing, spelled precisely the way they tell you.

 *You'll commonly see e-mail addresses that end in .com, .edu, .gov, .mil, .net, and .org. These are domain names that indicate servers that are (in order) commercial, educational, government, military, commercial network access, and nonprofit organizations.*

To enter a contact's e-mail address, click in the E-mail box and type the address exactly the way it was given to you. To enter a second or third e-mail address, click the drop-down arrow and choose a different E-mail field name, and then enter the e-mail address exactly as it was given to you.

If Outlook doesn't like the address you entered, the address won't be accepted and you'll be told to enter it again. (Sometimes, the error is something as simple as typing a comma instead of a period, or forgetting the @ symbol.)

 *CompuServe addresses have commas, and they work within the CompuServe system but not on the Internet. If someone gives you a CompuServe address that looks like 76543,1234, you need to enter it as 76543.1234@ compuserve.com.*

If you try to send someone an e-mail message and you get a User Unknown message in return, check the spelling of the e-mail name—and reenter it *exactly* the way it was given to you (except for CompuServe addresses, of course).

Web Page Addresses

If your contact has a home page on the Web, enter it in the Web Page Address

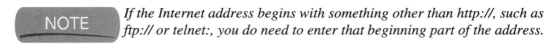 field so that you can surf directly to the Web site from the Contact dialog box. If it's an address on the Web, it begins with *http://*, but you don't need to enter that part; just type the part that begins after the two slash marks.

NOTE *If the Internet address begins with something other than http://, such as ftp:// or telnet:, you do need to enter that beginning part of the address.*

After you enter the Web address and click away from the box (or press ENTER

or TAB), Outlook inserts the http:// part, underlines the address, and makes the address blue; this means the address is now a hyperlink, so you can launch your browser and open the Web site by clicking the hyperlink.

After you create the hyperlink, you cannot click it to correct a misspelling (because when you click it, your browser launches). If you need to edit or change the hyperlink, right-click it and click Select All; then, retype the whole thing, or press DELETE to erase it.

Categories

You can apply as many categories as you want to an individual contact, to help you group and filter them into useful groupings later. To apply categories, click the Categories button to open the Categories dialog box. Then, mark check boxes for each category you want to apply to that contact, and click OK.

You can learn more about how to use categories in Chapter 2.

Privacy, Comments, and More Details

If your contacts are shared in a public folder on a network, you can keep specific contacts (such as private clients, your doctor, or your grandmother) hidden from others who have access to the public Contacts folder. Mark the Private box to keep a contact to yourself.

If you have miscellaneous comments about a contact (perhaps the date of a conversation and a few proposed contractual details, or the weekdays when they're in the office), enter them in the big box that has no label.

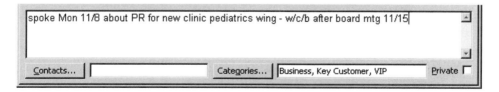

You can enter more details, such as a nickname, birthday, or assistant's name, on the Details tab, shown in Figure 3-4. After you enter all the detailed information you have about this contact, click the Save And Close button.

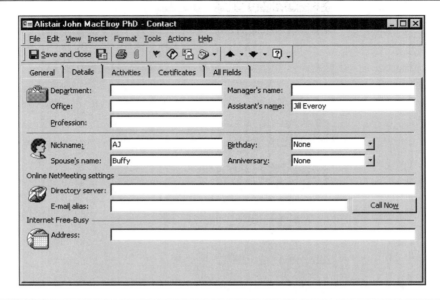

FIGURE 3-4   Enter more details on the Details tab

Group-Related Contacts

Later in this chapter, you'll learn how to switch views and group your contacts in useful ways. One useful grouping setup is to relate several contacts to a single primary contact, so that when you group by the Contacts field, all the related contacts appear in a single group in the list. You'll see this in action in the section "Group By Related Contacts," but before you can group them, you have to specify the related contacts. Start by opening or creating your primary contact (any name in your proposed set of related contacts is fine), and then click the Contacts button.

If you have just created the contact, you need to save it before you can add related contacts to it—click File | Save to save the new contact without closing it.

In the Select Contacts dialog box, click all the names of related contacts you want to be able to group (perhaps all of your contacts for a current project). Click the first name and then press CTRL while you click the remaining names. Then click OK; the names appear next to the Contacts button and will be useful if you organize your list by grouping.

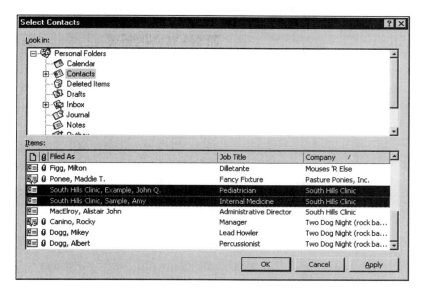

Add Another Contact from the Same Company

If you created at least one contact from a company and you have more contacts at the same company (same address, phone numbers, and so forth), you don't need to retype all the same company information. Instead, you can create a new contact with all that company information filled in automatically.

In the Contacts window, click the card for a contact at the company. Then, click Actions | New Contact From Same Company.

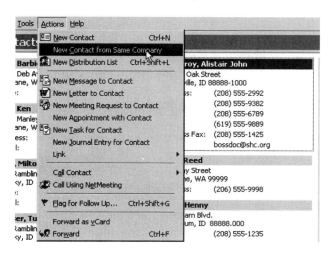

Fill in the individual details, and then save and close the dialog box.

Open a Contact

After you create and save a contact, you'll occasionally want to edit or add information or look up those notes to yourself that you typed in the big notes box.

To open a contact, double-click it. You can open more than one contact at a time, and switch between them easily by clicking their buttons on the Windows taskbar.

Delete a Contact

To delete a contact, you can do any one of these things:

- Right-click the contact and then click Delete.

- Click the contact and then click the Delete button on the Standard toolbar.

- Click the contact and then press the DELETE key.

- Click the contact and then choose Edit | Delete.

- Click the contact and then press CTRL-D.

You can delete a single contact, or delete several simultaneously by selecting them all before deleting them. Use the SHIFT key to select an adjacent list of contacts, or use the CTRL key to select nonadjacent contacts.

Create Distribution Lists

If you're working on a team or committee, you may find yourself addressing e-mail to the same group of people repeatedly. You can save yourself time by addressing messages to a single distribution list instead.

A *distribution list* is a group of contacts you can send an e-mail message to by addressing the message to a single name. Everyone in the distribution list gets the same message, and you don't have to click, click, click to add them all (or inadvertently forget someone).

To create a distribution list, do this:

1. Start in the Contacts window and click File | New | Distribution List.

2. In the Distribution List dialog box, type a name for the list and then click the Select Members button.

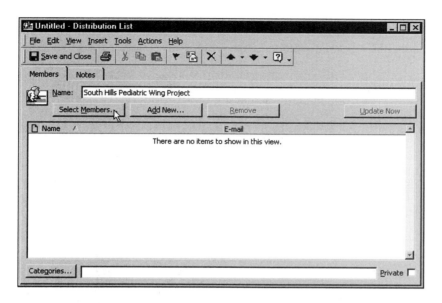

3. In the Select Members dialog box, double-click each contact name you want to add to your list, and then click OK.

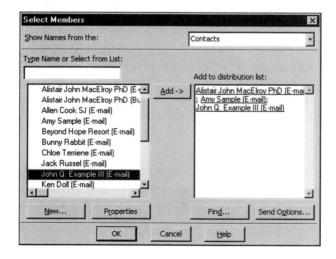

NOTE   *If you don't see any names, you may be operating in Corporate/Workgroup mode without an address book set up. See the next section, "Internet Mail Only vs. Corporate/Workgroup Setup," to learn how to set up an address book.*

4. If you haven't forgotten anyone, click Save And Close. You can use the list name like any other contact name when you send an e-mail message.

If the list of names changes, you'll need to change your distribution list. Start in the Contacts window, by double-clicking the distribution list name to open it.

Then do any of the following:

■ To add more members from your Contacts list, click the Select Members button; double-click contact names and then click OK.

■ To add new members who aren't in your Contacts list yet, click the Add New button; type their names and e-mail addresses in the appropriate boxes, click the Add To Contacts check box if you want to add them to your Contacts list also, and then click OK.

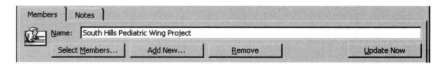

■ To remove a name from the distribution list, click the name in the Distribution List dialog box and then click the Remove button.

■ If someone's e-mail address changes, the list doesn't change automatically—you need to open and update it yourself. After you change the contact's e-mail address in your Contacts list, open the distribution list and click the Update Now button. All the names in the list are updated with any changed information (such as e-mail addresses).

When you're finished making changes, click the Save And Close button.

3

Internet Mail Only vs. Corporate/Workgroup Setup

If you have a standalone computer and Outlook is set up as Internet Mail Only, your Contacts list will be automatically available and you never need to think about profiles and address books. If your company's network administrators set up Outlook for you, they probably took care of the profile/address book business for you, and you don't need to worry about it. But, if you're setting up Outlook in Corporate/Workgroup mode yourself (and therefore are your own network administrator), you need to set up an address book before your contacts will be available to do any work for you. (*Hint:* If you try to create a distribution list or address an e-mail message but don't see your contacts' names, you need to set up an address book.)

> TIP
> *How can you tell whether you're working in Internet Mail Only or Corporate/Workgroup configuration? In Outlook, click Help | About Microsoft Outlook. A line at the top of the dialog box tells you Outlook's configuration.*

So, if you're working in Corporate/Workgroup configuration and haven't set up an address book yet, here's how you do it:

1. In Outlook, click Tools | Services.

2. In the Services dialog box, on the Services tab, click a profile (click your default profile—if you can click the Properties button and get a Properties dialog box, then the profile that's selected is fine).

3. Click the Add button.

4. In the Add Service To Profile dialog box, select Outlook Address Book and then click OK.

5. Click OK to close the Exit And Log Off message.

6. Click OK to close the Services dialog box.

7. In Outlook, click File | Exit And Log Off. Outlook closes.

8. Start Outlook again, and your contacts will be available wherever you need to use e-mail addresses (such as in e-mail messages and in distribution lists).

About Address Books

If you have an Internet Mail Only configuration, address books are easy—you have your Contacts folder and that's all you need. But if you're working in a Corporate/Workgroup configuration, address books are messy:

- **Outlook Address Book** automatically makes the contacts in your Contacts folder available to e-mail messages and distribution lists (but only those names that have e-mail addresses entered). To make the contacts in subfolders available, open the Folder list and right-click the subfolder name. Click Properties, and on the Outlook Address Book tab, mark the check box to Show This Folder As An E-mail Address Book. Then, click Apply, and click OK.

- **Personal Address Book** is a holdover from pre-Outlook days and contains any contacts you had if your computer used Exchange for mail before you upgraded to Outlook. If your copy of Outlook 2000 is freshly installed on a new computer, you may not need this at all (but if you want it, add it by following the same procedure as for the Outlook Address Book).

- **Global Address Book** is a list of all the e-mail addresses in your company that is maintained by the network administrator on the company server. It's available to everyone on the server (but you have to download it). See the section "Get the Company's Global Address Book," at the end of this chapter, to learn how.

Look Up Contact Information

If your Contacts list is short, you can find any contact yourself; but, when your list gets really long, you can search for names, instead.

Find It Yourself

When your contacts are displayed in the card view, you can locate a specific contact by jumping to the correct point in the alphabetical listing and then scrolling to bring the correct card into view.

Jump into the alphabetical listing by clicking a button on the right side of the Contacts window; scroll through the cards by using the horizontal scroll bar at the bottom of the Contacts window.

Conduct a Search

3

But, what if you can't remember a last name—just the first name, or just part of the name, like "van"-something? You can let Contacts do the searching for you.

Use the Find a Contact Box

The Contacts window's Standard toolbar has an unlabeled list box named Find A Contact (it searches the Full Name and File As fields only, so don't try to find a street name or city in this way). Type at least part of a first name or last name in the Find A Contact box and then press ENTER.

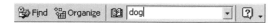

If a single contact fits the search characters, that contact opens. If more than one contact fits the search characters, a Choose Contact dialog box opens; double-click the likely contact to open it.

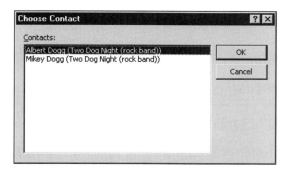

If you can't remember anything about the name but remember the city, or part of the company name, you can use the Find button to search, or switch to a table-type view and use sorting, grouping, or filtering to look for the bit you can remember.

Use the Find Button

Another button on the Standard toolbar, called Find, lets you search all the text in each contact entry (so, if all you remember is the company or the street name, you can still search for the contact). Click the Find button, and a Find Items In Contacts pane opens above your main Contacts pane.

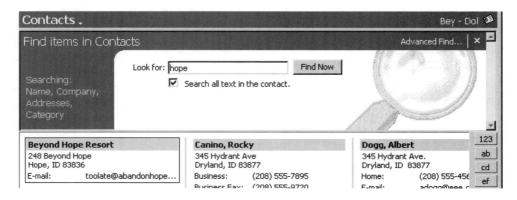

Type the bit you can remember in the Look For box and then click the Find Now button. Your Contacts list is filtered to show only the contacts that fit the search criteria.

If the search results don't give you the contact you're looking for, you can try again—click the Clear Search option that appears below the Look For box (or delete the existing characters in the Look For box), type a new text string in the Look For box, and click Find Now again.

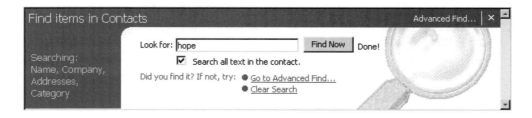

If you need to conduct a more specific search (such as contacts whose street address is "oak"-something), click the Go To Advanced Find option. The Advanced Find dialog box is exactly like the Filter dialog box, and works by filtering your list using criteria you set. You can learn how to use the Advanced Find dialog box in the "Filtering" section in Chapter 2.

To close the Find Items In Contacts pane, click the X in its upper-right corner.

Organize Your Contacts List

By default, your contacts are laid out in a card-type view, because that's usually the easiest way to use them. There are lots of table-type views, however, and for some tasks, a table view is easier to use. A more detailed card view also is available, and you can customize any of these views (and save them with custom names) so that you can quickly switch to whatever view is most useful for the task at hand.

Change the Card View Layout

Does your card view show you all the fields you want to see about your contacts? Or, does it show you too many fields when all you really want to see are names with all their phone numbers? You can change the layout of the card view to see just what you want. If you change a built-in layout, the changes are semipermanent; that is, the layout stays changed until you change it again or reset it to the original layout. If you want the benefit of being able to switch between custom views without having to re-create them each time, you can save your changed layout with a custom view name. Next, you'll learn how to change your layouts, and how to save your changes as custom views.

Add or Remove Fields from Cards

If you want to add or remove fields from your contact's cards (such as specific phone numbers, second e-mail addresses, and so on), this is how you do it:

1. Right-click an empty space in the Contacts main pane and then click Customize Current View. (Or you can choose View | Current View | Customize Current View.)

2. In the View Summary dialog box, click the Fields button. The Show Fields dialog box, shown in Figure 3-5, appears. The fields that are available for display are listed on the left, and the fields that are currently displayed are listed on the right.

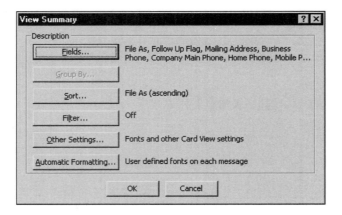

TIP

You can also open the Show Fields dialog box quickly by right-clicking an empty space in the Contacts pane and clicking Show Fields on the shortcut menu.

Double-click to add field   Double-click to remove field

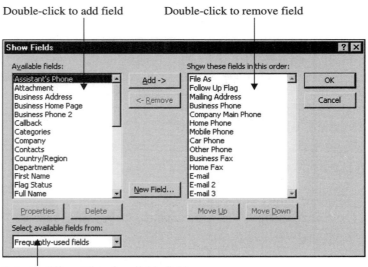

Select a different list of available fields

   Change the card display

3. In the Available Fields list, double-click the fields you want to add to your card display.

4. In the Show These Fields In This Order list, double-click fields you want to remove from the card display. For example, to create a names-and-phone-numbers card view, add the Full Name field and all the phone number fields, and remove all the other fields.

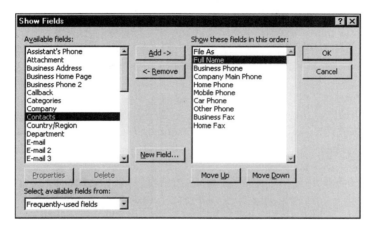

 *Earlier in this chapter, you learned how to add related contacts to a primary contact. To put the concept of related contacts to work, you can add the Contacts field to your card display, and all the related contacts' names will appear in the primary contact's card.*

Change the Displayed Field Order

Now that you have only the fields you want listed on the right, you can rearrange the order of the displayed fields, like this:

1. Click a field in the list on the right and then click the Move Up or Move Down button to move the field to a different position in the card.

2. Click OK twice to close both dialog boxes.

Save Your Changed Layout

The following is a custom view—just names and phone numbers—that I saved with the name Quick Cards. When you save a custom view, you can switch to it any time with just a few clicks or key presses. If you want to save a custom view, here's how:

1. Be sure the view you want to save is displayed in the Contacts window.

2. Choose View | Current View | Define Views.

3. In the Define Views For "Contacts" dialog box, shown in Figure 3-6, be sure that Current View Settings (at the top of the list) is selected and then click the Copy button.

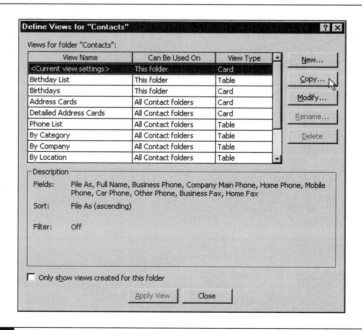

FIGURE 3-6   Save a custom view

4. In the Copy View dialog box, type a name for your custom view. If you create subfolders for your contacts (which you'll learn how to do later in this chapter), you can click the All Contact Folders option so you can switch to this view in your subfolders, too. Then click OK.

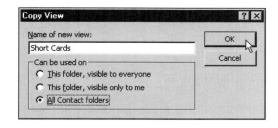

5. In the Define Views dialog box, click Close.

Your custom view is now available on a list of all the Contacts folder views.

Delete a Custom View

To delete a custom view, choose View | Current View | Define Views, and click the name of the custom view you want to delete. Then, click the Delete button and then click OK when asked if you're sure that you want to delete it.

You can delete and rename custom views, but not built-in views. Built-in views can be changed, however, by using the procedures previously described, and can also be reset to their original displays. When you click a view name in the Define Views dialog box, the buttons will change to show only what you're allowed to do with that view.

Change the Card Width

A quick way to see a card's details more fully, or to see more cards by partially hiding details, is to change the card width. You can make it narrower, to show  your cards in a dozen unreadable columns, or you can make the cards wide enough to show every detail completely, and the cards take up a single wide column in the Contacts main pane.

To change card width, point to one of the vertical borders between cards, and drag left or right until the view is exactly what you need.

Switch Views

Now that you've created custom views, you can switch between them and the built-in views rapidly.

Use the View Menu to Switch

Click the View menu, point to Current View, and click the name of the view you want.

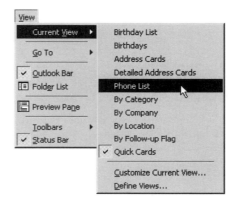

Some of the listed views are card views and some are table views; all the table views except for Phone List are pregrouped by a specific field. You can group table views yourself (the Phone List view is a good view to group because it's not pregrouped) using the grouping techniques explained in Chapter 2.

Use the Toolbar to Switch

The Advanced toolbar has a list box called Current View. If you switch views a lot (in any of Outlook's folders), this is a handy list box.

To switch views, select a view name from the Current View drop-down list box.

Use Grouped Views

A useful thing that you can do with grouped views is to transfer contacts between groups by dragging the entries from one group to another.

For example, if folks in your industry tend to change companies a lot, you can switch your display to By Company, and then quickly switch a contact from one company to another by dragging the contact from one company group to another.

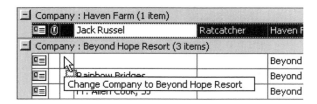

This technique works in all the grouped views.

Create Special Contacts Subfolders

All of your contacts are maintained in the Contacts folder, in one long list; but, what if you want to segregate your personal contacts from your business contacts? Or maybe you have contacts for a specific project and you want to be able to send faxes or mail-merge letters to the whole group without having to pick through the long list and select them each time.

Create a Subfolder

You can create subfolders for your Contacts folder, as many as you want, and you can quickly move or copy contacts between subfolders and the main folder. Better yet, you can create Outlook bar shortcuts to your subfolders (or leave them hidden in the Folder list).

NOTE *The procedure for creating subfolders is the same in all of Outlook's folders (not just Contacts).*

You create, rename, move, and delete subfolders using the Folder list. This is how:

1. Open the Folder list. Either click View | Folder List, or click the folder name in the Folder Banner and then click the pushpin to hold the Folder list open.

2. Right-click the name of the folder in which you want to create the subfolder, and click New Folder from the shortcut menu.

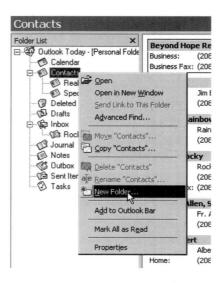

3. In the Create New Folder dialog box, type a name for your subfolder in the Name box.

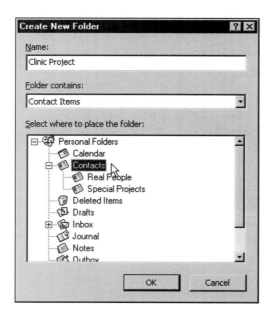

4. In the Folder Contains box, be sure the right type of item is shown, because each Outlook folder is designed to contain specific item types.

5. In the Select Where To Place The Folder list, click the name of the folder in which you want the subfolder to be kept. You can keep a subfolder in a main folder or in another subfolder, or create a new main folder by clicking the Personal Folders folder at the top of the list.

6. Click OK. You may see a message like the following, asking whether you want to add a shortcut icon to the Outlook bar. If you click Yes, a shortcut icon to the subfolder is added to your My Shortcuts group in the Outlook bar; if you click No, the new folder will be reachable only from the Folder list. If you mark the check box, you won't ever be asked about this again.

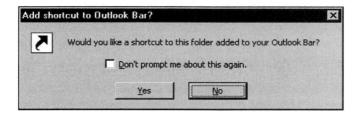

NOTE *In Chapter 15 you'll learn more about customizing your Outlook bar groups and shortcut icons.*

Move or Copy Contacts to the Subfolder

Now that you have a new subfolder, you need to put some contacts into it. You can move contacts if you want them in completely separate groups, or you can copy contacts so that the subfolder is a subgroup of the main folder.

To move or copy contacts from one folder to another:

1. Open the Folder list.

2. Show both the folder names (click the small plus symbol next to a main folder name to show its subfolders).

3. Click the name of the folder where the contacts are currently stored.

4. Select one or more contacts that you want to move, and drag them to the Folder list. If you want to move the contacts, just drag them with the left mouse button; if you want to copy them, drag them with the right mouse button.

5. Drop them on the name of the folder where you want to move them. If you dragged with the right mouse button, click Move or Copy on the shortcut menu.

Make the Contacts Subfolder Available As an Address Book

If you work in an Internet Mail Only configuration, all of your Contacts subfolders are always available, so you can ignore this section. But, if you work in a Corporate/Workgroup configuration, you have to do one more thing to make your Contacts subfolders available in your address books (for creating distribution lists and addressing e-mail messages):

1. Open the Folder list and right-click the subfolder name.

2. Click Properties, and click the Outlook Address Book tab.

3. On the Outlook Address Book tab, mark the check box to Show This Folder As An E-mail Address Book.

4. Click Apply, and click OK.

Now, when you create a distribution list or address an e-mail message, you can select the subfolder name in the Show Names From The address books list box.

Print a Portable Phone List

You'll learn a lot more about printing in Chapter 13, but here you'll learn how to quickly print an easy-to-use paper phone list, like the one shown in Figure 3-7, that you can use to find phone numbers for your contacts even when you're away from your computer.

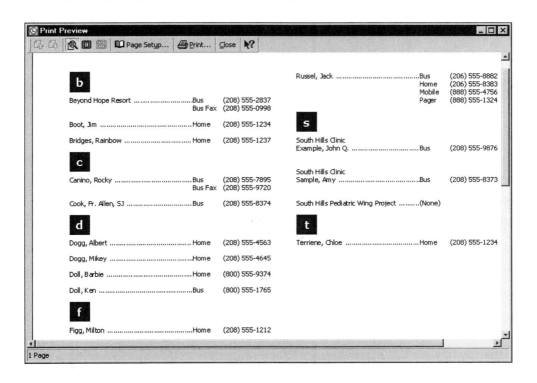

FIGURE 3-7 A phone list that's quick to print

If you want to print this phone list, here's how:

1. Open the Contacts folder or subfolder that has the contacts you want to print (only the contacts in the open folder will be included in the list).
2. Click File | Print.

3. In the Print dialog box, under Print Style, scroll down and select Phone Directory Style.

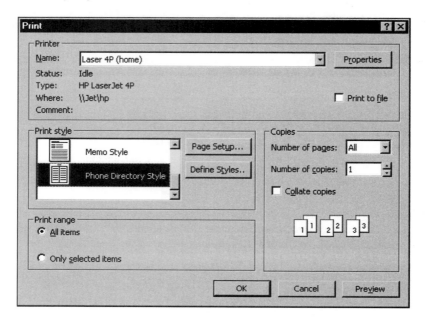

4. Click the Preview button to see what it will look like (it's always more efficient to preview before you print).

5. On the Print Preview toolbar, click the Print button.

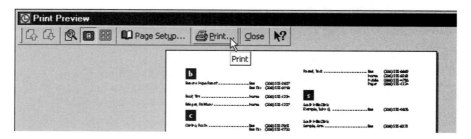

6. In the Print dialog box, click OK.

Get the Company's Global Address Book

This applies only if you're running Outlook in Corporate/Workgroup configuration, your company uses Microsoft Exchange Server as a mail server, and your network administrator maintains a Global Address Book on the company server. To copy the Global Address Book to your computer so that you can use those company addresses, click Tools | Synchronize | Download Address Book.

Dial a Contact on Your Speakerphone

Last but not least is something fun—you can have Outlook telephone your contacts for you! (Of course, you have to have the speaker and microphone hardware in your computer to do this, or have your telephone line running through your computer to your telephone.)

NOTE

You'll be talking on your computer's phone line, which is probably the same one you use for Internet access—so, don't plan on sending e-mail or surfing the Web while you talk on the speakerphone (get a headset telephone for your voice line instead).

1. Open your Contacts folder and right-click the contact you want to call.

2. On the shortcut menu, click Call Contact. The New Call dialog box appears. If you want to record the length of this call in Journal, click the Create New Journal Entry When Starting New Call check box before you call (you'll learn how to use Journal in Chapter 11).

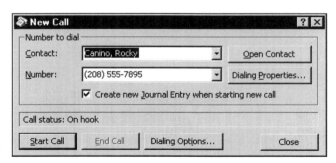

3. Make sure the correct number is shown in the Number box; if this contact has more than one number, select the correct one from the Number list box.

4. Click the Start Call button. The Call Status dialog box appears.

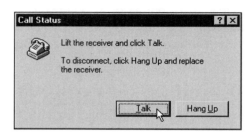

5. Lift the handset on your telephone and then click the Talk button. You'll hear the telephone being dialed like a normal telephone call. (If you're using your computer speakerphone system to make the call, see your system instructions about how to make voice calls.)

6. When you're finished, click End Call and then hang up the phone.

7. Click Close to close the New Call dialog box. If you created a Journal entry for the call, click Pause Timer to stop the clock when you hang up, and then click Save And Close to close the Journal entry.

That's it for this chapter. Now that you know how to create contacts, enter lots of them so that they'll be ready to send e-mail to. In the next chapter, you'll learn the basics of how to send e-mail from Outlook.

Chapter 4

Creating, Sending, and Reading E-Mail

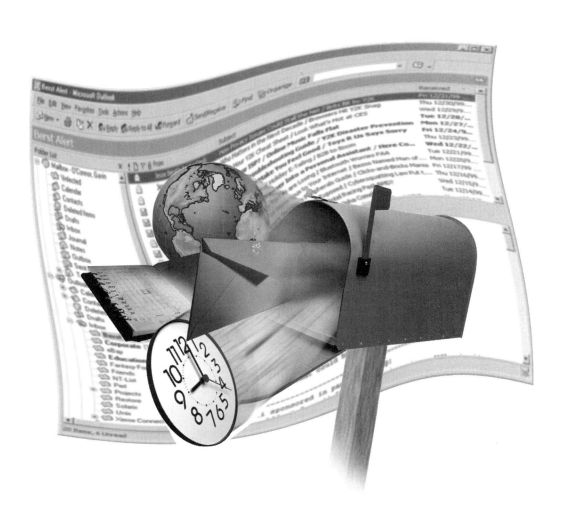

How to . . .

■ Create e-mail messages

■ Set e-mail message formats

■ Address e-mail messages

■ Send copies and blind copies of e-mail messages

■ Send e-mail messages

■ Receive e-mail messages

■ Reply to e-mail messages

■ Forward e-mail messages

■ Create message signatures

■ Create and send vCards

E-mail has changed the face of communication all over the world. More and more these days, if you don't have e-mail, you're out of the loop.

With Outlook, your e-mail communications can be as simple or as elaborate as you want them to be. In this chapter, you'll learn how to handle simple communications, such as creating, sending, receiving, replying to, and forwarding e-mail messages. You'll also learn how to use Outlook's e-mail bells and whistles, such as formatting your messages, tracking message delivery, and adding automatic signatures.

Creating Messages

The essential elements of creating an e-mail message are simple:

1. Open your Inbox, and then click the New button on the toolbar.

2. Enter an e-mail address in the To box, and type a few identifying words in the Subject line.

3. Type your message in the large message box, and click the Send button.

But, because this book is titled *How to Do Everything with Outlook 2000,* the rest of this chapter will show you how to use Outlook to create, format, send, receive, reply to, forward, and keep track of e-mail.

Create a Message

You've got contacts in your Contacts folder and words to share, so it's time to send e-mail. With Outlook, you can do more than merely send words—you can send words that have impact, because you can format them to look professional or threatening or clever, and you can send copies to as many people as you need to. You can mark messages as important (so they'll be read right away) or as private (so your recipient won't open the message when someone is standing over their shoulder).

Start a New Message

To start a new e-mail message, do any of these things:

- Open your Inbox, and then click the New button on the left end of the toolbar.

- Open any Outlook folder, click the down arrow next to the New button, and click Mail Message.

- Click File | New | Mail Message.

- In the Inbox, press CTRL-N.

- In any Outlook folder, press CTRL-SHIFT-M.

A new mail message like the one in Figure 4-1 appears.

Before you plunge into writing and addressing the new message, glance at the message format in the title bar and consider whether all of your recipients will be able to read it. There are three mail formats to choose from:

- **Plain Text** has no formatting at all, and is readable by any and all e-mail programs.

- **Rich Text** can be formatted like a Word document, with colors, bold text, different fonts, bullet lists, indents, and all that good stuff. Be careful with this—some older e-mail programs can't read Rich Text, and get a long message full of garbage characters.

- **HTML** is a Web page format and can include anything that can be placed on a Web page. Only the newest e-mail programs can read HTML format, so you're safest spending time formatting HTML messages that are going to others within your company's mail system. Recipients outside your company may have trouble reading them.

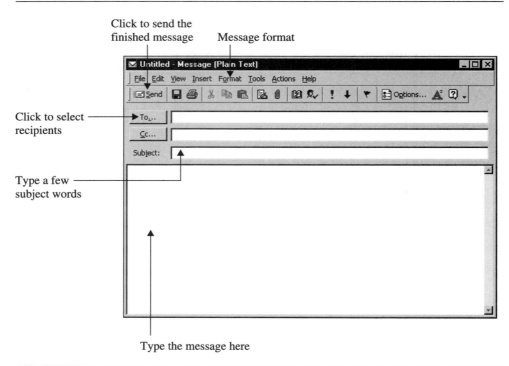

Click to send the
finished message   Message format

Click to select
recipients

Type a few
subject words

Type the message here

FIGURE 4-1   Create a new mail message

Select a Mail Format

You can set any of the three formats as your default message format, so that you'll only need to change the format occasionally, when you know a specific recipient wants messages to arrive in a different format than what you use as your default. When you need to change the format for a specific recipient, you can change the format for the new message when you create it.

SET THE DEFAULT MESSAGE FORMAT   To set the default message format:

1. Click Tools | Options, and click the Mail Format tab.

2. Under Message Format, select the format you want in the Send In This Message Format list box, and then click OK.

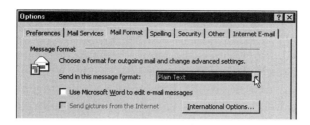

4

The other formatting options on the Mail Format tab change depending on the format that you select. For example, you can send Web-page-style pictures in your messages only if you use the HTML message format (and mark the Send Pictures From The Internet check box).

If you correspond with folks in a language other than English, and you have that language installed on your computer, click the International Options button and choose the language you want to send and receive messages in.

CHANGE THE FORMAT FOR A MESSAGE WHEN YOU CREATE IT   If you need to send a specific message in a format other than your default message format, you can switch that message to a different format, like this:

1. Create a new message.

2. On the message's menu bar, click Format.

3. Click the format you want.

SWITCH BETWEEN HTML AND RICH TEXT   You can switch a single message from Plain Text to either Rich Text or HTML, but you can't switch directly between Rich Text and HTML. So, what if your default format is HTML and you want to send a message in Rich Text format? Here's how (do this before you enter your message so you won't lose any work): First, switch the message to Plain Text format. Then switch to HTML. And if you want to switch from Rich Text to HTML, do the same thing—switch to Plain Text and then switch to HTML.

Entering E-Mail Addresses

Who are you sending the message to? The easiest way to address e-mail messages is to enter names from your Contacts folder, because the e-mail addresses are entered automatically (no inadvertent typing mistakes).

You can address e-mail by typing the recipient's e-mail address in the To box, and add the address to Contacts at the same time. After you type the address, move out of the To box; after the address is underlined (meaning Outlook recognizes it as an e-mail address), right-click the address and click Add To Contacts. A contact dialog box opens with the e-mail address filled in—finish the contact information and then click Save And Close. You'll never have to look up and type the e-mail address again.

USE AUTONAME   If you know that your recipient's name is in your Contacts folder, the fastest way to address a message to them is to have AutoName turned on. With AutoName turned on, you can click in the To box and type the name (first name, last name, partial name, whatever comes to mind), and then move out of the To box. Outlook looks up the name and enters it, underlined and in black, in the To box.

To turn AutoName on or off, click Tools | Options, and on the Preferences tab, click the E-mail Options button. Then click the Advanced E-mail Options button, and then mark or clear the Automatic Name Checking check box.

If Automatic Name Checking is not turned on, you can make Outlook look up the name by pressing ALT-K or CTRL-K after you type the name.

If there are a few name possibilities, or if there's a fax number and an e-mail address for a contact, you'll see the name with a wavy red underline or a green dotted underline. Right-click the name with the wavy green or red underline and select the correct name or e-mail address from the shortcut menu that appears.

To address a message to several recipients using AutoName, type each name or partial name, and separate the names with commas or semicolons.

TIP   *You can also create an e-mail directly from a contact entry: open Contacts and right-click the contact you want to send an e-mail to; then, click New Message To Contact in the shortcut menu.*

USE THE TO BUTTON   To enter an e-mail address from a Contacts folder, click the To button. The Select Names dialog box for Corporate/Workgroup configuration is shown in Figure 4-2.

The Select Names dialog box for Internet Mail Only configuration is shown in Figure 4-3. The difference is that in Corporate/Workgroup configuration, only names with e-mail addresses or fax numbers appear, whereas in Internet Mail Only configuration, all the names in the selected Contacts folder appear, whether they have e-mail addresses or not. If your list of names is long, but only a few names have e-mail

Select different Contacts folders and address books here

Double-click recipient names

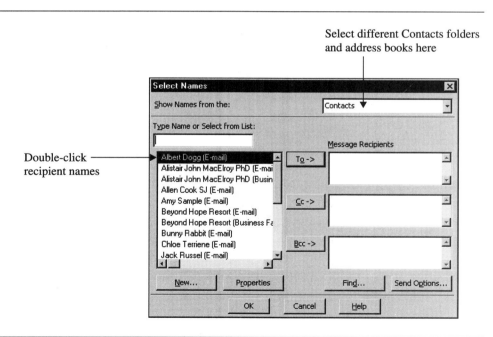

FIGURE 4-2   Selecting names in Corporate/Workgroup configuration

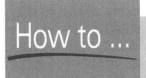

Switch the Select Names Listing to File As

By default, the names in the Corporate/Workgroup Select Names dialog box are listed first name first (as shown in Figure 4-2), but that's a difficult way to locate a name. If you'd like to switch the names to the display that you chose in the File As field for each contact, click Tools | Services. This will enable you to locate names alphabetically with ease. In the Services dialog box, click Outlook Address Book and then click the Properties button.

In the Address Book dialog box, click the File As (Smith, John) option, click the Close button, and click OK. Finally, close Outlook and open it again. Your Select Names dialog box will list all names in File As order.

Select different Contacts folders and address books here

Click to sort by column

Double-click recipient names

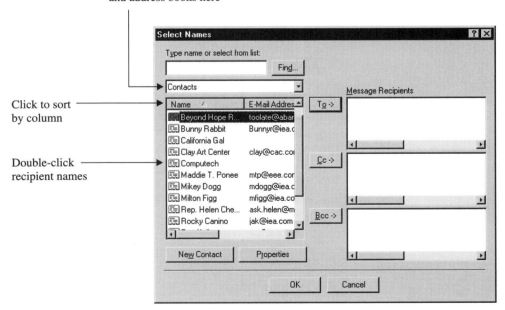

Selecting names in Internet Mail Only configuration

addresses, click the E-Mail Addresses column heading button to sort the list by e-mail address instead of by name; all the e-mail addresses sort to the bottom (click the button again to reverse the sort order and bring the names with e-mail addresses to the top).

> **TIP** *To see both columns better, point to the border between the column header buttons; when the pointer becomes a two-headed arrow, drag the column header to the left to narrow the names and widen the e-mail addresses.*

4

Although the dialog boxes are somewhat different in the two setup configurations, you use them to address messages in the same way. To enter names and e-mail addresses in your message:

1. Select the correct Contacts folder or address book in the Show Names From The list box.

2. Double-click each name you want to send the message to (the names appear in the upper Message Recipients box). You can send a message to as many recipients as you want, and to distribution lists. If you add a wrong name by mistake, click the name and press DELETE.

3. To send copies to other people (to keep them in the loop), click a name and then click the Cc button. Double-click more names and they'll also be added to the Cc box.

4. To send blind copies, click a name and then click the Bcc button. Double-click more names and they'll also be added to the Bcc box.

5. Click OK when you've added all the recipient names to the Message Recipient boxes.

> **NOTE** *If you want to add a new recipient to your Contacts folder and send them this message, click the New button below the list of names. Fill in the New Entry dialog box and click OK. Fill in the new contact dialog box that appears, and click Save And Close. When you see the Select Names dialog box again, add their name to the Message Recipients boxes.*

> **TIP** *If you enter a Nickname on the Details tab of a contact dialog box, you can type the nickname in the To box of a message, and AutoName will look up the contact's e-mail address.*

Write the Message Text

Enter a few words describing the subject of the message in the Subject line. The Subject line is a big clue to how urgently the message needs your recipients' attention, and it's helpful for a recipient when organizing their incoming messages (for example, when I sent messages to my editors about this book, I noted the book title and the chapter number in the Subject line).

Click in the large box in the lower half of the dialog box, and type your message. There's no limit on the size of your message. The text you type automatically wraps to a new line at the end of the current line, so press ENTER only to begin a new paragraph. If you're sending a Plain Text message, it's easier for your recipient to read if you press ENTER twice between paragraphs, to give the paragraphs good visual separation.

If you want to send a file with your message, such as a Word document or an Excel workbook, you can insert it in the body of the message (you'll learn how in Chapter 6).

If you want to use an elaborate closing line, perhaps your name, company name, and a favorite quote, you can create a signature that adds the whole thing automatically (you'll learn more about signatures at the end of this chapter).

Format Message Text

Your opportunities for formatting message text vary with the message format you've chosen (Plain Text, Rich Text, or HTML).

FORMAT TEXT IN PLAIN TEXT MESSAGES   To read your Plain Text messages (those you compose and those you receive) in a more pleasing font than Courier, do this:

1. Click Tools | Options and click the Mail Format tab.

2. Under Stationery and Fonts, click the Fonts button.

3. Under When Composing And Reading Plain Text, click the Choose Font button.

4. Set the font and size you want.

5. Consecutively click OK, OK, and OK to close all the dialog boxes.

Changing the font in a Plain Text message doesn't affect what your recipient sees; it only changes the font you see.

FORMAT TEXT IN RICH TEXT MESSAGES   If your message format is Rich Text, you have many font-formatting features available. To use all of Outlook's formatting features, display the Formatting toolbar (right-click any toolbar and click Formatting).

As in other Microsoft programs, you select the characters you want to format, and then apply the formatting. In the following message, I used Outlook's Formatting toolbar to apply a different font and red color to selected characters.

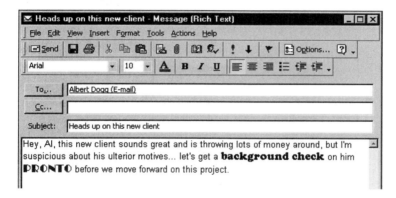

You can use all the formatting features in Microsoft Word in your messages if you turn on Microsoft Word as your e-mail editor. To do this, click Tools | Options and click the Mail Format tab; then, mark the Use Microsoft Word To Edit E-Mail Messages check box, and click OK.

Personally, I find Word formatting to be overkill for an e-mail message, but if you want to use highlighting and borders in your message, or write your message in Outline style, you can. Figure 4-4 shows a few formatting features that are available when Word is your e-mail editor.

Remember, not all e-mail programs can read all of your terrific Rich Text formatting.

FORMAT TEXT IN HTML MESSAGES   If you use HTML format for a message, you can make your message look like a Web page, and you

Choose backgrounds from
the Format menu

Borders Colors

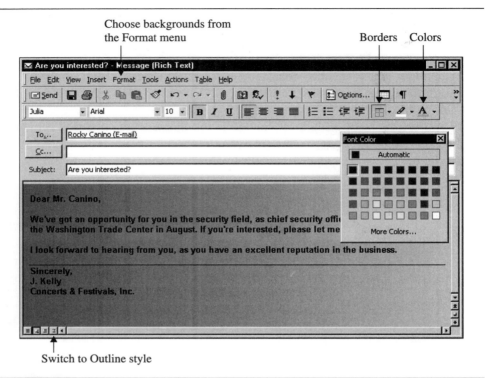

Switch to Outline style

FIGURE 4-4 Backgrounds and lots of colors are available when Word is your
e-mail editor

can add built-in backgrounds, called *stationery,* to add life to your message
(some are even animated).

Figure 4-5 shows an e-mail message formatted in HTML.

Horizontal lines are useful for separating sections of a message. To add a
horizontal line, click where you want the line to be located, and then click Insert |
Horizontal Line. To delete the line, click the line (your mouse will become a
four-headed arrow) and then press DELETE.

To add a picture that's stored on your hard drive, click where you want the
picture to be located, and then click Insert Picture. In the Picture dialog box,
click the Browse button to locate the picture file. Click OK to insert the picture
in your message.

*Messages with pictures can get pretty large and can be slow to send
and receive.*

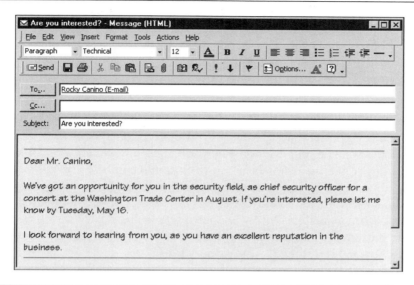

FIGURE 4-5   HTML messages can have all the elements of a Web page

Remember, not all e-mail programs can read that beautiful and lively HTML formatting.

USE E-MAIL STATIONERY   Stationery is a colorful background for messages that you can use with the HTML message format. You choose a stationery and set it as your default message format, and every new message you create will have that background.

Here's how to choose or change your stationery:

1. Click Tools | Options and then click the Mail Format tab.

2. Be sure you've selected HTML as your default mail format.

3. Under Stationery And Fonts, select a stationery name in the Use This Stationery By Default list box. To see what the different stationery styles look like, click the Stationery Picker button. You can then preview the different stationery styles.

4. When you see one you like, click OK. It becomes your default stationery. Click OK again to close the Options dialog box.

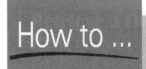 **How To Get More E-Mail Stationery**

In the Stationery Picker dialog box, click the Get More Stationery button. Your Internet browser is launched and goes to the Microsoft Office Update Web site, where you can preview and download lots more stationery styles.

Stationery can be found at non-Microsoft sites, too, which you can locate by using any of the various Internet browser search engines. Try Yahoo! (**www.yahoo.com**), Lycos (**www.lycos.com**), Infoseek (**infoseek.go.com**), or AltaVista (**www.altavista.com**), or one of the several other good search engines that are available. Once you open a search engine, try searching for **outlook stationery**. The sites themselves will give you instructions for downloading and installing their stationery files.

Check Spelling

If spelling isn't your strong suit, take advantage of Outlook's spelling checker before you send any important messages. You can turn on an automatic spelling checker that checks every message before you send it (so you never forget), or you can run the spelling checker yourself only when you want to.

TURN ON THE AUTOMATIC SPELLING CHECKER Here's how you turn on Outlook's automatic spelling checker so that every message is checked when you click the Send button:

1. Click Tools | Options and then click the Spelling tab.

2. Mark the Always Check Spelling Before Sending check box. (Clear this check box to turn it off.)

3. Click OK.

CHECKING SPELLING YOURSELF To run the spelling checker only when you want to, don't set the automatic feature. Instead, do this:

1. Write your message.

2. Click Tools | Spelling. If the Microsoft Office dictionary recognizes all the words, the following short message appears.

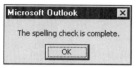

3. If there are any words that the dictionary doesn't recognize, the Spelling dialog box appears, which gives you several options:

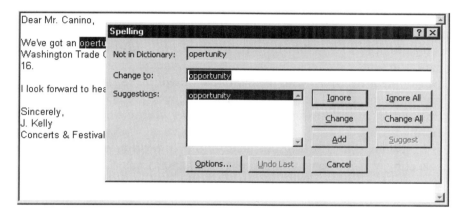

- If the unrecognized word is spelled the way you want it, you can add it to Microsoft's dictionary by clicking the Add button.

- If the unrecognized word is spelled the way you want it, but you don't want to add it to the dictionary, click the Ignore button to ignore the single occurrence, or click the Ignore All button to ignore every occurrence of the word in this message.

- If the word is spelled wrong and one of the suggested spellings is correct, click the suggestion you want, and then click the Change button to change the single occurrence. Click the Change All button to change every occurrence of the word in this message.

- If the word is wrong and none of the suggestions are correct, you can type the correct spelling in the Change To box and then click the Change or Change All button.

4. When all the words have been checked and dealt with, you'll see a message that the spelling check is complete. Click OK and you're done.

If you inadvertently add an incorrectly spelled word to your dictionary, you can remove it by clicking Tools | Options, clicking the Spelling tab, and clicking the Edit button. Your custom dictionary (all the words you've added to Microsoft's dictionary) opens in a Notepad file. Select and delete the wrong word and then save and close the Notepad file.

Sending Copies and Blind Copies

When you address a message, you can choose to send copies and blind copies of the message to people other than the recipient. A *copy* is an electronic carbon copy of the message sent to the recipient, and everyone who gets the message knows who else got the message. Copies are commonly used to keep supervisors "in the loop" and aware of what's being communicated about a project. A *blind copy* is an electronic carbon copy that's sent covertly—no one who gets the message knows who got blind copies.

There must always be at least one name in the To box (an original recipient). To send a copy of a message to others, put their names in the Cc box. To send blind copies, put the recipients' names in the Bcc box.

If you don't see the Bcc box in your message, click View | Bcc Field on the message menu bar.

Mark a Message As Private, Personal, Confidential, or Important

Nothing electronic is truly private, but marking a message with some level of confidentiality is a hint to the recipient that it's not for publication. And if you've found a really funny story on the Internet and want to share it with a colleague who's very busy, you can mark it as unimportant so that they'll know they don't have to read it right away.

To give a message a Sensitivity level, click the Options button on the message toolbar. In the Message Options dialog box, select Normal, Personal, Private, or Confidential in the Sensitivity box. Then click Close.

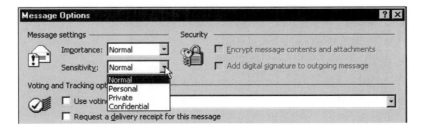

Setting an Importance level is easier—you can either set it in the Message Options dialog box or click one of the Importance buttons on the message toolbar.

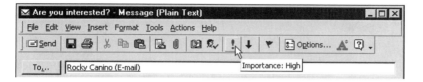

The Importance and Sensitivity settings appear in their own fields in the Inbox.

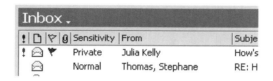

The Importance field (its heading looks like an exclamation mark) is displayed by default; if you want to see the Sensitivity field, you have to choose to display it. Right-click any column heading button, click Field Chooser, and drag the Sensitivity button to the column heading row; then, close the Field Chooser.

These settings also appear in the message, in case your recipient doesn't have the critical fields displayed in their Inbox.

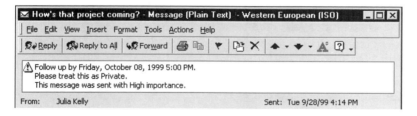

TIP

If you send a message marked Private, it can't be edited or changed by the person receiving it. This is one way to be sure no one alters your words in a message you've sent.

Flag a Message for Follow-up Action

If you want your reader to follow up on your message in some specific way (for example, telephone you), or not forward it, or respond (or not respond), you can *flag* the message with the follow-up action you want and a due date (if you have one). The flag appears brightly colored at the top of the message, so it's hard to miss.

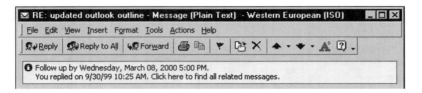

If you receive a message that isn't flagged but you want to remind yourself to follow up on it, you can flag it yourself.

To flag a message:

1. In the open message, click the Flag button on the message toolbar.

2. In the Flag For Follow Up dialog box, shown in Figure 4-6, select an action in the Flag To list box. If none of the listed actions is quite right, type your own action in the box.

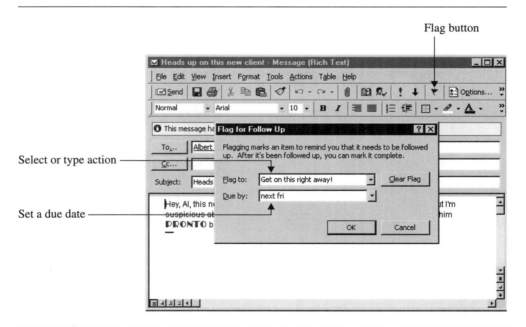

FIGURE 4-6   Flag a message as a reminder

3. If you have a due date for action, set it in the Due By box (click the list box arrow and click a date in the Date Navigator, or type **next Fri**, for example, and let AutoDate set the date for you). To remove the due date, open the Date Navigator and click the None button.

Flagged messages look like this in your Inbox:

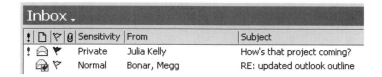

A red flag indicates a follow-up action that hasn't been completed yet; a white flag indicates that the follow-up action is marked complete. To mark a follow-up flag as complete, either right-click the closed message and click Flag Complete, or double-click the message to open it, click the Flag button on the message toolbar, mark the Completed check box, and click OK.

To remove the flag from the message (and from your Inbox display), right-click the closed message and click Clear Flag, or double-click the message to open it, click the Flag button on the message toolbar, and click the Clear Flag button.

Save an Unfinished Message Draft

Suppose you're halfway finished writing a complex message when you receive an urgent phone call and have to leave immediately. What can you do with the half-finished message? You can save it and close it. It will be automatically saved in the Drafts folder (which you'll find in the My Shortcuts group in your Outlook bar).

Close the message by clicking the X close button in its upper-right corner. You'll see a message asking if you want to save changes; click Yes, and the message will be closed and stored in the Drafts folder. When you're ready to finish the message, open your Drafts folder, double-click the message to open it, finish it, and send it.

Sending Messages

To send your message to your recipient, click the Send button on the left end of the message toolbar. What happens to the message after you click the Send button depends on your Outlook configuration.

Send a Message over the Company Intranet

If you're working in the Corporate/Workgroup configuration and are connected to a network mail server, your message will probably go directly to the network location for outgoing mail, and stay there until the network goes online to send and receive e-mail.

If you're in Corporate/Workgroup configuration but are not connected to a network mail server, your messages go to your Outbox and stay there until you connect to either the network or the Internet to send and receive e-mail. You can retrieve and open (or delete) messages from the Outbox any time before they're sent.

Send a Message over a Mail Service

If you're working in Internet Mail Only configuration, the message goes to your Outbox. How long it stays there depends on whether or not your Internet connection is active—if you keep the Internet connection open all the time, your message zips through the Outbox and out the phone line faster than you can blink. But, if you set Outlook to disconnect after sending/receiving mail, your message sits in the Outbox folder until you connect to send e-mail.

Send the Mail Out

To send the mail out onto the Internet, do any of the following:

- On the Outlook toolbar, click the Send/Receive button.

- Click Tools | Send/Receive and click your mail service (this is the right choice if you have more than one mail service).

- Press F5 (it's the same as clicking the Send/Receive button).

- Click Tools | Send if you want only to send outgoing mail and don't want to wait for incoming mail (this is good when you're dashing out the door in a hurry).

Outlook dials up your mail service, sends your messages, and picks up any waiting inbound mail. Then, it either hangs up or stays online waiting for more messages to send, depending on what you set up in your Mail Delivery options.

TIP   ***To keep your Internet connection open after you send e-mail,*** *click Tools |*
Options and click the Mail Delivery tab. Clear the Hang Up When Finished
Sending, Receiving, Or Updating check box. The next time you send e-mail,
it'll go immediately.

To keep Outlook off the phone when you're not actually sending e-mail,
mark the check box. Outlook will dial up the Internet connection each
time you send and receive e-mail, and will hang up when mail delivery
is complete.

Where's Your Outbox?

You'll find an Outbox icon in one of your Outlook bar groups, and the Outbox
folder in your Folder list.

Move Your Outbox

If you want to make your Outbox folder more convenient, you
can move it to a different Outlook bar group. For example, if
your Outbox icon is in the My Shortcuts group and you want it
in the Outlook Shortcuts group with all of your other icons,
open the My Shortcuts group and drag the Outbox icon onto the
button for the Outlook Shortcuts group. Hold it there for a
moment (don't release the mouse button), and the Outlook
Shortcuts group opens. Drag the icon to a position among the other icons and drop
it when the horizontal black line is where you want to locate the Outbox icon.

Save a Copy of Each Message You Send

It's a good idea to keep copies of your correspondence, whether paper or
electronic, because later on you may need to recall exactly what you wrote, or you
may need to resend the message because your correspondent's network was down
that day and they never got your message.

Outlook's default behavior is to save copies of all the messages you send in the
Sent Items folder. You can, of course, choose not to save them at all.

Find Your Sent Items Folder

You can always find your Sent Items folder in the Folder list, and there'll be a
shortcut icon for it in one of your Outlook bar groups. If you want to move your Sent

Items folder to a more convenient Outlook bar group, follow the procedure for moving your Outbox, which was just described in the "Move Your Outbox" section.

To Save or Not to Save

Do you think it's unnecessary to save copies of all the messages you send? To stop saving messages, click Tools | Options. On the Preferences tab, click the E-Mail Options button. Clear the Save Copies Of Messages In Sent Items Folder check box, and then click OK twice to close both dialog boxes.

If you decide not to save copies of all your messages automatically, you can save copies of individual messages as you create them. Click the Options button on the message toolbar and mark the Save Sent Message To check box. If you like, you can save it to a different folder (including custom subfolders) by clicking the Browse button and selecting a different Outlook folder in the Select Folder dialog box. Click OK to close each open dialog box.

Instead of not saving any messages, play it safe...save them and periodically clean out your Sent Items folder by deleting the messages you don't want to save. Open the Sent Items folder, select the messages you want to delete, and then either click the Delete button on the toolbar or press DELETE.

Set a Time Frame for a Message

Sometimes a message needs to be sent when you're out of the office, perhaps at a convention or on vacation. You can create your message and set a delayed delivery schedule, and the message stays in your Outbox until the scheduled delivery time. You can also set a time limit on a message so that if it's not delivered by a certain date, it doesn't get delivered at all (this is good when you need time-critical replies and some of your recipients are on vacation).

Delay Message Delivery

You set a delayed delivery schedule in the message when you create it, like this:

1. Click the Options button on the message toolbar.

2. In the Message Options dialog box, mark the Do Not Deliver Before check box.

3. To set the delivery date, click the arrow on the Do Not Deliver Before list box and use the Date Navigator to click a delivery date, or select the date in

the list box and type something like **week from mon** to let AutoDate set the date.

4. Click Close, and then finish and send your message.

You won't see the delayed delivery date unless you do one of two things: open the message, click the Options button, and check the delayed delivery date, or add the Defer Until field to your Outbox display. To display the Defer Until field, open Outbox and right-click any column heading button. Click Field Chooser and then select Date/Time Fields in the list box at the top of the Field Chooser. Drag the Defer Until button to the column heading row and then close the Field Chooser.

NOTE   *Your computer has to be turned on and Outlook has to be open for the scheduled delivery to take place.*

Expire a Message

You set a message expiration date in the message when you create it, like this:

1. Click the Options button on the message toolbar.

2. In the Message Options dialog box, mark the Expires After check box.

3. To set the expiration date, click the arrow on the Expires After list box and use the Date Navigator to click a delivery date, or select the date in the list box and type something like **2 wks** to let AutoDate set the date.

4. Click Close, and then finish and send your message.

If a message hasn't been received by a recipient by the expiration date, it won't be received at all.

Resend a Message

One really good reason to let Outlook save those Sent Items is that sometimes you need to resend a message. A recipient's network mail server may have been down the day the message was sent, and the message is lost forever; or another colleague may need to see a copy of the message you sent; or you may have sent the message to the wrong e-mail address; in short, there could be any number of reasons why you'd want to recover that message and send it again.

When you resend a message, you can change anything that needs changing—change the text, add attached files, change the recipients, whatever you want.

Resending a message essentially saves you from having to re-create the message from scratch. To resend a message, do this:

1. Open your Sent Items folder and double-click the message to open it.

2. Make any changes you need to make.

3. On the message menu bar, click Actions | Resend This Message. A copy of the message, with a Send button on the left end of the toolbar, appears.

4. Click the Send button.

5. Close the original message.

The new copy goes to your Outbox (or gets sent straight out, depending on your e-mail setup), and both the original and the re-sent copy are saved in your Sent Items folder.

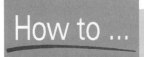 **Turn Off the Dialing Noises**

When your computer is new and you've just hooked up your Internet connection, it's nice to hear the dialing noises and connection static while your computer is dialing to connect to the Internet, because you know that your system is working properly. But after a while, those dialing noises can become downright annoying. Want to turn them off? Here's how:

Click Start | Settings | Control Panel and then double-click Modems. On the General tab, select the modem that dials your Internet connection, and click Properties. In the Properties dialog box, on the General tab, under Speaker Volume, slide the pointer to OFF.

Finally, click OK, click Close twice to close both dialog boxes, and close your Control Panel dialog box. Now, your computer will dial up any and all Internet connections silently.

Recall or Replace a Message You've Already Sent

If you're working in Internet Mail Only configuration, ignore this section.
Messages can only be recalled (pulled out of the Inbox) or replaced by Outlook in
the Corporate/Workgroup configuration, and then only if your network uses
Microsoft Exchange Server.

If your message has been sent and hasn't been opened and read by a recipient
yet, you can delete or replace the message, like this:

4

1. Open your copy of the sent message.

2. On the message menu bar, click Actions | Recall This Message.

3. Read the wording in the Recall This Message dialog box, mark your
choices, and click OK. If a dialog box choice isn't clear, right-click it to
see a brief explanation.

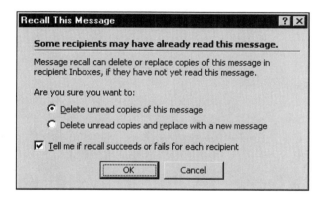

4. Close the copy of the message that you opened in step 1.

A recall instruction is sent out immediately if you're online, or appears in your
Outbox until you go online (even though it looks like an Outbox message, you
can't open the recall instruction).

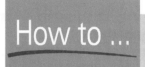 **How To Keep Your E-Mail Private**

First of all, understand that e-mail is never truly private. Just because you've deleted a message from your computer doesn't mean it no longer exists.

In a network environment, data (including e-mail messages on the network) is regularly backed up and can live on for many years. Messages you've sent to someone not on your network can be saved by that person, electronically or on paper, forever, or can be inadvertently or intentionally forwarded to other people. Marking a message as Personal, Private, or Confidential is pretty much only a hint, because anyone lacking integrity who has access to your e-mail account can open the message (and some e-mail systems don't recognize those Sensitivity settings). SO: If you wouldn't write it down on paper, don't write it down in e-mail.

Receiving Messages

If you can send e-mail, you can receive it, too. At its most basic, when you send and receive e-mail, new messages arrive in your Inbox. New message headers (the From and Subject lines in your Inbox) are in bold type until you read them, so you know which ones you haven't read yet. And in the Outlook bar, your Inbox icon shows you the number of unread messages that are awaiting your attention.

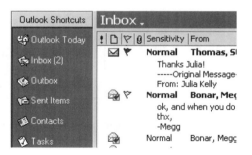

Changing What You See When Messages Arrive

When new messages arrive, their From/Subject lines will always be bold, and you may or may not see a three-line AutoPreview of each new message. After you open a message, the line is "unbolded" (and the AutoPreview disappears).

Preview New Messages with AutoPreview

AutoPreview is a terrific efficiency tool—often, you can tell immediately whether or not you need to open a message. If the message is a single-line reply to your message, it will read <end> in one of the three blue AutoPreview lines, and you'll know there's nothing more to read in that message.

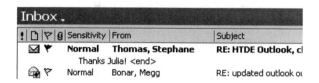

To avoid opening and closing a message you don't need to read, right-click the message and click Mark As Read. To call your later attention to a message you've already opened and closed, right-click the message and click Mark As Unread.

To have new messages arrive without AutoPreview (just the bold From/Subject lines), switch your Inbox view. With your Inbox open, on the Outlook menu bar, click View, point to Current View, and click Messages. To switch back to AutoPreview, click View, point to Current View, and click Messages With AutoPreview.

Preview New Messages in the Preview Pane

The Preview Pane (shown in Figure 4-7) is another efficiency tool for reading messages. It saves you time spent opening and closing messages by letting you read a whole message instead of just three lines.

To use the Preview Pane, open your Inbox and click View | Preview Pane. Do the same to close the Preview Pane.

When the Preview Pane is open, you can right-click the pane header and customize it. In the shortcut menu, click Preview Pane to close the pane, click Header Information to hide or show the From and Subject information in the pane header, and click Preview Pane Options to alter Preview Pane behavior or change the Preview Pane font.

Click the message

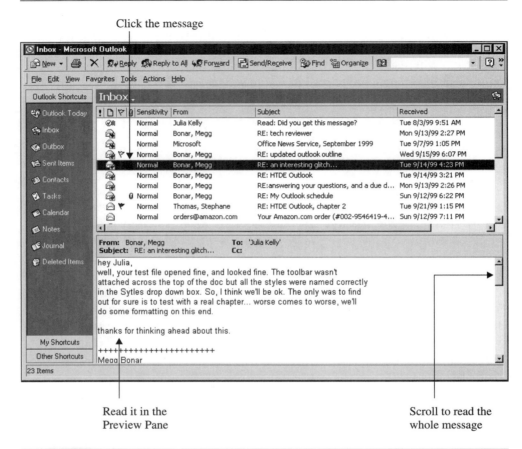

Read it in the
Preview Pane

Scroll to read the
whole message

FIGURE 4-7 Read messages in the Preview Pane without opening them

Delete a Message Without Reading It

Some messages you don't need to open or read at all—like the ones that are
clearly *spam*, or bulk-marketing junk mail. In Chapter 5, you'll learn how to create
rules that take care of much junk mail automatically, but there will always be those
that slip through.

To delete a message without reading it, do one of the following:

■ Click the message line to select it, and then click Delete on the
Outlook toolbar.

■ Click the message line to select it, and then press DELETE.

4

■ Right-click the message line and click Delete.

The message is moved into your Deleted Items folder, from where you'll have to delete it again to get rid of it completely.

Open and Read New Messages

When messages come in and accumulate in your Inbox, they remain in bold type until you open or delete them.

Open New Messages

To open a message, double-click the message line. To close a message and keep it in your Inbox, click the X close button on the right end of the title bar. To keep a

message open but minimize it so that you can see another window, click the Minimize button.

The message is minimized to a button on your Windows taskbar; click the taskbar button to resize the message.

Delete Open Messages

If a message doesn't warrant keeping, you can delete it. Click the Delete button on the message toolbar.

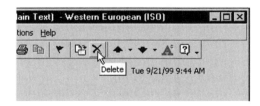

The message goes to your Deleted Items folder and stays there until you empty the Deleted Items folder.

NOTE   *Chapter 5 covers deleting e-mail and emptying your Deleted Items folder in greater detail.*

Add a Sender to Contacts

The best way to get a correspondent's correct e-mail address into your Contacts folder is to lift it directly from a message they send you. Here's how:

1. Open a message from the correspondent you want to save as a contact.

2. Right-click the correspondent's name in the From line.

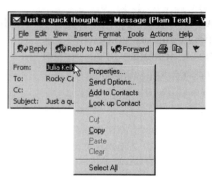

3. Click Add To Contacts. A new Contact dialog box opens, filled in with your correspondent's name and address.

4. Fill in any other information you want to save about the new contact. If there's information such as a mailing address or telephone number in the message, or items you want to save in the notes section, resize and/or drag the contact dialog box and message so that they're side by side or somewhat overlapped, and then select and drag the information from the message and drop it in the appropriate box in the contact dialog box.

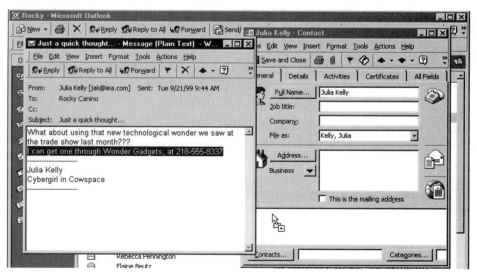

5. Click the Save And Close button to save the contact.

Divert Incoming Replies to a Coworker

Suppose you sent a message to a large group of people requesting, say, background data on a potential new employee. You're in charge of compiling the dossier, and it's time-critical data, but you're going out of town for a week. You can let the incoming replies accumulate in your Inbox until you get back, or you can divert the replies to a coworker who will deal with them in your absence.

Here's how you can divert replies to your message:

4

1. When you create your original message, click the Options button on the message toolbar.

2. In the Message Options dialog box, mark the Have Replies Sent To check box.

3. Click the Select Names button, and double-click each name the replies should go to. You might to leave your own name in the list so that you'll have a record of all the replies that arrived in your absence.

4. Click OK to close the Have Replies Sent To dialog box, and click the Close button to close the Message Options dialog box.

5. Finish and send your message.

Be sure you tell your coworkers that replies to your message are coming their way.

Replying to Messages and Forwarding Messages

Most of the messages you receive probably will need a reply (even if it's only "Thanks!") and many will need to be shared with someone else. Replying and forwarding are even simpler than sending new messages.

Briefly, to reply or forward an open message:

1. Click the Reply or Forward button on the message toolbar.

2. Add your responses or intro to the original message text.

3. Click Send.

In the next few sections, you'll learn how to reply or forward messages in much greater detail.

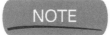 *Attachments that you receive won't be included in your reply, but are included in forwarded messages.*

Reply to a Message

Most messages deserve replies. Your reply might be as quick as "Thanks, see ya later!" or it might be an in-depth response to a series of high-level legal questions. Either way, sending a reply is a quick procedure.

To send a reply, do one of these things:

■ Click the Reply button on the message toolbar to reply only to the sender.

■ Click the Reply To All button on the message toolbar to send your reply to the sender and to every name in the To and Cc lists.

If the message isn't open, you can right-click the message line in your Inbox and click Reply or Reply To All.

A copy of the original message opens, as shown in Figure 4-8, with the address filled in and RE: added to the subject line to indicate a reply. You can change the Subject line if you want to, and you can add more recipients for your reply by clicking the To and Cc buttons.

You can type a quick reply at the top of the message, or you can type pieces of your reply anywhere within the message. A handy and polite way to reply to specific statements in a long message is to delete everything except the specific statements, and reply to those wherever they occur.

You can change the format of message replies, so that original message lines are prefixed by a specific symbol (a common one is ">"), or not, or you can choose not to include original message text in your replies at all—you'll learn how to change reply formats in the section "Change the Format of Replies and Forwarded Messages," later in this chapter.

After you edit and add your reply, send it like normal mail, by clicking the Send button on the message toolbar. It goes out with your regular e-mail delivery.

 After you reply to a message, its Inbox symbol changes from an opened envelope to an opened envelope with a left-pointing arrow in the corner.

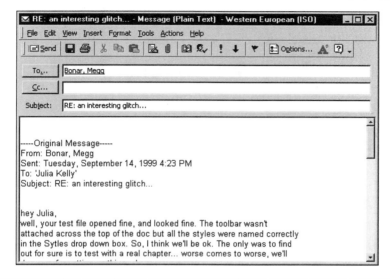

FIGURE 4-8   Replies contain the original message

And if you open an original message that you replied to, there's a notation across the top of the message that tells you when you replied.

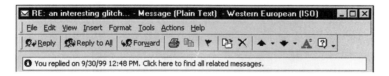

As for message format (Plain Text, Rich Text, or HTML), whatever format the original message arrived in will be used in the reply (and if someone sent you a message in Rich Text format, you know they'll be able to read your reply in Rich Text format). So, if you have extra formatting options in the reply format, you can use them to your advantage—for example, you can color your own responses bright red so that they don't get overlooked.

Forward a Message to Someone Else

Suppose you receive a message from someone outside of your company—or band of colleagues—that contains information that all of them ought to have. Forwarding a message to propagate it to a wider circle is easy, and in fact is how Internet legends like the famous (but unsubstantiated) Nieman-Marcus $250 cookie recipe got started.

To forward a message, click the Forward button on the message toolbar.

 *If the message isn't open, you can right-click the message line in your Inbox and click Forward.*

A copy of the original message opens with information about it at the top of the message. You can add your own note at the top (perhaps something like "This looks important" or "What do you think?") and edit the forwarded message for spelling or brevity. If the message has been forwarded through several addresses before it got to you, it's polite to delete the lengthy lists of addressing at the top of the message.

Send the message like any other: address it and then click the Send button to add it to your stack of outgoing mail.

Edit a Message Before Replying or Forwarding

Sometimes, the message you receive needs to be edited, or its Subject line needs to be changed, because you want to clean it up and keep it for future reference, regardless of whether you reply or forward it. But, you'll often find that messages you receive apparently can't be edited or changed.

Well, they can be edited, and here's how: in the open message, click Edit | Edit Message. Make any changes you want and then click File | Save and close the message.

 If the message was sent marked Private, you won't be able to edit it.

Change the Format of Replies and Forwarded Messages

The classical reply to a message has each line of original text prefixed by a symbol, such as >, to denote original text (the same applies to forwarded messages). If the message is in Plain Text (as they all were until just a few years ago), that symbol pretty much is the only way to differentiate original text from your additions and responses. Now, however, you can choose much more aesthetically pleasing formats for replies and forwards, especially if the message is in Rich Text or HTML.

Choose a Format

To change the format for replies and/or forwards, select Tools I Options, and on the Preferences tab, click the E-Mail Options button. In the E-Mail Options dialog box, shown in Figure 4-9, choose the formats you prefer for replies and formats.

You have the same four format choices for both replies and forwards, except that you can choose to not include the original message text in replies. When you

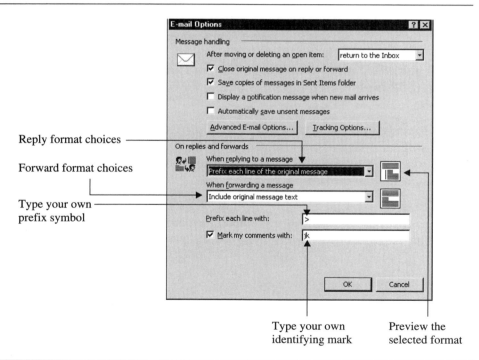

Reply format choices

Forward format choices

Type your own prefix symbol

Type your own identifying mark

Preview the selected format

FIGURE 4-9   Choose formats for your replies and forwards

choose a format in one of the list boxes, a preview of that format appears in the small sketch next to the list box. Here are a few more details about each choice:

```
Do not include original message
Attach original message
Include original message text
Include and indent original message text
Prefix each line of the original message
```

- **Attach Original Message**   The original text isn't displayed in your reply/forward, but is attached as a separate message that your recipient can double-click to open. If you're forwarding a message that's been through several mailboxes already, think twice about forwarding it as an attachment. Recipients will have to double-click a half dozen forwarded attachments just to get to the original message you want to share with them.

- **Include Original Message Text**   There's no differentiation between the original text and text you type unless the message you received is in Rich Text or HTML (in which case your responses or additions are in a different color). This isn't a good choice if most of your correspondence is in Plain Text format, but it's the best choice if most of your correspondence is in Rich Text or HTML.

- **Include And Indent Original Message Text**   This is supposed to indent the entire original message about one inch to the right, and enter your added text at the far-left side of the message. Sometimes it works and sometimes it doesn't.

- **Prefix Each Line Of The Original Message Text**   There's a column of symbols (your choice) down the left side of the original text because each line is prefixed. This is the most obvious way to differentiate between original text and your additions if the message is in Plain Text format. The classic prefix symbol is >, but you can choose any prefix symbol you want by deleting the existing symbol and typing your choice.

What Should Outlook Do with the Original Message?

You can choose to have Outlook close or leave open original messages after you open a reply or forward; closing the original automatically generally is more efficient, because if you leave it open, you have to close it yourself after you send a reply or forward.

To set or change this particular behavior, mark or clear the Close Original Message On Reply Or Forward check box in the E-Mail Options dialog box.

If you work in Internet Mail Only configuration, you'll also see the Automatically Put People I Reply To In check box at the bottom of the E-Mail Options dialog box, which automatically adds the e-mail addresses of your correspondents to your Contacts folder.

Message Tracking

If you send a message to someone, how do you know if the person received it? Well, you can ask Outlook to notify you when your message has been delivered. This works sometimes out in the real world, and works really well within your company if your company policy is to send read receipts.

You can set Outlook to request read receipts from your correspondents' e-mail programs. If their program is capable of responding to the request, and if they have their program set to respond to those requests, you'll get a short e-mail message back telling you when the message was delivered (it can't tell you whether the message was read, deleted, or shuttled automatically to junk mail, however).

Be Notified when Messages Are Delivered and Read

You can track all of your sent messages by setting up default tracking, or you can track only specific messages by setting tracking in the message when you create it.

It's more polite to request read receipts only in individual messages when you need to know whether or not the message was received—if you request them by default for all messages, some people think it's rude and others are confused because they don't know what a read receipt is.

Set Up Notification

To set up default tracking for all of your outgoing mail:

1. Click Tools | Options, and on the Preferences tab, click the E-Mail Options button.

2. In the E-Mail Options dialog box, click the Tracking Options button.

3. Mark the appropriate check boxes in the Tracking Options dialog box, and then click OK.

Figure 4-10 shows the Tracking Options dialog box for Outlook in Corporate/Workgroup configuration; in Internet Mail Only configuration, you cannot request a delivery receipt (just read receipts), and you can tell Outlook to ask you before it sends a response (so you can respond to those you choose and ignore others).

Get Notified

When you get a receipt that tells you when your message was delivered or read, it arrives in your Inbox. You can keep it, delete it, or move it to another folder.

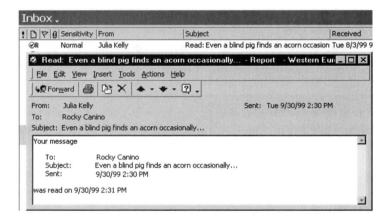

After you open the receipt, a Tracking tab is created in your copy of the original message (in the Sent Items folder). The receipt information is recorded on the Tracking tab, so that you can delete the receipt itself and still keep a record of the date and time the message was read. All the recipients to whom the message was addressed appear in the Tracking tab.

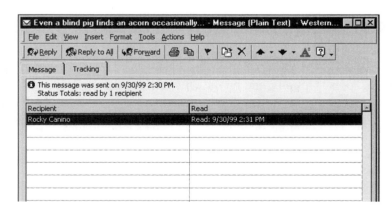

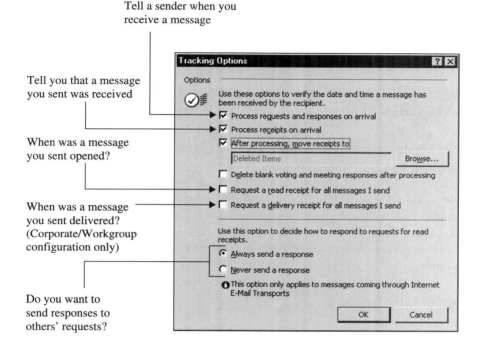

Tell a sender when you receive a message

Tell you that a message you sent was received

When was a message you sent opened?

When was a message you sent delivered? (Corporate/Workgroup configuration only)

Do you want to send responses to others' requests?

FIGURE 4-10   Handling tracking requests that you send you receive

When someone requests a read receipt from you, and you have Outlook set to respond to requests, a receipt addressed to the sender appears automatically in your Outbox when you open a new message.

Track Delivery Automatically

You can avoid the accumulation of read receipts in your Inbox by having the receipt recorded and the Inbox receipt deleted automatically. When you open a receipt, the receipt date and time are recorded in the Sent Items copy of your original message (in the Tracking tab), and after you close the receipt, it's moved to the Deleted Items folder.

To record and delete receipts automatically:

1. Click Tools | Options, and on the Preferences tab, click the E-Mail Options button.

2. In the E-Mail Options dialog box, click the Tracking Options button.

3. Mark the After Processing, Move Receipts To check box, and then click OK.

Eventually you'll find an accumulation of read receipts in your Deleted Items folder.

Using Signatures

Have you ever gotten e-mail that ended in a paragraph of information about the sender? Maybe a list of credits and accomplishments, the mailing address of their company, or a clever quote of the week? People generally don't type those each time they send a message; instead, they use a *signature,* which is set up once and then inserted in its entirety into the message, either selectively in individual messages or automatically in every message.

You can create lots of signatures and insert different ones for different message recipients (one you'd send your best friend might not be appropriate for sending to your supervisor).

Create Signatures

Here's how you can create your own signatures:

1. Click Tools | Options and click the Mail Format tab.

2. Under Signature, click the Signature Picker.

3. In the Signature Picker dialog box, click the New button.

4. In the Create New Signature dialog box, type an identifying name for the signature, and then click Next.

5. In the Edit Signature dialog box, type your signature. Use the ENTER key to space the lines, and include characters that create a separation from the body of your message. Click the Font button to format selected characters.

6. Click Finish and then click OK to close each dialog box.

To edit an existing signature, follow the preceding steps, but in step 3, click the name of the signature you want to edit, and click the Edit button. Then, make your changes and finish the steps.

To delete a signature, follow the preceding steps, but in step 3, click the name of the signature you want to delete, and click the Remove button. When asked if you're sure, click Yes and then click OK to close each dialog box.

Insert Signatures

Once you've created a signature or two, you can insert them when you need them, or have one inserted automatically into each new message (you can always delete a signature when you create the new message).

To set one signature as a default that's automatically inserted in every new message, do this:

1. Click Tools | Options and click the Mail Format tab.

2. Under Signature, select the signature you want in the Use This Signature By Default list box. If you want to include it by default in your replies and forwarded messages, too, clear the Don't Use When Replying Or Forwarding check box. If you don't want any of your signatures inserted by default, select <None>.

3. Click OK.

To insert a specific signature in a message when you create the message, click Insert, point to Signature, and click the signature you want. If you've created a really long list of signatures and don't see the one you want on the menu, click More. Select the signature from the Select A Signature dialog box, and click OK.

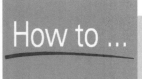

How To Write Clear, Professional E-Mail

Here's a bit of personal philosophy regarding e-mail messages (some people disagree with me about this point, but I can always tell who they are when I read their e-mail...).

People tend to write e-mail casually, but they read it very seriously, so be careful what you write and how you phrase your thoughts. It's easy to misinterpret words that aren't accompanied by a tone of voice or facial expressions.

Spell check and proofread your messages before you send them. People who dash off messages in a hurry and send them with misspellings and missing words tend to be seen as unprofessional by folks who read their messages; the fact that e-mail is fast is no excuse for grammatical sloppiness and miscommunication.

Separate your paragraphs and be concise. An endless, wordy e-mail message can be really irritating to a reader, especially on Friday evening at the end of a long and busy week.

Sending vCards for Contacts

A vCard is a virtual business card, so you can swap cards with someone over the Internet as easily as you can face-to-face. To use vCards, recipients need to have a contact management system that can handle them, and Outlook's Contacts folder can. Symantec's ACT and Lotus Organizer, among others, can also handle vCards.

When you receive a vCard, you add it to your Contacts folder. It creates a new contact automatically, without typing or copying/pasting the contact's information. It arrives in a message as an attached file, and you drag its icon to your Outlook bar and drop it on your Contacts icon. A new contact dialog box opens, with all the information filled in, and you can add anything else you like (such as notes to yourself), and then save and close the new contact.

When you create a vCard for yourself or your own company, you can send it to other people (you can even include it in a signature).

Create Your Own vCard

The entries in Contacts are used to create vCards. To create a vCard for yourself or your company, first create and save a contact for yourself or your company.

Then, in the contact dialog box, click File | Export To vCard File. In the VCARD File dialog box, check the filename (change it if you need to) and click the Save button. Then, click Save And Close in the contact dialog box.

Create a vCard for One of Your Contacts

If you get an e-mail asking who your company's cleaning service is, or asking whether you can recommend a good pediatrician, you can create a vCard for the person or company you want to recommend, and send the vCard in reply to the question.

Create a vCard for any contact by using the same procedure as for creating a personal vCard, described in the preceding section.

Make a vCard Part of Your Signature

When you create a signature, you can include a vCard with it. When you get to the Edit Signature dialog box, select the vCard from the Attach This Business Card (vCard) To This Signature list box. If you haven't created the vCard yet, click the

New vCard From Contact button and follow the procedure described in the preceding section. Then, select the vCard name from the list box and click OK to close each dialog box.

Send a vCard in a Message

You can send just the vCard, or you can include it in a message.

To send just the vCard, open Contacts. Click the contact whose vCard you want to send, and then click Actions | Forward As vCard. A new message opens, containing the vCard as an attachment and ready to be addressed and sent (you should probably add a few words, just to be polite).

To attach a vCard to a message as you create the message, click Insert | File in the message menu bar. Navigate to the Signatures folder. It's probably in the path C:\Windows\Application Data\Microsoft, but you can search for it by clicking Start | Find | Files Or Folders. Your vCards have little contact icons (and a .vcf extension, if you have extensions in view).

Chapter 5

Deleting E-Mail and Managing Your E-Mail Flow

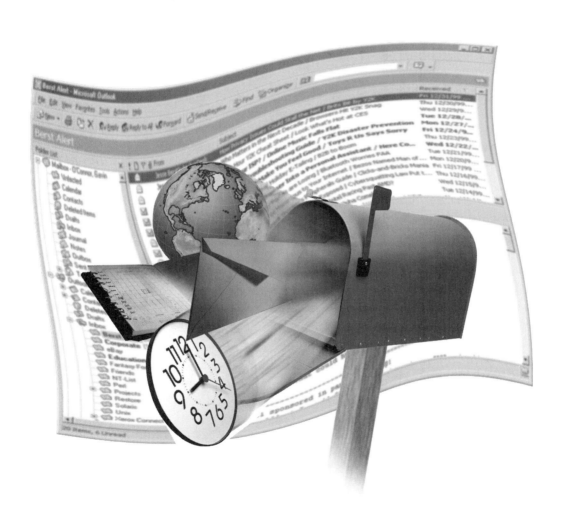

How to . . .

■ Delete messages

■ Manage mail flow by creating rules

■ Create subfolders

■ Move and copy messages to subfolders

■ Find a specific message

■ Follow a message thread

■ Use digital signatures and encryption for secure e-mail

This chapter shows you how to carry out many very efficient activities with e-mail messages, such as how to get rid of them, move them around, manage them automatically, find a specific message, find all the messages in a particular *thread* (or e-mail conversation), and encrypt your messages for security.

Deleting Messages

Messages are easily deleted, except for the sarcastic one you wrote to a coworker with a joke about your boss (that one will exist somewhere forever, and will come back to haunt you). You can delete messages as you read them, before you read them, or automatically before you ever see them. (In Chapter 4, you learned how to delete messages, both open and unopened.)

When you delete a message by any method, it goes into your Deleted Items folder, where you have one last chance to retrieve it. It's a good idea to clean out your Deleted Items folder regularly and ruthlessly, because those messages can eat up a lot of your hard drive space (and if your messages exist on the company network server, your allowable space for e-mail may be even more limited than on a standalone computer's hard drive).

Retrieve a Deleted Item

All the Outlook items you delete (messages, notes, contacts, and so forth) go into the Deleted Items folder. To retrieve any item, open the Deleted Items folder by clicking its icon in the Outlook bar.

Double-click the item to open it and make sure it's the one you want to retrieve. Then, close it and drag the closed item to the appropriate icon in the Outlook bar. For example, to retrieve a message, drag it to the Inbox icon to move it to your Inbox. If it's a copy of a message you sent, drag it to the Sent Items icon, and so forth.

A new feature in Outlook 2000 is that you can reply to, forward, and resend messages that are in the Deleted Items folder (you don't have to drag them to the Inbox first).

5

Empty the Deleted Items Folder

When you're sure the items in the Deleted Items folder are trash, right-click its Outlook bar icon, and then click Empty "Deleted Items" Folder. You'll be asked whether you are sure you want to permanently delete the items. Click Yes, and the entire folder will be emptied, with all the items gone irretrievably.

If you know some of the items are trash but are unsure about others, you can open the Deleted Items folder and permanently delete individual items without emptying the folder. Delete them the same way you deleted them from their original folders: click items to select them (use the SHIFT or CTRL key to select multiple items), and click the Delete button on the toolbar.

If you want Outlook to empty the Deleted Items folder every time you exit, click Tools | Options, and on the Other tab, mark the Empty The Deleted Items Folder Upon Exiting check box.

Setting Rules to Manage Mail Flow

As soon as you start giving people your e-mail address—especially if you order some product on the Internet—you'll start getting mail you don't want, referred to as *spam*. Spam is the electronic equivalent of junk mail, and it's almost as annoying as telemarketing phone calls that come just as you're sitting down to dinner.

If you keep getting personal messages from some specific person or company that you sincerely don't want to hear from, you can automatically delete those items by creating a *rule* that deletes them automatically when they arrive. An Outlook rule is similar to a macro in Excel, Word, or Access; it's an automated procedure that uses behind-the-scenes programming that you don't have to write. The Rules Wizard helps you build the automated procedure and writes the programming for you.

How Does Outlook Filter Junk and Adult-Content Mail?

Outlook looks for specific words and phrases that are typical of junk mail and adult-content mail, such as "advertisement," "money back," "100% satisfied," and "over 18," and also looks for combinations of phrases, such as "more info," "visit," and "dollars" all in the message body. It's worth taking a look at this list, because you could send out an important internal message to your colleagues that says "About our latest TV advertisement" in the Subject line, or "Last year we did over 18 million dollars' worth of business in that region" somewhere in the body, and your colleagues who have the junk mail filter turned on won't ever see your message. You can get around the filter phrases, however, by creating rules that accept messages from specific people regardless of the words and phrases in the messages. What you can't get around is a happy client whose message says "I am 100% satisfied with the service I received from your company;" because you won't know these messages are coming, you can't set a rule to accept the message.

To see the whole list of filter criteria, open the file filters.txt (it's in the folder where Outlook is installed). To find it quickly, click Start | Find | Files or Folders and search your hard drive (including subfolders) for **filters.txt**. You can double-click the filename in the Find Files dialog box to open the filters.txt file. This is a simple text file, and you can delete criteria from the list if you want to (but you can't control what your colleagues have in their filters lists).

You can also create rules that separate your incoming mail messages into groups based on their attributes, such as the sender's name; marked urgent; sent only to you; sent by someone on a distribution list; containing specific words in the address, subject, or body of the message; and much more. Rules will help you fine-tune your junk mail filter, too.

Avoid Junk and Adult-Content Mail

If you want to turn on the Junk Mail or Adult Content filters which will filter your incoming mail with built-in criteria, here's how:

1. Open Inbox and click Tools | Organize.

2. In the Organize pane, shown in Figure 5-1, click Junk E-Mail on the left side of the pane. If you see a Turn Off button in either the Junk or the Adult Content option, it means the filter is already turned on. The option tells you what the rule does; to change the rule, click the Turn Off button so that you can reset the rule.

3. To set the actions for a rule, select Move or Color in the left drop-down list box; then, select a folder or a color in the right drop-down list box.

4. Click the Turn On button.

5

When the Junk Mail and/or Adult Content rules are turned on, the rules use the Junk or Adult Content filter criteria to automatically screen your incoming e-mail, and either color or move any new messages that meet the criteria. If you color the messages, they'll stay in your Inbox so that you can glance at them before you delete them. If you move them automatically to the Deleted Items folder, you may never see them at all.

If you get a message that you consider junk mail but which slipped through the filter, you can add it to your Junk Senders list, which is a list of senders you don't want to read mail from.

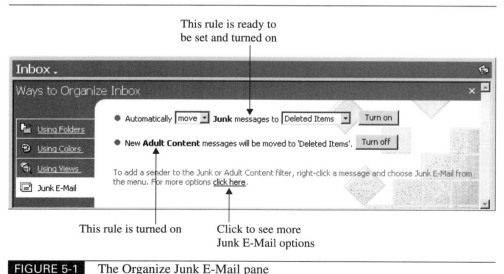

This rule is ready to
be set and turned on

This rule is turned on   Click to see more
Junk E-Mail options

FIGURE 5-1   The Organize Junk E-Mail pane

 *Unfortunately, you can only screen mail as it comes into your Inbox; if you pay connect-time charges to your Internet service provider, those unwanted messages will still take up connection time while you pick up your mail.*

Add Senders to the Junk Senders or Adult Content Senders List

Outlook provides a Junk Senders list and an Adult Content Senders list to which you can add the names of unwanted senders. To see more Junk E-Mail options, click the Click Here link at the bottom of the Organize Junk E-Mail pane previously shown in Figure 5-1. The pane shown in Figure 5-2 appears.

If you click the Edit Junk Senders or the Edit Adult Content Senders link, an Edit Junk Sender dialog box appears.

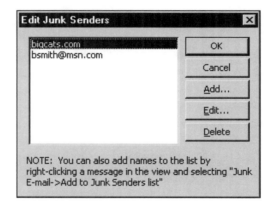

■ **To type an e-mail address or domain name that you *don't* want mail from,** click the Add button. The domain name is the part that comes after the @ symbol; typing just a domain name, such as **Microsoft.com**, will treat all messages from anyone at that source as junk mail.

■ **To remove a name you added to the list in error,** click the name to select it and then click the Delete button.

■ **To edit an address** (for example, if you added an address and mistyped it), select the address, click the Edit button, edit the address, and click OK.

Edit the Senders lists

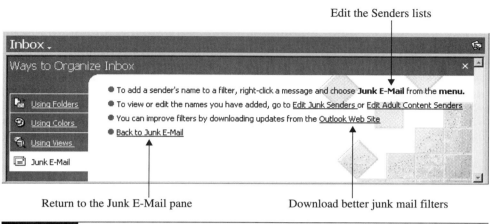

Return to the Junk E-Mail pane   Download better junk mail filters

FIGURE 5-2   The Organize Junk Senders pane

Add Senders the Easy Way

When a junk message arrives and you know it's junk mail before you open it, right-click the message line, point to Junk E-Mail, and then click one of the Add To commands.

When a junk message arrives and you've opened it, click Actions, point to Junk E-Mail, and click one of the Add To commands.

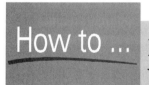 **Handle Junk Mail that Arrives Without a Sender**

Clever spammers (those nasty beasts) have figured out how to send you messages with no entry in the From field, and when you try to add them to your Junk Senders list, Outlook tells you there's no sender to add. Harrumph.

If this happens to you, you can scan the message for a word or a phrase (in the Subject or the body) that's not likely to appear in nonjunk messages, and create a rule to delete messages containing that word or phrase. Look especially for words that are spelled wrong, and be sure you use the precise incorrect spelling in your rule. These folks tend to send the same message out over and over again, and a rule to catch and delete that particular message saves you the irritation of seeing it again and again.

Create Message Rules

Would you like to automatically flag messages you get from your supervisor with a Follow Up in 2 Days flag? Or move messages that read "ABC Project" in the Subject automatically into your custom ABC Project subfolder? Or maybe you don't want to hear any more about a specific topic, and you'd like to automatically delete any message that has specific topical words in the Subject field. You can do all of these things, and even create a custom message that pops onto your screen whenever you receive a message that was sent with High Importance.

There are lots of rules you can create, and the Rules Wizard (shown in Figure 5-3) helps you to create them. You also can edit rules (to add or change specific names or words) after you create them.

NOTE *Rules run from your own copy of Outlook when your computer and Outlook are turned on and open, so you can't use rules to reply automatically when you're out of the office. If, however, you get your mail through a company network that uses the Microsoft Exchange Server, you can use the Out Of Office Assistant to automatically reply to e-mail while you're out. You'll learn how to do that in Chapter 18.*

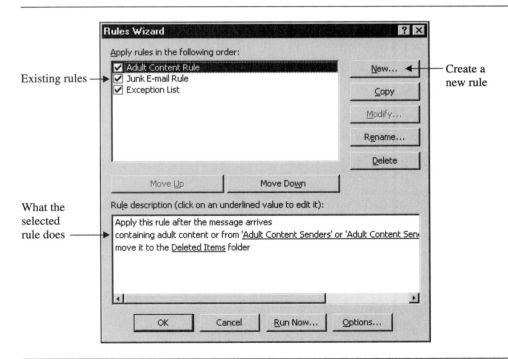

FIGURE 5-3   Create a new a mail rule

Create a New Rule

If you want to create a new rule, follow these steps:

1. Open any mail folder (Inbox, Sent Items, or Outbox) or the Outlook Today window.

2. Click Tools | Rules Wizard. The Rules Wizard dialog box appears and shows a list of existing rules. If you click an existing rule in the upper pane, the rule itself appears in the lower pane.

3. Click the New button to start the wizard. There will usually be at least three parts to a rule, and each selection you make in the wizard determines what options are available in the next step.

4. In each wizard step, scan the list of options in the upper pane, and click the one that seems appropriate. When you click a selection, the rule wording appears in the lower pane, and may have one or more blue, underlined words that need your input.

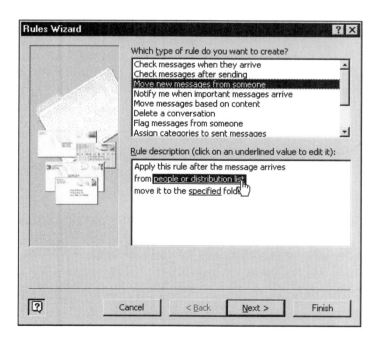

5. If there are blue, underlined words in the lower pane, click one and then make selections from whatever dialog box appears. In this example, I'm creating a rule to move new messages from all members of the South Hills Pediatric Wing Project distribution list to a custom subfolder named Clinic Project.

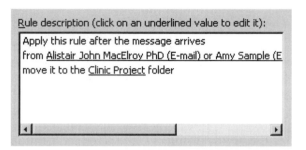

NOTE *If you try to add a distribution list to a rule, you may see a message that says you can't do so; but, the message asks if you want to add the members of the distribution list, which is what you wanted in the first place, so click OK and all will be well.*

6. Click Next to move to each new wizard step, and continue selecting pieces of your rule in the upper pane and setting the specifics for that piece in the lower pane. Sometimes, you'll have a list of check boxes—you can check as many as you like, or none at all if you don't want to apply any of the conditions in that list.

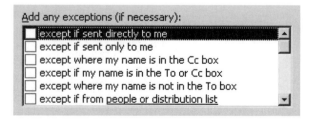

7. In the next-to-last wizard step, you can add exceptions to the rule, so that in specific cases, Outlook will ignore the rule (if you have no exceptions to add, just click Next).

8. In the last wizard step, type a name for the rule so that you'll recognize it in the Rules Wizard list that you saw in Figure 5-3. If you want to run the rule retroactively on messages you've already received, click the Run This Rule Now check box; if for some reason you don't want to turn on the rule yet, be sure you clear the Turn On This Rule check box. Then click Finish.

The Rules Wizard dialog box appears again, and this time your new rule is listed in the upper pane.

Create a No-Sender Junk Mail Rule

Now, suppose you get a message that says "Free Universety Degree" in the Subject field (I got one of these, and the misspelling is real), and there's nothing in the From field, so you can't add it quickly to your Junk Senders list. You don't want to have to delete this message every time it comes in (and it will probably come in again two or three times); instead, you can create a rule that looks for the misspelled word "universety" and deletes those messages. (And you'll want to create an exception to the rule for mail from your nephew who's a mathematical genius but doesn't spell very well.)

1. Create a new rule, and select Check Messages When They Arrive in the first wizard step.

2. In the second wizard step, mark the check box for With Specific Words In The Subject Or Body.

3. In the lower pane, click the blue, underlined "specific words." In the Search Text dialog box that appears, type the misspelled word you'll use to identify the unwanted message (for this example, I'll type **universety**) in the Add New box, click Add, and then click OK.

4. In the next wizard step, mark the Delete It check box.

5. In the following wizard step, mark the Except If From People Or Distribution List check box, and in the lower pane, click the blue, underlined "people or distribution list." In the Rule Address dialog box, double-click the names of senders you want the rule to ignore (such as your nephew, the poor speller) and then click OK to be returned to the wizard step. Then click Next.

6. In the final wizard step, type a name for the rule (the misspelled word itself would be good) and click Finish.

7. Click OK to close the Rules Wizard dialog box.

Any repeats of this message will automatically accumulate in your Deleted Items folder. Be sure you clean out your Deleted Items folder regularly so that these worthless messages don't eat up valuable disk space.

 In Chapter 16, you'll learn how to set archiving rules that automatically empty your Deleted Items folder on a regular basis.

Edit a Rule

Suppose you discover that your retired uncle, who recently discovered the joys of e-mail, also doesn't spell very well, and you want to add him to your list of exceptions for your junk message rule. Here's how to do it the easy way:

1. Open a mail folder, and click Tools | Rules Wizard.

2. Click the rule you want to edit so that its description appears in the lower pane.

3. Click the blue, underlined name (your nephew's name in step 5 of the previous example) in the Except If From line, and add your uncle's name by double-clicking it in the Rule Address dialog box.

4. Click OK to close the Rule Address dialog box, and then click Finish to finish editing the rule. Click OK to close the Rules Wizard dialog box.

If you need to alter major parts of the rule, open the Rules Wizard, click the rule name, click the Modify button, and go through each wizard step, making your changes where needed.

Delete or Turn Off a Rule

Rather than undertake a major editing procedure, you may find it easier to simply delete the rule and create a new one; you can also turn a rule off without deleting it and turn it on again later.

■ **To delete a rule** Open the Rules Wizard dialog box, click the rule name, and click the Delete button.

■ **To turn a rule off (without deleting it)** Open the Rules Wizard dialog box and click the check box next to the rule name.

Clearing the check box turns the rule off; marking the check box turns the rule on.

Moving and Copying Messages

Rules are great because they automate your mail flow, and when you deal with lots of messages, rules are a real time-saver. But you don't need to create rules to move or copy messages to other locations; you can do that yourself.

Create Subfolders

Subfolders are very handy places to hold specific messages while you're using them. For example, you can copy or move a set of messages about a specific project into a subfolder, to keep them together and easy to find. Or you might need to temporarily segregate a set of messages in a message thread, so that you can move between them easily until you're finished with them.

Create a New Mail Subfolder

In Chapter 3, you learned how to create subfolders for Contacts; you use the same procedure to create subfolders for your Inbox or other mail folders. Open the Folder list (click the pushpin in the upper-right corner to hold it open, if you need to). Right-click in the Folder list and click New Folder. Type a name for the new subfolder, make sure the Folder Contains list box reads Mail Items, and click the Outlook folder in which you want to create the new subfolder.

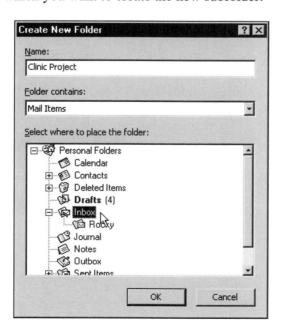

Click OK. You'll be asked if you want to create an Outlook bar shortcut; a shortcut icon in the Outlook bar makes the subfolder quicker to get to if you plan on using it a lot. If you click Yes, a new icon appears in the My Shortcuts group in the Outlook bar.

Delete a Subfolder

If you decide to delete the new subfolder, move its messages into another folder, if you want to save them. Then, open the Folder list and right-click the subfolder. Click Delete and then click Yes.

Move Messages

You can move closed messages quickly by dragging them, or you can use a menu command to move an open or closed message.

Drag Closed Messages to Move Them

You can drag closed messages to shortcut icons in the Outlook bar or to a folder in your Folder list (if you didn't create a shortcut icon for a new subfolder, you'll need to open the Folder list to display the subfolder).

Open the list of messages and drag one or more to the folder or shortcut icon where you want to move them. To drag multiple messages, use the SHIFT or CTRL key to select them, and then drag the selected set of messages. If you drag with the left mouse button, the messages will be moved into the new folder; if you drag with the right mouse button, click Move when you drop them.

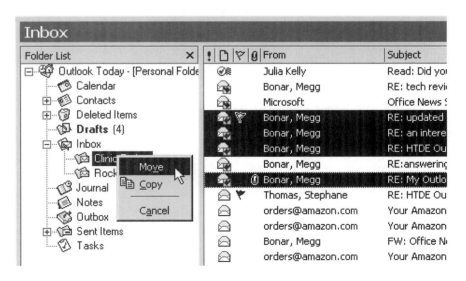

Move Messages with a Menu Command

If the message(s) are closed, right-click the selected message(s) and click Move To Folder. In the Move Items dialog box, click the folder you want to move them into, and click OK.

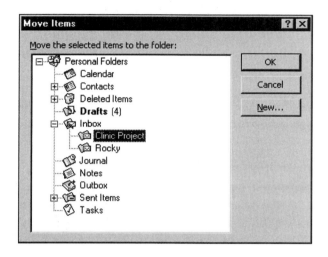

If a message is open when you decide to move it, click File | Move To Folder on the message's menu bar. In the Move Item To dialog box, click the folder you want to move it into, and click OK.

Copy Messages

Suppose you've sent messages to several outside associates asking for their feedback on a new advertising campaign. Their replies have trickled in over time, and now you want to segregate the replies temporarily so that you can find and work with them easily while you compile your report about responses to the ad campaign. You can place them into a single custom subfolder, for temporary ease of access, without losing them from your Inbox (which could happen if you move them to a subfolder and forget to move them back when you're finished with the project).

Instead of moving them, copy them to a subfolder. Then you can change, delete, or generally mangle them, and you'll still have the original messages safe in your Inbox.

You can copy closed messages quickly by dragging them, or you can use a menu command to copy an open message to another folder.

Drag Closed Messages to Copy Them

You can drag closed messages to shortcut icons in the Outlook bar or to a folder in your Folder list (if you didn't create a shortcut icon for a new subfolder, you'll need to open the Folder list to display the subfolder).

Open the list of messages, and use the right mouse button to drag one or more to the folder or shortcut icon you want to copy them into. When you drop them, click Copy.

Copy Messages with a Menu Command

If a message is open when you decide to copy it, click File | Copy To Folder on the message's menu bar. In the Copy Item To dialog box, click the folder you want to copy it into, and click OK.

Decide What Happens After You Delete or Move a Message

Outlook can do one of three things after you move or delete a message that's open: it can open the next message in your list of new messages, open the previous message (which you've probably already read), or return to the Inbox and let you open your own messages. Also, Outlook can close the original message after you've replied to it or forwarded it, or it can leave the original message open (your choice).

To switch Outlook's response to a moved or deleted open message, click Tools | Options, and on the Preferences tab, click the E-Mail Options button. In the E-Mail Options dialog box, select a message-opening behavior from the After Moving Or Deleting An Open Item list box.

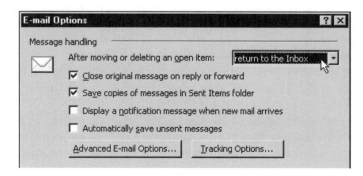

To automatically close an original message after you have replied or forwarded it, mark the Close Original Message On Reply Or Forward check box; to keep an original message open (and close it yourself when you're finished with it), clear the check box.

Finding a Specific Message in a Mail List

When you've used Outlook for even a short while, you'll discover that you have so many messages that finding a specific one is quite a task. If you can think of a particular word or phrase that the message is likely to contain, you can ask Outlook to search the messages for you. Outlook filters the messages in the folder and displays all messages that contain your search word or phrase anywhere in them.

To conduct a message search, follow these steps:

1. Open the folder or subfolder that you want to search (Outlook can only search one folder at a time).

2. On the Outlook toolbar, click the Find button (or click Tools | Find).

3. In the Find pane that appears, type the search word, partial word, or phrase in the Look For box. To search all the text in every message, be sure the Search All Text In The Message check box is marked; if you clear the check box, only the From and Subject fields are searched.

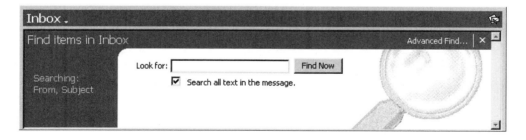

4. Click the Find Now button. The list of messages is filtered to show only those that contain the word, partial word, or phrase. If you choose a specific enough search word or phrase, the search will be narrowed considerably.

To change your search criteria, select the text in the Look For box and type new search text. To remove the filter and display all of your messages again, click the Clear Search option.

To set up a more complex filter, click Advanced Find in the upper-right corner of the Find pane. The Advanced Find dialog box is just like the one in Chapter 3, except for the Messages tab. You can fine-tune your search by setting several criteria—perhaps a search word or phrase, in the subject and body, from someone specific, received last month. To search all the message folders rather than just one, let the In box (in the upper-right corner) read Personal Folders. Click Find Now to run the search.

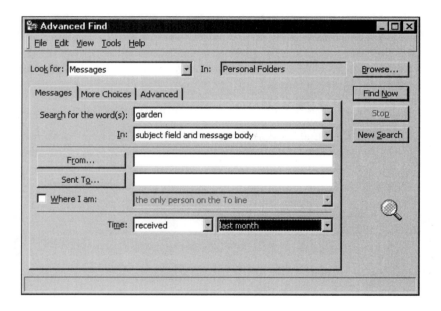

The results of your search appear in a list at the bottom of the Advanced Find dialog box instead of in the Outlook window. You can either open any of those messages by double-clicking it, or drag one or more into a subfolder where you can find them easily.

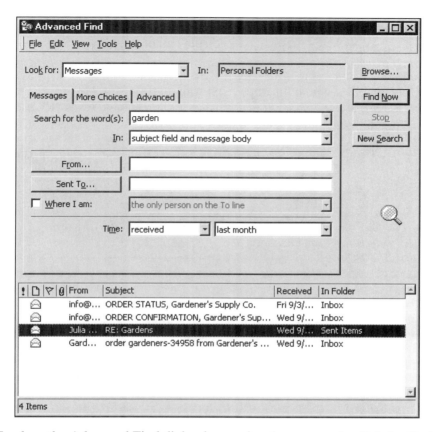

To close the Advanced Find dialog box and end your search, click the X close button in the upper-right corner of the dialog box. To close the Find pane, click the X in its upper-right corner.

If you're sure you didn't delete a particular message that you can't find, it may have been archived. See Chapter 16 to learn about archiving and how to recover archived messages.

Threading Your Way Through a Conversation

Suppose you've been carrying on an e-mail conversation with someone, replying back and forth through several generations of messages, and you want to take a look at what each of you wrote several letters back. The chain of related messages is called a *message thread,* and you can quickly locate all the messages in a thread, as follows:

1. Open any message in the thread you want to trace. If there are related messages, a yellow banner near the top of the message reads "Click here to find all related messages." Click the banner.

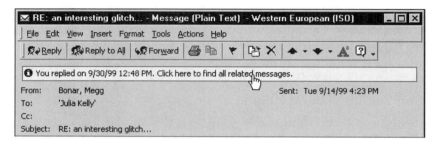

2. An Advanced Find dialog box opens and displays a list of all the related messages in the thread, in any message folder. You can either open individual messages in the list by double-clicking the message, or move or copy them into another folder so you'll have them all in one place.

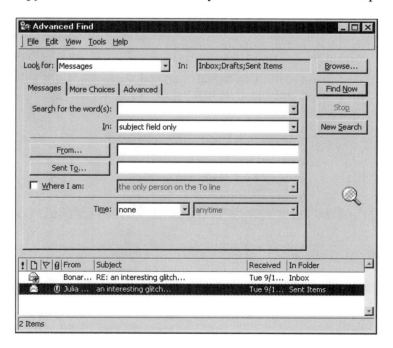

3. To close the Advanced Find dialog box, click the X close button in its upper-right corner.

Sending Messages Securely

Most of us don't need to send messages securely, but if you work in an environment where there's sensitive material (like the Justice Department or the Securities & Exchange Commission), you may well have messages that need extra protection from prying eyes. There are a couple of ways to send secure messages in Outlook e-mail:

- **Use a digital signature**   Assures your recipient that the message has come unaltered from you

- **Encrypt the message**   Prevents anyone but your recipient from reading your message

Both security measures require digital IDs.

Digital Signatures

A digital signature is proof to your recipient that a message really came from you and hasn't been altered or tampered with along the way. To add a digital signature to a message, you need to get yourself a digital ID.

NOTE   *Your recipients don't need to have Outlook to recognize digital signatures; they only need to have any e-mail system that's capable of reading S/MIME (Secure Multipurpose Internet Mail Extensions) encoded messages (such as Eudora Pro, Netscape Messenger, Outlook Express, and others). If your recipient isn't using an S/MIME-capable e-mail program, they can still read your message without verification, and your digital signature shows up as an attachment to the message (that's how they can tell whether their mail program is S/MIME-capable—the digital signature icon won't appear if their program isn't S/MIME-capable).*

A message that arrives with a digital signature has an icon in the Inbox list.

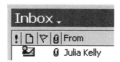

When a signed message is open, this icon is in the lower-right corner of the address pane.

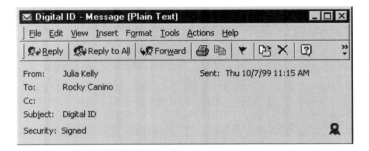

Get a Digital ID

Getting a personal digital ID is easy. There are companies that issue digital ID security certificates, both for individuals and for large companies. One such company is VeriSign, and you can go to its Web site to get more information and get your own personal digital ID. You can get a free 60-day trial ID from VeriSign, and if you decide you want to keep using it, a full-featured one-year subscription costs less then $15 (at least, that's what it cost when I wrote this book).

To get a digital ID from VeriSign, click Tools | Options, and then click the Security tab. Click the Get A Digital ID button at the bottom of the dialog box; Outlook launches your browser and goes to Microsoft's Where To Get Your Digital ID information page.

From there, click the VeriSign Get Your ID Now button to go to the VeriSign Web site and get your own ID. At the VeriSign site, read the instructions to get and install your digital ID.

While you're at the Microsoft site, click the Outlook 2000 Keeps Your Mail Secure link in the upper-left corner of the page and read about Outlook security in greater detail.

Use Your Digital ID

You can add a digital signature to all of your outgoing messages, or you can add a digital signature to individual messages as you create them.

To add your digital signature to all of your messages automatically, click Tools | Options and click the Security tab. Mark the Add Digital Signature To Outgoing Messages check box and click OK.

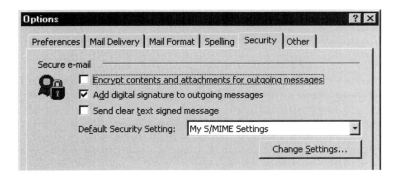

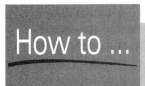

Install Your New Digital ID in Outlook 2000

The VeriSign site has instructions for installing your digital ID in Outlook 98, and by the time you read this, it may have added instructions for Outlook 2000. But if not, after you receive your digital ID, the instructions for Outlook 98 tell you to open Tools | Options, click the Security tab, and click the Change Settings button. Instead, click the Setup Secure E-Mail button (on the Security tab of the Options dialog box). When your ID has been installed, there will be lots of information in the Change Security Settings dialog box; click OK to accept the data and close the dialog box, and your security check boxes will be available for sending secure e-mail.

 *This check box becomes available only when you actually have a digital signature to add.*

To add your digital signature to an individual message, open and create your new message. On the message toolbar, click the Options button. In the Message Options dialog box, mark the Add Digital Signature To Outgoing Message check box, and then click the Close button to close the dialog box.

Understanding Encryption and Digital IDs

Security is the new Internet dilemma. Consider paper security, which has many centuries of practice behind it: when you type or write a message on paper, you can sign it at the bottom to provide proof of its source and verity, and your signature can easily be checked against permanent records (the same way that a bank can check the signature on a check). Beyond that, you can seal the document in an envelope, sign again over the flap, and cover that with cellophane tape to ensure tamper-free transmission. As a final measure, you can send it via certified delivery, and have proof that your correspondent received the document intact. Given these precautions, we've had faith in paper-based messaging systems for a very long time. But how can you have that same degree of faith in electronic transmissions, especially when they're sensitive or involve your credit card number?

S/MIME, or Secure MIME, is a new e-mail standard that attempts to ensure confidential, secure delivery by using a combination of encryption and digital signatures to protect against snooping, tampering, and forgery. There are a number of levels of encryption and different kinds of digital signatures, and S/MIME-capable e-mail systems can negotiate the appropriate encryption algorithms between themselves. This negotiation between e-mail systems involves an encryption key—a secret number that's used in an algorithm (a mathematical formula) to encrypt data. Outlook uses public key encryption, which requires a pair of keys, called public and private keys.

In a public/private key encryption system, two different (but mathematically related) numerical keys are used. When one key encrypts something, the other can decrypt it. You send your public key to your correspondents, and keep the private key. (It's safe for you to give your public key to others, because it's quite difficult to figure out a private key from a public key.) When they send you a message, they can encrypt it using your public key (which you sent them ahead of time). The only person who can decrypt their message is you, because you hold the private key. For you to send them an encrypted message, they must send you their public key ahead of time so that you can encrypt your message.

Even though you can encrypt a message to prevent snoopers from reading it, you still need a way to prove to your correspondents that the message came from you and that the message was not tampered with during transit. To do that, you send the message with a digital signature, which is transmitted to your correspondent along with the message. For a digital signature to mean anything, there has to be a way to verify that people are who they say they are. The way this happens is through a digital certificate, a public key that's signed with the private key of a trusted third party (such as VeriSign, from whom you can get your own digital ID).

Encryption

Encryption is James Bond stuff. It uses a mathematical algorithm to scramble your message, and only a recipient with the key can unscramble and read the message. To send an encrypted message to someone, they must have a digital ID (which contains an encryption algorithm), and you must have a copy of their digital ID in your Contacts list. If you don't have a copy of their digital ID in your Contacts list, you'll see the following message when you try to send encrypted mail to them.

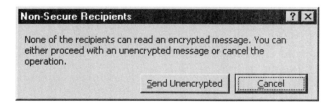

 When you get your own digital ID, you'll have an encryption algorithm of your own that you can send to your contacts. Then, they can send you encrypted messages.

To get someone's digital ID into your Contacts list, ask them to send you a digitally signed message. Open the message and right-click the From field, and then click Add To Contacts. The new contact that's created will include their digital ID and encryption algorithm (you'll see the certificate entered in the Certificates tab of their Contact dialog box).

To encrypt a single message, click the Options button on the message toolbar. In the Message Options dialog box, mark the Encrypt Message Contents and Attachments check box, and then click the Close button to close the dialog box.

To encrypt automatically all the messages you send, click Tools | Options, and click the Security tab. Mark the Encrypt Message Contents And Attachments For Outgoing Messages check box, and click OK. If you automatically encrypt every message, you can deliberately unencrypt specific messages by opening the message's Message Options dialog box and clearing the Encryption check box.

When you receive an encrypted message, you'll see this icon in the message

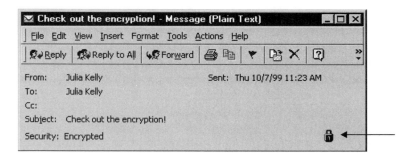

and this icon in your Inbox list:

In this chapter, you learned how to manage your e-mail flow. (Chapter 17 covers some specialized features for those of you who use Outlook in Corporate/Workgroup configuration *and* use the Microsoft Exchange Server as a network mail server.) The next chapter covers sending files with e-mail, receiving files in your e-mail, and sending your friends hyperlinks directly to Web sites.

Chapter 6

Sending Files Through E-Mail

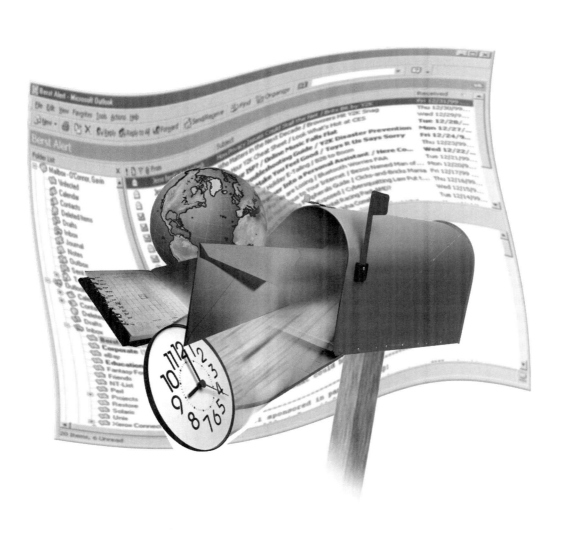

How to . . .

■ Send Files in your messages

■ Receive files in messages

■ Send Web hyperlinks in messages

■ Write a Microsoft Word letter in Outlook

Lots of people never use e-mail to send anything more than typed messages to friends, family members across the country, military spouses overseas, or their representatives in Congress. But, if you use Outlook as a work tool, sooner or later you'll need to send someone an entire electronic file, such as an Excel spreadsheet or a WordPerfect document. Even if your colleague is located just two doors away in another department, sending a file in an e-mail message is more efficient than carrying it on a floppy disk or making them find their way through the company intranet labyrinth to the folder where the file is saved.

The capability to send written material, such as the pages and pictures in this book, over telephone wires has changed many industries dramatically. For example, in the not-so-distant past, I'd have printed out each chapter of this book and mailed it to my publisher, who'd mark it up with red pencil and mail it back to me. I'd retype the whole messy chapter with the changes (and would probably add new typing errors), and mail it back to my publisher, where it would be entirely retyped for printing. The capability to send the same chapter back and forth electronically and edit it in a word-processing program has saved incalculable time, paper, and postal charges for everyone (and has reduced the inevitable typographical errors considerably).

If you need to send files, either within your workplace or across the world, you can use Outlook to send them. Outlook gives you a variety of options for sending files, so that no matter what sort of e-mail system your correspondent uses, you can still send files back and forth. One very big advantage of sending files in e-mail is that you can share files cross-platform (for example, if you use a Windows-based PC and your colleague works on a Mac, sharing files via floppy disks can be a big headache, whereas files sent in e-mail are easy to share).

Sending Files in Your Messages

There are three ways to send a file in Outlook: as an *attachment*, as *text* in the body of the message, and as a *shortcut* to the location of the file on your network.

When you send a file as an attachment, a copy of the entire *binary* file (the Access database, the Windows Paint picture, the WordPerfect document, and so forth) is attached to, and rides along with, the message. The attached file appears as an icon in the body of the message, and your recipient can either double-click the icon to open the file from within the message or copy the file to a more permanent location by dragging the icon to another folder or their Windows desktop. Figure 6-1 shows a Plain Text message with two attached files.

NOTE *To be able to open the attached file, your recipient must have a program that's compatible with the program in which you saved the file (for example, a correspondent who has Access 95 won't be able to open an Access 2000 database).*

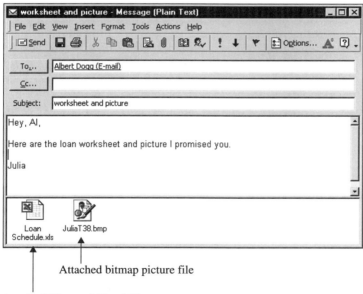

FIGURE 6-1   A Plain Text message with two attached files

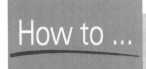 **Send Large Files and Multiple Files**

If you're sending large files, especially database and picture files, don't try to send more than 2MB (2000K) in a single message, because many mail servers can't handle more than that. Messages that are loaded with large and/or multiple files take a long time to send and receive, and are capable of crashing a recipient's mail service if they're too big. Here's my advice about how to get those large files to your recipients.

To check the size of an outgoing message, add the Size field to your Outbox. To compress a file down to a more efficient size, use a common file-compression program, such as WinZip (you can find it at **www.winzip.com**), and send the compressed file. You can also compress multiple files into a single "zipped" file. Zipped files not only reduce file sizes by quite a lot, they also tend to carry files through the different mail gateways with fewer encoding problems.

If you find that your message is too large because you're sending multiple files (more than 1.5MB is awfully large), send several smaller messages, each with a single file. And if you zipped several files into a single zipped file that's too large, divide the files among a few zipped files and send each zipped file in its own message. If worse comes to worse and you absolutely can't reduce the size of a file adequately, contact your recipient and investigate using a computer-to-computer connection, such as Windows HyperTerminal, to transfer the file directly between your two computers.

Another way to send a file is as *text* in the body of your message, which is a good solution if you need to send a file type that your correspondent can't open (and if the file isn't tremendously lengthy). A text file is like text you typed in the message, except that you don't have to type it; because it's already in electronic form, you can insert or drag the existing text into the message. Files sent as text are not limited to word processing documents; you can send other files, such as the following snippet of an Excel worksheet.

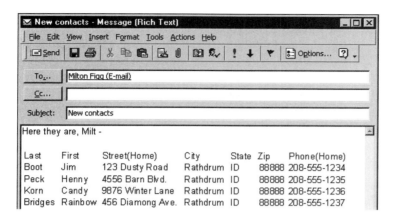

How the text appears in the message depends on the format of the message (Rich Text, Plain Text, or HTML).

The third way to send a file is to send a *shortcut* to the file rather than the file itself. For example, if you and a co-worker are working on the same Excel spreadsheet, you can send a shortcut so your co-worker can find and open the file quickly. The shortcut appears as an icon in the message.

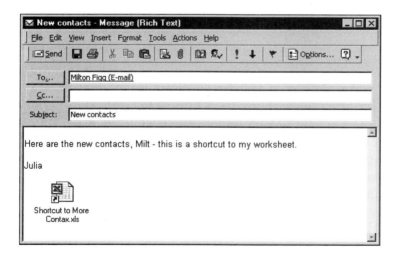

This only works if the file is located in a folder that your coworker has access to, such as a shared or public folder on a company network, and your message is created in Rich Text Format (you won't be able to create a shortcut in a Plain Text or HTML message).

> **TIP** *Sending a shortcut to a file gives your coworker access to your original file rather than a copy, so be sure you protect the file, or create a copy and send a shortcut to that, if you want to protect your work.*

Sending a File As an Attachment

Suppose you're drafting a major financial report for the Budget Committee, and it's going to be a polished, professional Excel workbook. You want input on your work from a colleague who's not on your network, and you want them to see the

What Are Binary Files?

A binary file (a file created in a specific program, such as Microsoft Word or Excel) contains a lot more than the text you typed. The file also contains all the formatting you see on your screen, such as the font type and size, page breaks, margins, bullets, page numbers, and so forth. Essentially, any file you can format to look good and be easy to read is a binary file.

The opposite of a binary file is a text file. A good example of a text file is any file you create and save using Windows Notepad—it has no formatting at all, just the characters you type. Text files aren't good-looking, but they are small and can be opened in just about any program. For example, the size of my draft of Chapter 2 in Word was 38K, but when I copied and pasted it into a Notepad file, it was only 23K.

Text files are useful for information when no formatting is required. Databases of information, such as long customer lists, are often stored as text files to save space and then opened in a program such as Microsoft Access or FoxPro when someone wants to use the information.

fully formatted file, so the best way to send a copy of the file is as an attachment. To attach a file to a message, follow these steps:

1. Create the new message. It can be any format (Plain Text, Rich Text, or HTML).

2. Click the Insert File button on the message toolbar. The Insert File button looks like a paper clip.

3. In the Insert File dialog box that opens, navigate to the folder where the file is stored, and double-click the filename. An icon for the attached file appears in your message.

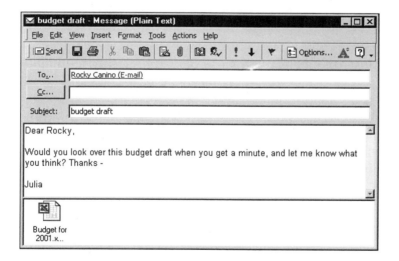

If your message is formatted as Rich Text, the icon appears within the message body, at the location of the insertion point (so if you want the icon in the middle of the message, or at the end, click there before you click the

Insert button). If your message is formatted as Plain Text or HTML, the icon appears in a separate pane below the body of your message (refer to Figure 6-1).

4. Finish your message and send it.

If your recipient has a copy of the same program in which you saved the file, they can double-click the icon to open the file. If you're not sure about which programs they use, check with your correspondent before you send the file. Most word processing and spreadsheet programs can be saved as different or multiple file types so that you can share them more easily.

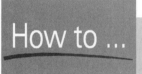 **Change the Mail-Encoding Format**

When you send a binary file, Outlook encodes the file so that it travels to its destination rapidly and intact. When the file arrives, most e-mail programs automatically decode the file, regardless of the encoding format. Occasionally, however, you'll have a correspondent who cannot receive and open your attached files, and they might tell you it's because of the encoding type (some e-mail programs and commercial mail services are not truly up to date).

The most common file-encoding type is MIME, and an older file type still in use is UUEncode. There's no need to remember what they mean, but if you're curious: MIME stands for *Multipurpose Internet Mail Extensions,* and UUEncode stands for *Unix-to-Unix Encode.* MIME is newer and supports the transfer of a wider range of file types (such as audio, video, and graphics, as well as e-mail); UUEncode was the standard for a long time, and was originally designed primarily to support the transfer of text-based files. The "best" one is whichever one works for you and your specific correspondent, but in most cases, MIME will be the correct choice.

If you need to switch your encoding type for a specific correspondent, make the switch, create and send their message, and then switch back (so you won't upset your other correspondents with your changed encoding). To change the encoding type (which of the following procedures you use depends on your Outlook configuration), click Tools I Options, and then:

- If you have Internet Mail Only configuration, click the Mail Format tab, select Plain Text formatting, and then click the Settings button. Choose an encoding option (MIME or Uuencode) and then click OK twice to close both dialog boxes

- If you have Corporate/Workgroup configuration, click the Internet E-Mail tab, choose an encoding option (MIME or UUENCODE), and click OK. In the Corporate/Workgroup configuration, you can also change the encoding for a single message when you create the message: click File | Properties on the message's menu bar, click the Internet E-Mail tab, click the Override Default Setting And Use option, click the encoding option you want, and then click OK.

6

Sending a File As Text

Suppose you need to send an electronic document to someone who can't open files you create in your word processing program. As long as they need just the information and don't care about the formatting of the document, you can send them the information as a text file, and the text will appear in the message. Your correspondent won't have to open anything but your e-mail message to read the information.

Insert the Entire File

If you insert a binary file, such as a WordPerfect document, into a message as a text file, you'll see pages of garbage characters, because the binary file carries its underlying formatting with it. However, binary files in just about any program can be saved as a Text File type, and those text files can be inserted directly into the message.

To insert a file into a message as text, follow these steps:

1. Create a new message.

2. Click the Insert File button on the toolbar. The Insert File dialog box appears.

3. Navigate to the folder where the file is saved, and click the filename to select it. *Don't* double-click the filename, because that inserts an attachment by default.

4. In the Insert File dialog box, click the arrow next to the Insert button, and click Insert As Text.

The text of the entire file is inserted in the body of the message.

Drag Text into the Message

You can send a binary file as text without saving the file as a text type, if the software in which the file was created is Object Linking and Embedding (OLE)-compliant (which means you can drag and drop information from one window into another). Microsoft Word and Excel are OLE-compliant; if you use a different program, you can find out whether it's capable of drag-and-drop transfers by trying the following procedure.

TIP *This procedure is most helpful when you want to send a short portion of a file in your e-mail message. For example, if someone wants to know what books I've written, instead of sending them my whole resume, I can drag or copy and paste just the list of titles from my resume document into the message.*

To insert a file as text using this technique, open the file and drag the text from the file window into the message. The file (or whatever part of it you select) is inserted as text without all the extra formatting characters. To drag and drop text into a message, follow these steps:

1. Create a new message.

2. Open the file you want to insert in the message, and arrange the file and message windows side by side or overlapping.

6

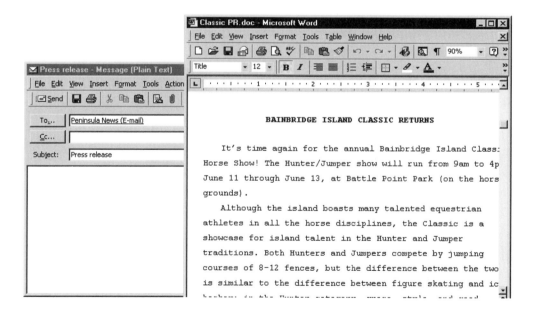

3. In the file, select the text you want to insert in the message (in most programs, you can select the entire file by pressing CTRL-A).

4. Drag the selected information from the file window, and drop it in the message.

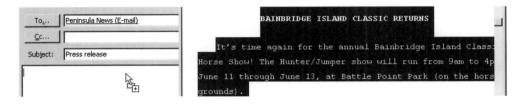

5. Finish the message and send it.

Sending a Shortcut to a File

If you're sharing a file with a coworker on your network, you can save them time by sending a shortcut to the file instead of the file itself. The advantage of sending a shortcut is that it doesn't create a copy of the file, so there's no need to compare or merge copies of the file later. Or, suppose you keep a list of supplies that need to be ordered, and it's most efficient to have everyone in your organization add the items they want to the same list. Sending everyone in your organization a shortcut to that file is a good way to centralize and simplify the process.

NOTE *Be sure that recipients of your shortcut have network access to the folder where the file is stored.*

To send a shortcut in a message, follow these steps:

1. Create a new message. The message must be in Rich Text Format to be shortcut-capable (if Rich Text isn't your default message format, click Format in the message toolbar, and click Rich Text to switch).

TIP *If your default message format is HTML, switch the message to Plain Text format and then switch the message to Rich Text Format.*

2. Click the Insert File button on the message toolbar. The Insert File dialog box appears.

3. In the Insert File dialog box, navigate to the folder where the file is saved. Be sure the file is saved in a folder your correspondent is allowed to access.

4. Click the filename to select it (don't double-click, because that inserts an attachment by default).

5. Click the arrow next to the Insert button in the lower-right corner of the dialog box and click Insert As Shortcut. The shortcut is an icon that reads "Shortcut to" the filename.

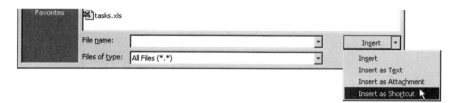

6. Finish your message and send it. You can send the message to any number of recipients, or to distribution lists, and they'll all receive the shortcut.

Sending Outlook Items

If your correspondents have Outlook, you can send them copies of your Outlook items. You can send any sort of Outlook item, such as messages you've received, contacts, notes, tasks, and calendar appointments. For example, if you already have all the details of the annual departmental picnic recorded in your Calendar (and your correspondent has Outlook), it's faster to send the appointment than to copy all the details into a message. If your correspondent doesn't have Outlook, you can send the information in an Outlook item as text. To send an Outlook item, follow these steps:

1. Create a new message.

2. On the message menu bar, click Insert | Item. The Insert Item dialog box appears, as shown in Figure 6-2.

Click an Outlook folder   Click an insert option

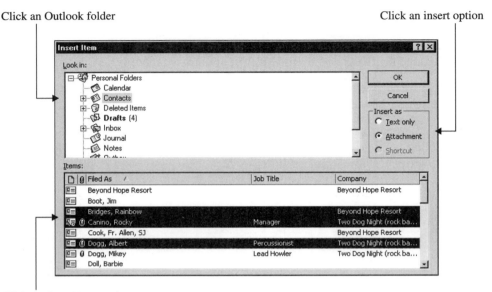

Click the item(s) to send

FIGURE 6-2 The Insert Item dialog box

3. In the upper pane, click the Outlook folder where the item is saved. If the item is in a subfolder, click the plus symbol next to the main folder to display its subfolders, and then click the subfolder. If you're sending a shortcut to the item, be sure you select a shared or public folder so that your correspondent has access to the item.

4. In the lower pane, click the item(s) you want to send. You can select multiple items by using the SHIFT or CTRL keys.

5. In the Insert As option group, select whether you want to send Text Only (for correspondents who don't have Outlook), Attachment (for correspondents who have Outlook but no access to your copy of Outlook), or Shortcut (for correspondents who have Outlook and have access to the selected Outlook folder).

6. Click OK.

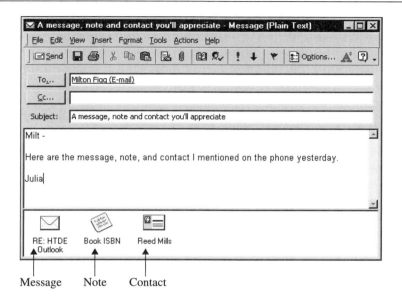

FIGURE 6-3 A message with attached Outlook items

The message in Figure 6-3 has a message, a note, and a contact inserted as attachments. My recipients have Outlook, and can drag the icons from the message into the folder icons in their Outlook bars.

Receiving Files in Messages

If you can send files in your e-mail, you can receive them, as well. You may get messages with attached files, text, shortcuts, or Outlook items, and here's what you can do with them.

Receiving Attached Files

If you receive a message with an icon in it (and the icon doesn't read "shortcut to"), you've got an attached file. You can do any of these things with the icon:

■ Double-click the icon to open it and leave it in the message.

■ Click the icon to select it, and then click the Delete button on the message toolbar (if you know you don't want the file, but want to keep the message).

■ Drag the icon to the appropriate folder icon in your Outlook bar, if the icon is for an Outlook item. For example, if a correspondent sends you a contact, drag the item's icon to the Contacts icon in your Outlook bar.

■ Drag the icon to the appropriate folder icon in your Outlook bar, if the icon is for a non-Outlook file and you've got a shortcut to the hard-drive folder displayed in your Outlook bar (you'll learn how to use Outlook to work with folders on your hard drive in Chapter 12).

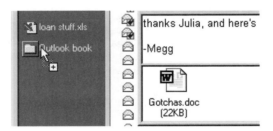

■ Drag the icon to a folder on your desktop to save it in the folder, and open it from there.

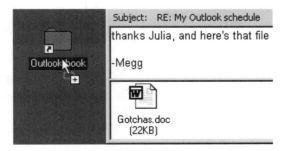

When you drag an icon from a message to a new location, the file is copied—which is useful if you inadvertently mess up or delete the file, because you'll still have an untouched copy in your message.

TIP   *If your correspondent writes "Here's that file..." in a message, and you don't see an icon for the file, one of two things has probably happened: either they forgot to include the file, or they sent the file but for some reason your mail server couldn't handle it. Ask your correspondent to try changing the encoding type (MIME vs. UUEncode), and see if that does the trick.*

6

Receiving Text Files

If you receive a message with a text file, it will be text in your message. All you have to do is read it.

Receiving Shortcuts

If you receive a message with an icon that reads "shortcut to...," it's a shortcut to a file on your correspondent's network. If you have access to the network folder that the shortcut points to, double-click the icon to open the file. If the file is one that you need to open fairly often, you can drag the shortcut icon to your desktop or into another folder to keep it handy. If the shortcut icon won't open the file, contact your correspondent—you may need to be granted access to the folder where the file is saved.

Sending Web Hyperlinks in Messages

When you find a great and useful Web site on the Internet, you can share it with friends and coworkers by sending them a direct *hyperlink* in a message. A hyperlink is the blue, underlined text that you've probably seen in software help files or in Web pages—it contains the Web address of a specific Web page, and if you click the underlined words, your Internet browser finds and opens that Web page. To add a hyperlink to a message, follow these steps:

1. Create a new message.

2. At the point in your message where you want to place the hyperlink, type the hyperlink address, as shown in Figure 6-4. You can type a hyperlink anywhere in the body of your message; Outlook recognizes what you've typed and turns it into a hyperlink.

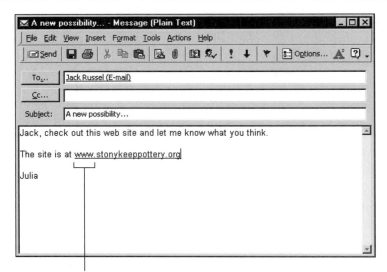

Type the URL prefix first

Typing a hyperlink in a message

What happens when you type your message varies depending on what your message format is:

- In a Plain Text or Rich Text message, begin by typing the **www.** portion of the address. As soon as you type the next letter, the hyperlink turns blue and is underlined. Continue typing the address, and press ENTER or type a space to complete the hyperlink. If you make a mistake, use the BACKSPACE key to delete the error, and then continue typing.

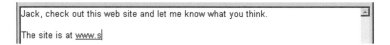

- In an HTML message, you can type the hyperlink, beginning with **www.**, and after you complete the address and press ENTER or type a space, the hyperlink will turn blue and be underlined. You also have the option, in an

HTML message, of clicking Insert | Hyperlink on the message menu bar. The Hyperlink dialog box appears. In the Type list box, you can select from a number of different Internet address prefixes, such as gopher, news, or telnet, and then finish entering the address in the URL box.

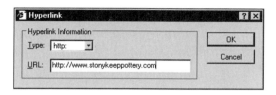

NOTE *URL is an acronym for Uniform Resource Locator, which is an address for a location on the Internet. The WWW, or World Wide Web, is one region of the Internet.*

6

No matter what your message format is, if the Web address doesn't begin with "www." (and many new ones don't), type the address beginning with **http://** and Outlook will recognize and create the hyperlink to the Web site. If the address is a different type of Internet site, such as gopher or telnet, you can type those, too. They don't all use the same punctuation, however, so check whether the address needs the "//" characters before you enter the address.

If you notice an error after you finish typing the hyperlink, you can't click the hyperlink to edit it, because clicking the hyperlink launches your browser. Instead, select the entire hyperlink and at least one character or space adjacent to the hyperlink, and press DELETE. Then retype the hyperlink.

To avoid typing errors when entering a hyperlink, you can select and copy the hyperlink from your browser's Web address toolbar (while you have the Web page open), and then paste the copied characters into a message.

When your recipients receive a hyperlink, or when you receive one from them, all they (or you) need to do is click the link. Outlook automatically launches the computer's default browser, and the browser finds and displays the Web or Internet site.

TIP *You can launch your own browser and go to a Web site quickly by typing the Web address in a new message and then clicking it. Delete the message without saving it when you're finished.*

Writing a Microsoft Word Letter in Outlook

If you use Microsoft Word, Outlook provides a Letter Wizard to help you create a formally formatted letter to a specific contact. After you write the letter, you can send it as an attachment to an e-mail message, as a fax, or print it and send it via snail mail.

 This only works if you have Microsoft Word 2000 installed on your computer.

To use the Letter Wizard, open your Contacts folder and click the contact to whom you want to address the letter. Then, click Actions | New Letter to Contact. Microsoft Word opens, and the Letter Wizard appears.

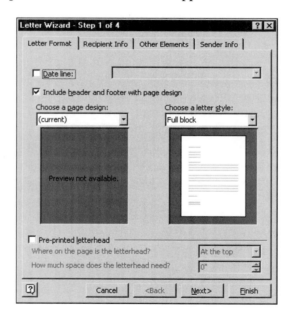

The Letter Wizard is fairly self-explanatory; each time you click the Next button, a different tab in the wizard's dialog box opens (so you can switch between tabs instead of clicking the Next and Back buttons). The wizard helps you add all the correct elements and lay them out properly. When you click Finish, the prepared letter opens in Microsoft Word and you can type the body of your letter.

When you finish the letter and want to send it as an e-mail message, click File | Send To, and then click either Mail Recipient or Mail Recipient (As Attachment).

If you select Mail Recipient, an e-mail addressing header appears at the top of the Word document.

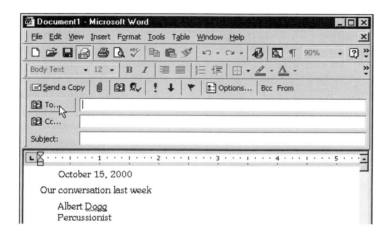

Fill in the boxes in the addressing header just as if the letter were an e-mail message, and click the Send A Copy button at the left end of the toolbar. The letter goes to your Outbox to await mailing, and is sent as an HTML message.

If your recipient's mail program can't open and read HTML messages, select Mail Recipient (As Attachment) instead. A new e-mail message appears, in your default message format, and the letter (a Word file) is included as an attachment. Address and send the e-mail using normal e-mail procedures.

After you set up the e-mail message and send it to your Outbox, close Word. Save the letter if you want to, but even if you don't save it, a copy of the letter remains in your e-mail message.

In this chapter, you've learned how to use Outlook to send files and hyperlinks to other people, and what to do with files and hyperlinks when others send them to you. The next chapter will finish up the subject of communication in Outlook by showing you how to set up and send faxes from Outlook, and how to run mail merges from your Outlook Contacts folder.

Chapter 7

Sending Faxes and Running Mail Merges

How to . . .

- ■ Set Up a Fax Program in Outlook
- ■ Send a Fax
- ■ Receive and Open a Fax in Outlook
- ■ Run a Mail Merge from Contacts

When you have to send written communications, especially in a business environment, you need to be able to take advantage of all the techniques available. This chapter completes your collection of techniques for written communications with Outlook.

When you use Outlook to communicate, you're not limited to e-mail; Outlook can also help you fax (send facsimiles of) files from your computer, and use mail-merge techniques to send bulk e-mail messages and faxes. Faxes come in really handy when you need to send information to someone who doesn't have e-mail (or even a computer), but has a fax machine. You can use Outlook's mail-merge feature to set up printed documents and mailing labels for Outlook contacts.

The fax software in your computer won't completely replace a separate fax machine, because you can't feed sheets of paper (like order forms or contracts with your signature) into your computer as quickly and simply as you can feed them into a fax machine. On the other hand, if your document is already electronic, it's faster to fax from Outlook than to print and fax separately.

Another advantage of Outlook's fax capability is that you can receive faxes as electronic images (no more running out of fax paper in the middle of a fax). As long as Outlook is open and set up to receive, incoming faxes go directly to your Inbox.

NOTE *To send and receive faxes, your computer must have a fax/modem installed and be connected to a telephone line.*

Mail-merging a document to a large number of addresses (to send form letters or to create mailing labels) is a fairly common procedure in word processing programs, and many word processing programs can use Outlook's Contacts as a data source of addresses. But from within Outlook, you can use mail-merge procedures and Contacts folders to do more: you can merge Contacts addresses to send bulk e-mail messages (like spammers do), and if you're set up in Corporate/Workgroup configuration, you can send mail-merge documents as bulk faxes.

Setting Up a Fax Program in Outlook

There are two fax programs for Outlook:

- If you're set up in Internet Mail Only configuration, you'll use the Symantec Fax Starter Edition.

- If you're set up in Corporate/Workgroup configuration, you'll use Microsoft Fax from Windows 95 or Windows 98.

NOTE *If you don't know what configuration you have, click Help | About Microsoft Outlook, and you'll find the configuration at the top of the message.*

Installing Symantec Fax for Internet Mail Only Configuration

If you're running Outlook in Internet Mail Only configuration, the Symantec WinFax Starter Edition Setup Wizard automatically starts the first time you attempt to send a fax.

NOTE *If you installed and set up the Symantec Fax Starter Edition when you installed Outlook, you can skip this section. Whether you install the fax program when you first install Outlook, or later when you try to send your first fax, this is the procedure for using the Setup Wizard.*

This is how to run the wizard and set up the Symantec Fax Starter Edition:

1. Open your Inbox and click Actions | New Fax Message. When you see a message that Symantec Fax Starter Edition is not installed, and asking if you want to install it now, click Yes.

2. The wizard installs several files and then tells you that you must restart Outlook. Click OK and then quit Outlook and restart it.

3. When you restart Outlook, you'll see the starting message from the wizard. Click Next.

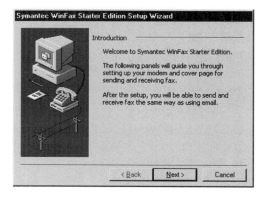

4. In the next step in the wizard (shown in the following illustration), fill in the requested information. The Station Identifier is the text that's printed on the faxes your recipients see, telling them who sent the fax. You can enter your name, your company name, or your fax telephone number as the station identifier. After you fill in all the information, click Next.

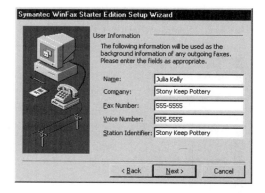

5. In the next step, fill in your address information. This information is automatically entered in cover sheets for outgoing faxes (and you can delete it from a cover sheet before you send a fax, if you prefer). Filling in the information here spares you the effort of typing it in on cover sheets; then, click Next.

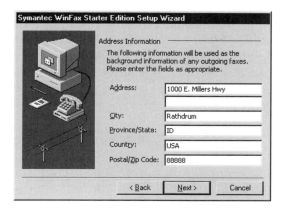

6. The next wizard step asks for your preferences for receiving and sending faxes. If you want your computer to automatically receive faxes when a fax machine dials in (for example, to accept faxed product orders), click the Automatic Receive Fax check box; if you don't want to be bothered by random faxes and want to receive only those that you know are inbound from associates, leave the check box clear. Under Retries, set your preferences for dialing a fax number that's busy.

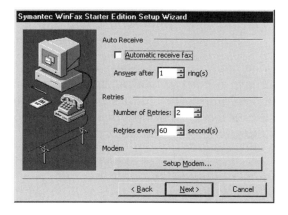

7. Click the Setup Modem button to check and set your modem for sending and receiving faxes. The Modem Properties dialog box appears. If you have more than one modem listed, click the name of the fax/modem you'll use to send faxes. Then click the Properties button. When you see a message saying that the selected modem has not been configured, and asking if you want to run the Modem Configuration Wizard now, click Yes.

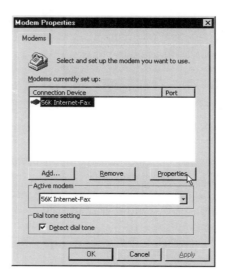

8. The Modem Configuration Wizard starts. Read and follow the steps in the wizard. If you have an external modem, be sure it's turned on; if you have an internal modem, you can assume it's turned on. Be sure your browser and Outlook are not using the modem (they should not be connected online). Then click Next.

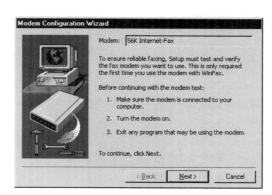

9. The wizard spends a few moments checking the specifications of your modem, and when it's finished, it shows a list of results, and the Next button becomes available again. Click Next to continue.

10. In the final step, the wizard tells you that your modem is configured. Click Finish. A Properties dialog box for your fax appears. On the General tab, you can safely leave the default settings, or you can set a faster initialization speed and you can silence the modem noise (slide the Volume marker to Off if you don't want to listen to the modem dialing and connecting to fax machines when it sends faxes). Then, click the Fax tab.

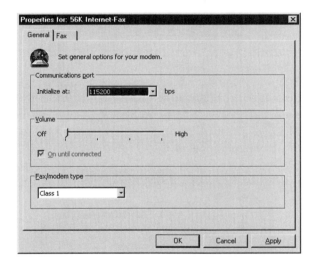

11. On the Fax tab, take a look at the fax transmission settings, but don't make any changes unless you are an expert in this area (you could easily wind up with a nonfunctional fax). Then, click OK to return to the Modem Properties dialog box.

7

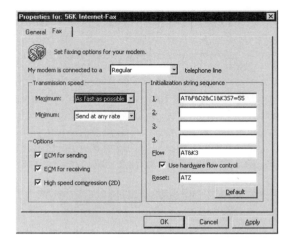

12. Click OK again to close the Modem Properties dialog box. You'll see a message saying you've changed the active modem and that you need to restart Outlook before you use the modem. Click OK to return to the Symantec WinFax Starter Edition Setup Wizard, and click Next. The cover page step of the wizard appears.

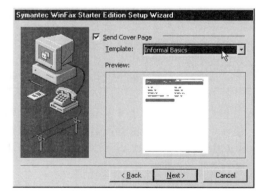

13. If you want to use a default cover page with each fax, leave the Send Cover Page check box marked, and then select a cover page style from the Template list box.

14. Click Next, and then click Finish. Quit and restart Outlook, and send someone a fax to test your setup.

 *When you restart Outlook, a Symantec Registration dialog box appears—you don't have to register unless you want future e-mail from Symantec. If you don't want to register, click Skip.*

See the section "Sending a Fax," later in this chapter, to learn how to send faxes after you set up your fax program.

Change Your Cover Page

Suppose you discover, when you look over the cover page for your first fax, that you spelled your address or station identifier incorrectly. Here's the easy way to change these settings:

1. Click Tools | Options.

2. On the Fax tab (which appears after you install your fax program), click the Edit button and change any cover page information that needs changing. Click the Template button if you want to choose a different default cover page.

3. Click Apply to make your changes take effect immediately, and then click OK to close the Options dialog box.

7

Can't Find Your Symantec Fax Setup Wizard?

Occasionally the Symantec WinFax Starter Edition Setup Wizard gets lost—for example, if you begin the setup procedure and quit before it's finished, the wizard might not start automatically again. Or, someone else might have done that on your computer, and the wizard won't start automatically. The wizard does a lot of behind-the-scenes setup work for you, so it's important that you use the wizard to set up your fax, instead of trying to do it yourself.

If the Setup Wizard doesn't start automatically when you follow the installation procedure, you can locate the wizard file and start it manually.

First, quit Outlook. Then, click Start | Find | Files Or Folders. Search for the file named OLFSETUP.EXE on the drive where you installed Outlook. In the Search Results list, double-click the OLFSETUP.EXE file to start the wizard, and then follow the steps in the section "Installing Symantec Fax for Internet Mail Only Configuration," starting at step 3.

Change Your Dialing Setup

Perhaps you decide that Outlook should try each fax number five times before giving up, instead of the default two times. Here's how to make the change quickly:

1. Click Tools | Options.

2. On the Fax tab, under Modem, you can change dialing settings for sending and receiving faxes. If you need to change any modem properties, click the Modem button and make your changes.

3. Click Apply to make your changes take effect immediately, and then click OK to close the Options dialog box.

Installing Microsoft Fax for Corporate/Workgroup Configuration

If you're running Outlook in Corporate/Workgroup configuration, you use the Microsoft Fax program that comes with Windows 95 and Windows 98. The Microsoft Fax program is already on your computer if you use Windows 95, and is on the Windows 98 CD-ROM if you use Windows 98. If you already had Microsoft Fax installed on your computer before you installed Outlook 2000 in the Corporate/Workgroup mode, then Outlook 2000 will have configured itself to use Microsoft Fax. To check, click Outlook's Help menu; if you see a Microsoft Fax Help command, then Microsoft Fax is already installed and you can skip this section. If you don't see the Microsoft Fax Help command, use one of the following installation directions to install Microsoft Fax for Outlook in Corporate/Workgroup configuration.

Install Microsoft Fax for Windows 95

If you're using Windows 95, Microsoft Fax is available (you may need to have your Windows 95 CD-ROM ready, however). To install Microsoft Fax for Windows 95, follow these steps:

1. Close Outlook and any other open programs.

2. Click Start | Settings | Control Panel.

3. In the Control Panel dialog box, double-click Add/Remove Programs.

4. In the Add/Remove Programs dialog box, on the Windows Setup tab, click the Microsoft Fax check box to mark it, and then click OK and allow Windows to install the new files. (If the Microsoft Fax check box is already marked, that means it's already installed—click Cancel to exit the Add/Remove Programs dialog box).

5. Close the Control Panel dialog box, and then follow the steps in the upcoming section "Add Microsoft Fax to Your Mail Profile."

Install Microsoft Fax for Windows 98

If you use Windows 98, you need to install the Microsoft Fax files from your Windows 98 CD-ROM and follow these steps:

1. Close Outlook and any other open programs.

2. Put your Windows 98 CD-ROM in the CD-ROM drive. If the CD-ROM automatically opens a window, click the Browse This CD button. If the CD doesn't open a window, double-click your My Computer icon to open the My Computer window of your file system, and then double-click the CD-ROM drive icon. Either way, a list of the folders and files on your CD-ROM appears.

3. In the list of folders, double-click the Tools folder, double-click the oldwin95 folder, double-click the message folder, and then double-click the us folder.

4. Double-click the awfax.exe file to install the fax program files.

5. The License Agreement that appears doesn't specifically mention Outlook 2000, but that's okay. Click Yes to continue. If asked about keeping current versions of files, click Yes.

6. When a message asks if you want to restart your computer, click Yes. After Windows restarts, close any open windows, remove the CD-ROM from your CD-ROM drive, and then follow the steps in the next section.

Add Microsoft Fax to Your Mail Profile (for Windows 95 and Windows 98)

After you install the Microsoft Fax files, you need to add Microsoft Fax to your Mail Profile, and then reinstall Outlook 2000. (Remember, these procedures are for the Corporate/Workgroup configuration of Outlook 2000.)

1. Click Start | Settings | Control Panel.

2. Double-click the Mail icon (if you have a Mail And Fax icon, double-click that). The Microsoft Outlook Internet Settings dialog box appears.

3. On the Services tab, click the Add button. The Add Service To Profile dialog box appears.

4. Click Microsoft Fax, and click OK. A message appears asking if you want to enter important fax information now. Click Yes, and the Microsoft Fax Properties dialog box appears.

5. In the Microsoft Fax Properties dialog box, fill in all the information you can in each of the dialog box tabs:

   ■ On the User tab, fill in your phone number and address information.

   ■ On the Modem tab, click the Set As Active Fax Modem button. If you have more than one modem listed, click the one you'll use to send faxes, before you click the button.

   ■ On the Dialing tab, you can change the number of retries for sending faxes, or keep the default settings. Click the Dialing Properties button and check the dialing properties for your phone line to be sure they're correct, and then click OK.

   ■ On the Message tab, the default settings are safe to keep, and you can select a different default cover page if you want to (or clear the Send Cover Page check box to avoid sending cover pages at all).

6. Click OK when you finish filling in the dialog box. Microsoft Fax appears in your Microsoft Outlook Internet Settings dialog box list. Click OK to close the dialog box, and then close the Control Panel window.

Next, and last, you need to reinstall Office 2000 (or Outlook 2000, if you installed Outlook separately).

Reinstall Office (or Outlook) 2000

The last part of setting up Microsoft Fax for Corporate/Workgroup configuration is to reinstall Outlook; when you reinstall Outlook, it configures itself to use Microsoft Fax automatically. To reinstall, follow these steps:

1. Click Start | Settings | Control Panel and double-click the Add/Remove Programs icon.

2. In the Add/Remove Programs dialog box, on the Install/Uninstall tab, click Microsoft Office 2000 (or Microsoft Outlook 2000, if you installed it separately) and then click the Add/Remove button. The Microsoft Office 2000 Maintenance Mode dialog box appears.

3. Click the Repair Office button. The Reinstall/Repair dialog box appears.

4. Click the Reinstall Office option, and then click the Finish button. All of your Office files are checked, reinstalled, and reconfigured while you wait. No changes will be made to your installed programs and preferences, except that Outlook will incorporate the Microsoft Fax feature.

5. When a message tells you that the setup has completed successfully, click OK and then click Yes in the next message to restart your computer.

 After you install Microsoft Fax, a fax icon appears in your Windows taskbar whenever Outlook is open—it's the icon that looks like a desk telephone. The fax icon shows you the status of your fax reception, and you'll use it to handle incoming faxes.

Now you're ready to send faxes. To learn how, go to the section "Send a Fax Using Microsoft At Work Fax (Corporate/Workgroup Configuration)," later in the chapter.

Sending a Fax

So, your fax program is set up and you're ready to test it. Faxes are sent as images—they're not editable files, which means that if you fax a document created from word processing software, your recipient will be able to read and print the image, but won't be able to open it in their own word processing program and make edits. If you send a quick message, the text of your message is sent on a fax cover page. If you fax a document, the document appears to be attached to the message when you send it, but the fax actually sends the full document as a series of page images.

The procedures for sending a fax are different in Outlook's two different configurations, so be sure you read the section that's appropriate for your configuration.

Send a Fax Using Symantec Fax Starter Edition (Internet Mail Only Configuration)

If you're using the Symantec Fax Starter Edition because you have Outlook set up in the Internet Mail Only configuration, this is how you send a fax with an attached file:

1. Close your Internet connection, if it's open. Outlook can't dial anyone's fax number if it's already online with your mail service.

 *If you set up and send faxes while your Internet connection is open, the faxes will sit in your Sent Items folder until you break your Internet connection, and then Outlook will start to dial your outgoing fax numbers automatically.*

2. Open your Inbox (or any of your e-mail message folders) and click File | New | Fax Message. A new message opens—it looks much like an e-mail message.

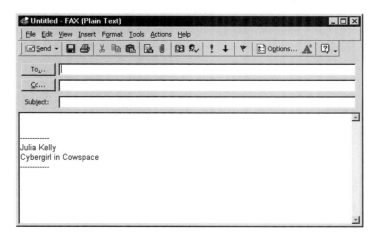

3. In the To box, enter the recipient name(s). It's easiest if you can look up names in your Contacts folder, because Outlook automatically uses contacts' fax numbers.

If you create a new subfolder and keep copies of all contacts that have fax numbers in that subfolder, you'll know that any name you select from that subfolder in the Select Names dialog box has a fax number.

If you don't have a recipient entered in your Contacts folder, you can type a name in the To box, using the following format: **fax@*name***. For example, to send a fax to your colleague Bill York, at 213-555-8999, you would type **fax@bill** (you can type anything as a name—it's the "fax@" part that tells Outlook this is a fax, and the name identifies it for you). After you finish and send the fax, you'll see a dialog box asking you to verify the fax number, and you can type the fax number in the Number box.

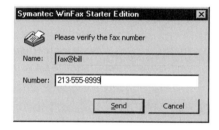

If you have the recipient entered in your Contacts folder without a fax number, the same dialog box appears, but with the recipient's name in the Name box, and you need to enter only their fax number (without the "fax@" part) in the Number box.

*If you need to dial a number to get an outside line, type **w** before the fax number. For example, if you have to dial 9 to get an outside line, you'd type a fax number like this: **9w213-555-8999**.*

4. In the large message box, type the message you want to appear on the cover page. Fax messages are Plain Text by default, but if you want to format the text (fonts, sizes, bullets, and so forth), you can switch the fax message to Rich Text and then use the Formatting toolbar to format the body of your message. If all you want to fax is a message, skip the next step and go to step 6 to send the fax.

7

5. To fax a document, click the Insert button on the fax/message toolbar. In the Insert File dialog box that appears, navigate to the folder where the file is saved, and double-click the filename. The file appears as an attachment to the fax/message. You can attach as many files as you want to the fax.

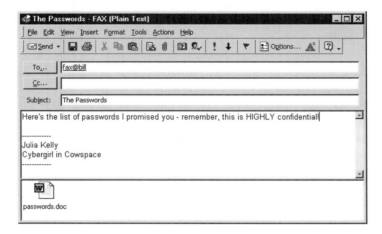

6. When your fax is ready, click the arrow next to the Send button, and click Symantec Fax Starter Edition.

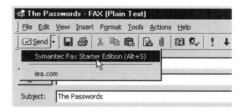

If the fax is going to someone who isn't in your Contacts folder, or who is but doesn't have a fax number entered there, you'll see the dialog box shown in step 3—type the number and click Send. If the fax is going to a contact with a fax number in your Contacts folder, Outlook dials the fax number automatically and sends your fax—you'll know the fax is being sent when you see the progress window.

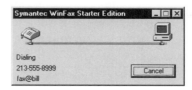

Send a Fax Using Microsoft At Work Fax (Corporate/Workgroup Configuration)

After you set up Microsoft Fax in Corporate/Workgroup configuration, Outlook uses the Compose New Fax wizard to set up faxes for sending. These are the steps to send a fax:

1. Open any mail folder or the Contacts folder.

2. Click Actions | New Fax Message. The Compose New Fax wizard starts.

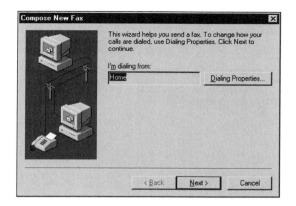

3. If you need to change the dialing properties (for example, if you're using your laptop computer from an airport terminal), click the Dialing Properties button and make the appropriate changes. If the default settings are correct, click Next.

4. In the next wizard step, select recipient names and fax numbers. To send a fax to someone not in Contacts, type the name in the To box and a number in the Fax# boxes, and then click the Add To List button.

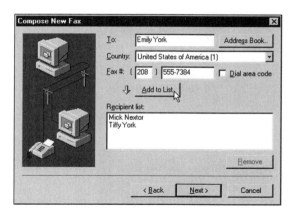

If a recipient is in your Contacts folder, click the Address Book button, and double-click names in the Address Book dialog box to add them to the recipient list for the fax. In the Address Book dialog box, you can select a Contacts folder or subfolder in the list box at the top of the dialog box, and the list of names tells you if the name has a fax number entered. Click OK when you finish adding names from your Contacts folders.

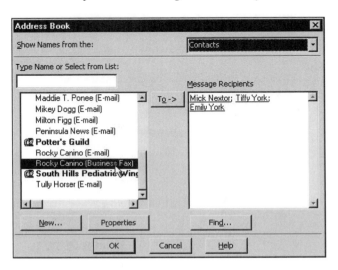

5. When recipient names have all been added, click Next. The next wizard step gives you cover page and scheduling options. To delay sending the fax until phone rates are better, click the Options button, set a specific time for sending, and click OK to return to the wizard. Then click Next.

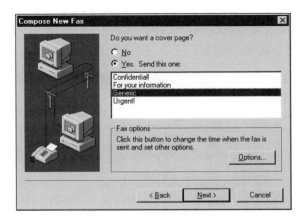

6. In the next wizard step, type a Subject and whatever message you want to
appear on the cover page, and then click Next.

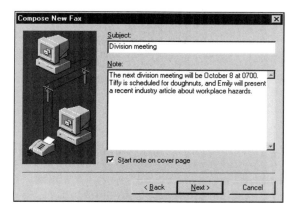

7. If you want to fax any documents, this is the step where you attach them.
In this wizard step, click the Add File button. Browse to locate the file, and
double-click the filename to add it. You can add as many files as you want;
click Next when all the files you want to fax are listed.

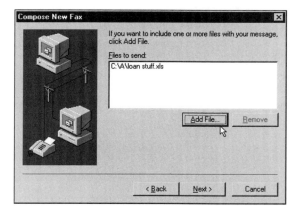

8. The final wizard step tells you the fax is ready to send. Click Finish to send it.

7

 *Remember that Outlook won't send your fax if your browser or Outlook is online, because it needs the phone line free to dial out.*

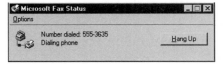

The Microsoft Fax Status dialog box appears and tells you what the fax program is doing at each step of the way. If you need to cancel a call to a specific recipient, you can cancel that call by clicking the Hang Up button when that recipient's name is displayed; Microsoft Fax continues to call the remaining recipients.

Receiving and Opening a Fax in Outlook

How you receive faxes in Outlook depends, again, on what your Outlook configuration is. All faxes that you receive through Outlook arrive in your Inbox.

Keep in mind that you don't have to receive incoming faxes through Outlook. If you have a standalone fax machine that shares the phone line with your computer, you can continue to receive paper faxes at all hours on your fax machine, and use Outlook only to send faxes.

Receiving and Opening Faxes in Symantec Fax Starter Edition (Internet Mail Only Configuration)

To receive faxes through the Symantec Fax Starter Edition, you need to have fax reception turned on in Outlook. Outlook itself needs to be open to receive faxes, and your computer needs to be turned on.

If you expect faxes to arrive without notice at all hours (for example, catalog orders or memos from your supervisor about an urgent project), you can turn on automatic fax reception and leave it on all the time. As faxes are sent to your computer's phone line, they are automatically accepted and accumulated in your Inbox.

NOTE

If you don't want to leave your computer open for business at all times, you can turn on fax reception when you're expecting a fax. Click Tools | Receive Fax. Outlook opens a connection to receive any incoming faxes, and closes the connection when no transmission has occurred after a specified period of time.

To turn on automatic fax reception, follow these steps:

1. Click Tools | Options and click the Fax tab.

2. Click the Automatic Receive Fax check box to mark it, and set a number of rings in the Answer After box. The default number 1 is a good choice if you want the computer to answer before any other telephone equipment on the line can answer. Then click OK.

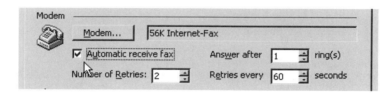

3. When a fax arrives, the following message appears on your computer screen.

When the fax transmission is complete, a fax message appears in your Inbox. When you double-click the message line to open the fax, the first thing you'll see is a window like the one in Figure 7-1.

If you see a macro virus warning, click the Open It option and then click OK. (Windows programs are sometimes extra-cautious about incoming files.)

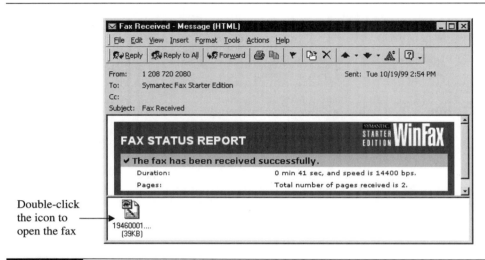

Double-click
the icon to
open the fax

A newly arrived fax

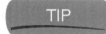

Files sent as faxes cannot contain viruses. If you don't want to be bothered with this message whenever you receive a faxed file, clear the Always Ask check box before you click OK. You'll still be asked about other types of files, but not about faxed files.

Your fax pages open in the Quick Fax Viewer window, shown in Figure 7-2. Use the buttons on the viewer's toolbar to read the fax, and click File I Print to print the fax.

Click File I Exit to close the Quick Fax Viewer. The fax remains an attachment to the fax message in your Inbox.

To turn off automatic fax reception, click Tools I Options and, on the Fax tab, clear the Automatic Receive Fax check box, click Apply, and then click OK.

Receiving and Opening Faxes in Microsoft Fax (Corporate/Workgroup Configuration)

To receive faxes through Microsoft Fax, your computer needs to be turned on and Outlook must be open. And, you need to have fax reception turned on as either automatic or manual.

Click a zoom button to   Rotate   Show a different
change magnification.   pages.   page.

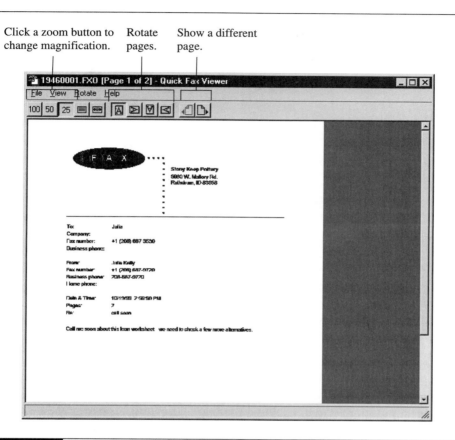

FIGURE 7-2   A new fax in the Quick Fax Viewer window

To turn on automatic fax reception so that Outlook answers incoming calls
after a specific number of rings, follow these steps:

1. Click Tools | Microsoft Fax Tools | Options.

2. In the Microsoft Fax Properties dialog box, on the Modem tab, select the
name of your fax modem and click the Properties button. The Fax Modem
Properties dialog box appears.

3. In the Fax Modem Properties dialog box, click the Answer After option under Answer Mode, and set the number of rings after which Outlook should answer the phone.

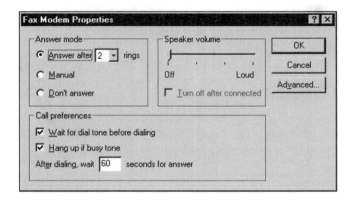

When a fax arrives, Outlook answers the phone after the specified number of rings, and receives the fax into your Inbox.

4. Click OK twice to close both open dialog boxes.

If you use the same phone line for voice calls and computer connections, you'll want to receive faxes manually instead of automatically, so that you can receive both incoming voice calls and faxes. To set manual fax reception, follow the preceding steps, but in step 3, click the Manual option under Answer Mode. When a fax arrives, your phone will ring and you'll see a message asking whether you want to receive a fax now.

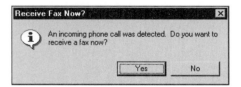

Click Yes, and Outlook answers the phone; if you're not expecting a fax, pick up your voice line to answer the phone.

When you open a fax that you received through Microsoft Fax, you'll see the message warning you about macro viruses (which faxed files cannot contain); click the Open It option and then click OK. The fax opens in an Imaging window like the one shown in Figure 7-3.

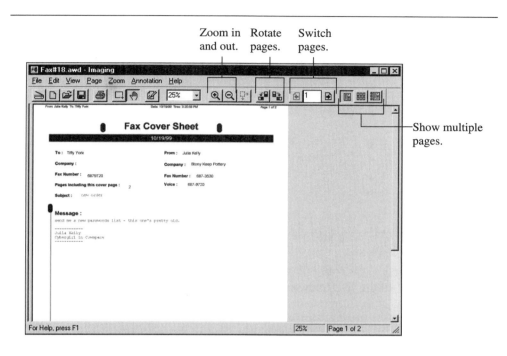

Zoom in and out. Rotate pages. Switch pages.

Show multiple pages.

FIGURE 7-3   A new fax through Microsoft Fax

Running a Mail Merge from Contacts

A *mail merge* is the process of setting up a single document—a form letter, or perhaps a set of mailing labels—and *merging*, or combining, several addresses into one document. The result is a single document that contains many copies of the file you merged, each with a different address and separated onto its own set of pages. For example, a set of mailing labels is a single document with a different mailing address on each label; a merged letter is a single document that contains several copies of the letter, each with a different address in the recipient's Address fields, and each printing on a separate page when you send the file to your printer.

Any mail-merge operation requires a *data source,* a file in which all the names, addresses, and other individual information are located. If you run a mail merge from a word processing program, the data source is usually a table of contact data in another word processing document or in a database file, such as an Excel worksheet or an Access table. If you keep all of your contact data in Outlook, you have a ready-made data source: your Contacts folder (and any contacts subfolders you create).

You can run a mail-merge operation from Outlook, using documents created in Microsoft Word. If you use Outlook in the Corporate/Workgroup configuration, you can also mail-merge documents for faxing.

> **NOTE** *If you use a word processing program other than Microsoft Word, you'll need to export your contacts data to a text file, Excel worksheet, Access table, or FoxPro database and use that file as your data source to run the mail merge from within the word processing program. (Save the exported-data file and reuse it for repeated mail-merge operations in your word processing program.) You'll learn how to export Outlook data in Chapter 16.*

Starting a Mail Merge in Outlook

Suppose you regularly have the task of sending an update on a current project to a long list of contacts. You could place all the contacts on a distribution list and send the e-mail update to the list, but using a mail merge instead offers the following advantages:

- A distribution list has to be updated whenever you change a contact's e-mail address, and it's easy to forget to do the update (which means someone won't get your message); but when you change a contact's e-mail address, the address will be current for the mail merge.

- If the list of message recipients changes temporarily, you can filter your set of contacts, or even select the individual contacts to receive the mail-merged message, instead of sending the message to the entire group.

- All mail-merge documents are created in Microsoft Word, so you'll be sending a letter even if you send it via e-mail.

To mail-merge a document, start by selecting the contacts to whom the document will be addressed. You can select them by using the SHIFT and CTRL keys to select a group of contacts in the Contacts folder, or you can create a new subfolder and move or copy all the mail-merge contacts into that subfolder. If you use a subfolder, you don't need to select any of the contacts, because you can mail-merge the entire subfolder. Then, follow these steps:

1. Click Tools | Mail Merge. (Be sure you're in a Contacts folder or subfolder, or you won't see the Mail Merge command on the Tools menu.) The Mail Merge Contacts dialog box, shown in Figure 7-4, appears.

2. If you've selected specific contacts for the merge, click the Only Selected Contacts option under Contacts; if you've created and opened a subfolder of contacts for the merge, click the All Contacts In Current View option.

3. If you want to merge data fields that aren't displayed in your contacts view (perhaps Birthday or Spouse's Name), click the All Contact Fields option under Fields To Merge. If all the merge fields you need for the merge are displayed, click the Contact Fields In Current View option (this makes the list of fields to choose from much shorter).

> TIP *You can make field insertion simpler by changing your Contacts view to show only the Contacts fields that your document will need for individual contacts (such as name, address, e-mail address, and any other contact information that you want your document to include automatically). See Chapter 3 to learn how to change the Contacts view.*

4. Under Document File, click the New Document option if you haven't created the letter or mailing labels yet. If the Word document you want to

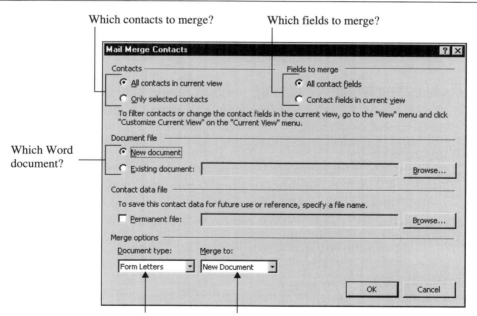

Which contacts to merge?   Which fields to merge?

Which Word document?

What kind of document?   Where do you want to send it?

FIGURE 7-4 The Mail Merge Contacts dialog box

send has already been created and saved, click the Existing Document option; then, click the Browse button, locate the file in the Open dialog box that appears, and double-click the filename. The file and path appear in the Mail Merge Contacts dialog box.

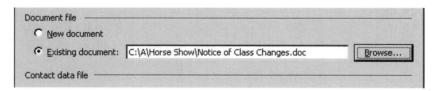

5. If you need to send updates to this particular set of contacts on a regular basis, you can click the Permanent File check box to save the set of contacts as a Word data source for use again.

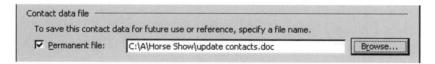

Then, click the Browse button, locate an appropriate folder in the Open dialog box to save the file, give the file a name, and click OK. If you don't need to save this set of contacts as a Word data source, leave the check box clear.

6. Under Merge Options, select the sort of document you want to create in the Document Type list box (Form Letters, Mailing Labels, Envelopes, or Catalogs).

7. In the Merge To list box, select New Document to create a new document in Word, select Printer to send the new merged document directly to your printer, select Electronic Mail to send the merged document as e-mail, or select Fax to send it as a fax (if you are working in Corporate/Workgroup configuration). If you choose E-Mail, a box appears for a Message Subject Line.

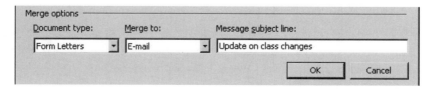

8. Click OK. Word opens, and your document opens in Word, along with the Mail Merge toolbar.

Finishing a Mail Merge in Word

At this point, Word mail-merge procedures take over. Use the Insert Merge Field button on the Mail Merge toolbar to add contact data to the document, if you need to.

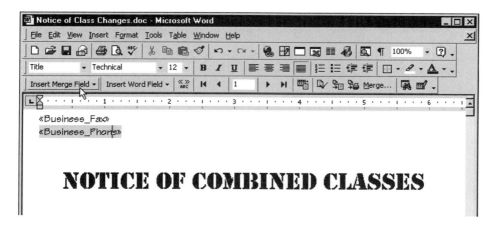

1. Click the Merge button (at the right end of the Mail Merge toolbar) to start the merge. A Merge dialog box appears.

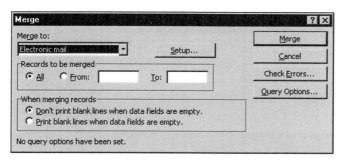

2. In the Merge dialog box, you have another opportunity to select New Document, Printer, Electronic Mail, or Fax (if you are in Corporate/ Workgroup mode) from the Merge To list box. When you're ready to create the final merged document, click the Merge button.

Your merged document is created. If you merged to e-mail, only those contacts with e-mail addresses will get messages, and all the messages appear in your Outbox, ready to be delivered with the outgoing mail.

If you also want to print the merged copies of the document, or save them as a Word file, switch back to the document in Word and click the Merge button on the Mail Merge toolbar again. The Merge dialog box appears, and you can select a different output in the Merge To list box. Figure 7-5 shows a merged new document in Print Preview. I selected five contacts when I began the merge, and added the Business Fax and Business Phone merge fields in the upper-left corner of the document. The fax and phone numbers appear only in the documents for contacts who have those numbers in my Contacts folder. I can save this merged document as a Word file and edit it or print it later.

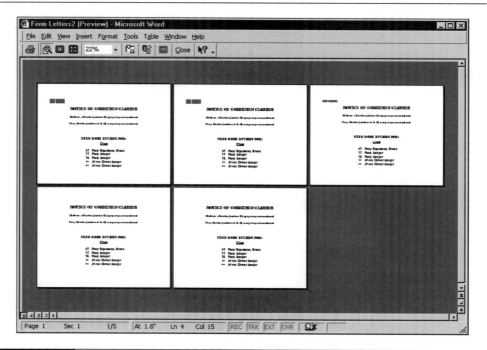

FIGURE 7-5   A new document merged from five selected contacts

When you're finished with the merging procedure, you'll have two Word documents to close: the finished, merged document, and the merge template (the document you inserted the merge fields into). Save the finished document if you want to print it later, and close the documents and Word.

This chapter rounds out the methods you can use in Outlook to communicate with your associates, contacts, colleagues, and friends. In the next chapter, you'll learn how to use Outlook's Notes (a remarkably simple efficiency tool), and after that, you'll learn how to use all the rest of Outlook's folders.

7

Part III

Organization

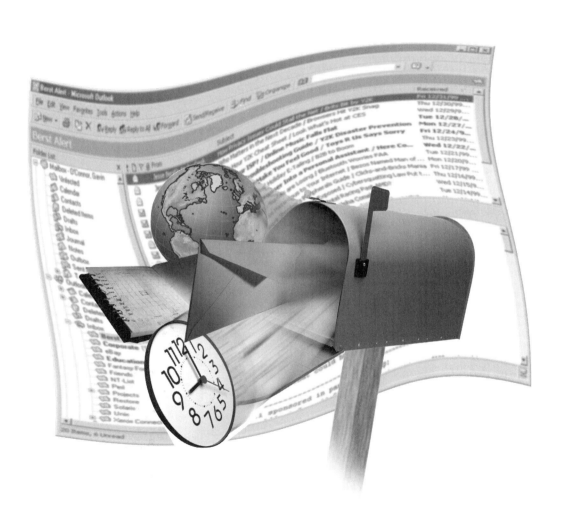

Chapter 8

Taking Notes with Outlook

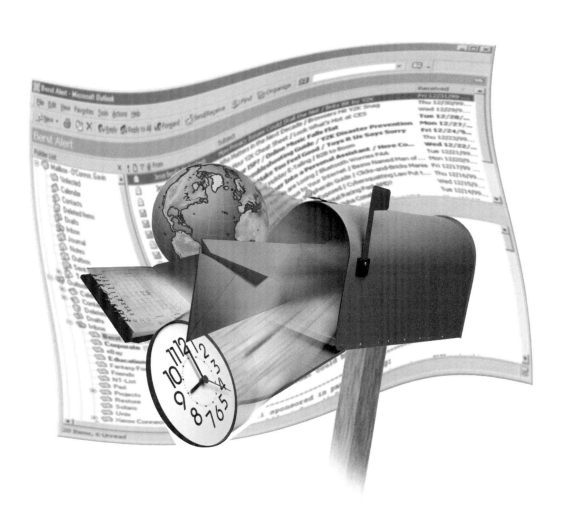

How to . . .

- ■ Type notes

- ■ Create notes without typing

- ■ Resize notes

- ■ Organize notes

- ■ Change note color

- ■ Change note font

- ■ Add categories to notes

- ■ Associate a note with specific contacts

Notes are designed to be used for important information that doesn't fit neatly anyplace else. Odd bits of information, such as your password for an Internet site, flight information for a business trip, or perhaps a quote that you want to hang on to but don't know where to stash for easy retrieval later, can be conveniently stored as notes. The kind of information that folks often jot down on a scrap of paper and then lose somewhere on their desk is the kind of information that Outlook's Notes were made for.

> TIP   *Open notes stay open on your Windows desktop even after you close Outlook.*

Every Outlook note is automatically date- and time-stamped when you create it, and the date/time stamp is updated every time you change it. A note can remain open on your desktop all day long, as shown in Figure 8-1, and can be brought to the top of your open windows by clicking its button on the taskbar.

Notes can be organized in many layouts, and can be colored in five different colors to help you quickly locate the one you need. They're simple to create, and very handy.

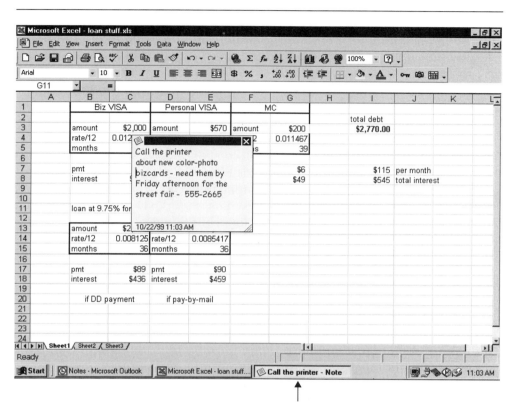

Click its Taskbar button to bring a note to the top

FIGURE 8-1   Notes can remain open on your desktop

Creating Notes

You can create a new, empty note in any of the following ways:

- In any window, click File | New | Note.

- In the Notes window, click the New toolbar button.

- In a non-Notes window, click the arrow next to the New toolbar button, and then click Note.

- In the Notes window, double-click in an empty area.

- In the Notes window, right-click in an empty area and click New Note.

- In the Notes window, press CTRL-N.

- In a non-Notes window, press CTRL-SHIFT-N.

Each of these techniques creates a new, blank note.

The new note is date/time stamped at the bottom, and by default is colored yellow. You'll learn how to change the default color and the color of an individual note in the section "Changing Note Color and Font," later in this chapter.

You can add text to your note by typing it (for example, if you're on the phone asking for someone's phone number, you can jot it quickly in a note), or you can add text by dragging it or copying and pasting it from another Outlook item or another file on your computer. No matter how you get text into your note, the note is automatically saved when you close it.

Notes can be a word or two, or they can be very long (for example, I put a 15-page Word document into the long note in Figure 8-2 without any difficulty). There's no scroll bar in a note, however; to scroll back and forth through a long note, drag through it with your mouse or use your arrow and page keys to move up and down.

 *If you inadvertently double-click a note's title bar, it maximizes to fill your screen; double-click the title bar again to resize it to its original size.*

Typing a Note

To type a note, open a new note by any of the ways listed above and begin typing. A note acts like a text file with word-wrap turned on—you can't format the text except to separate paragraphs by pressing ENTER and to indent by pressing TAB. Whatever the size or shape of the note, the text in a note automatically wraps to fill the note's area.

Type a Title

It's a good idea to type a title or subject heading as a first line, press ENTER, and then begin typing the actual note text. The first line will be the icon's title, and you'll find that organizing and finding your notes is easier if they all have short titles.

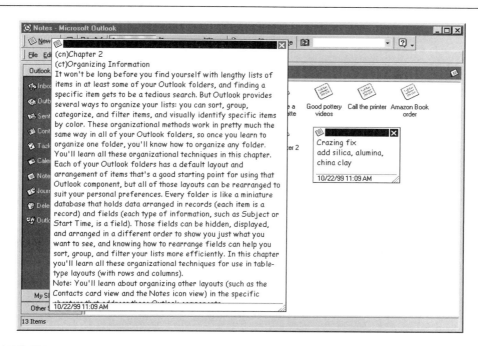

FIGURE 8-2 Notes can be very short or very long

8

If you don't type a title, the whole text of the note appears below the icon. In the following example, the note on the left has a short title and the note on the right has no title.

Type the Note Text

Spodumene

Call the printer about new color-photo bizcards - need them by Friday afternoon for the street fair - 555-2665

While you type, press ENTER once (or twice) at the end of each paragraph to separate the paragraphs and make the note easier to read. If you need to edit your typing, you can select text and then delete it or type new text to replace it, and you can drag selected text to a new position in the note. You can also cut, copy, and paste note text, just like in any other Outlook item or word processing document (but you're stuck with typing errors, because you can't spell check notes).

Close a Note

When you finish typing, you can leave the note open on your Windows desktop while you work in other programs (click the Note button on the taskbar to bring it back on top), or close the note by clicking the X (close) button in its upper-right corner.

 *You can leave notes open all over your Windows desktop, even after you close Outlook; and you can still edit and delete open notes when Outlook is closed.*

Type a Hyperlink

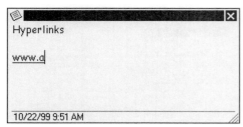

You can type functional Internet hyperlinks into a note. For example, if you're on the telephone with an associate who gives you the URL of a specific Internet site for information about a project, you can type the URL into a note as they spell it for you, and Outlook will turn it into a functional hyperlink.

To type a hyperlink to a Web site, begin by typing **www.**; when

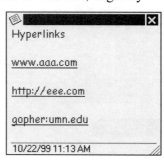

you type the next letter, the new hyperlink turns blue and is underlined. Continue typing the URL and press ENTER or type a space when you finish.

If the Web site doesn't begin with www, start by typing **http://** and then type the Web address. If the site is not a Web site but is instead a gopher, news, or some other type of Internet site, type the entire URL. Outlook recognizes all the standard URL prefixes.

Creating a Note Without Typing

Suppose you receive an e-mail message with a colleague's flight arrival information that you want to keep handy. You know that when you close the message, it will disappear into a long list of messages, and locating it again will take you extra time. You want to put the flight information into a note with a clear heading so that you can find it quickly, but if you type the information into the note, how much time have you saved? And, what if you make a typing mistake, and go to meet your colleague's 8 P.M. flight at 3 P.M.?

Drag Text to a Note

Outlook can help. To put the e-mail information into a note without typing it, select the details for the note and drag the selected text onto the Notes icon in the Outlook bar.

A new note is created, and you can type a short heading at the top for a title.

You can drag text from any Outlook item (messages, tasks, appointments, other notes, and so forth). If the text you want to save as a note is in a program that's drag-and-drop-capable with Microsoft software, such as Microsoft Word or Microsoft Excel, you can drag selected text from the file and drop it on the Notes icon in the Outlook bar, as shown in Figure 8-3.

Drag selected text

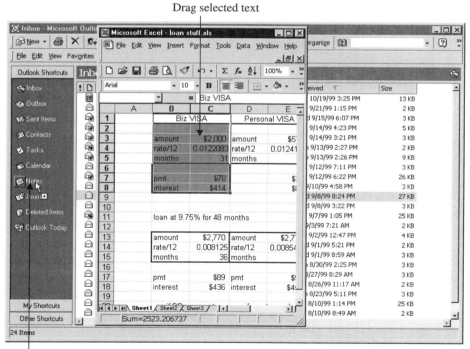

Drop text here

FIGURE 8-3 Drag text from another file to create a note

If you drag text from an Excel worksheet, it appears as a table with borders.

If you receive an e-mail message with a hyperlink in it, you can drag the message text, including the hyperlink, into a note, and the hyperlink remains active in the note.

Biz VISA	
amount	$2,000
rate/12	0.0122083
months	31
pmt	$78
interest	$414
10/22/99 11:21 AM	

Turn an Entire Outlook Item into a Note

You can create a note that contains an entire Outlook item—an appointment, for example—by dragging the closed item to the Notes icon in the Outlook bar. For example, in Figure 8-4, I'm creating a note from an appointment.

Drag the appointment from Calendar

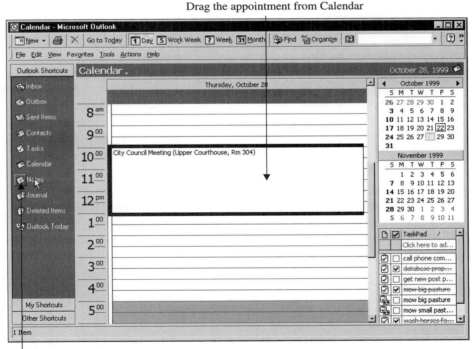

Drop it on the Notes icon

FIGURE 8-4   Turn any Outlook item into a note by dragging it

The resulting note contains all the information in the Calendar appointment.

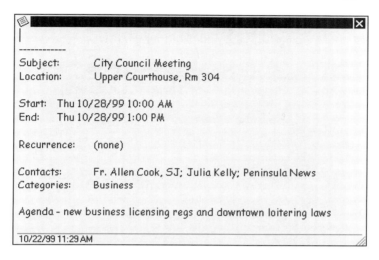

```
------------
Subject:       City Council Meeting
Location:      Upper Courthouse, Rm 304

Start:   Thu 10/28/99 10:00 AM
End:     Thu 10/28/99 1:00 PM

Recurrence:    (none)

Contacts:      Fr. Allen Cook, SJ; Julia Kelly; Peninsula News
Categories:    Business

Agenda - new business licensing regs and downtown loitering laws
```
10/22/99 11:29 AM

Copy and Paste Text to a Note

If the text you want to save as a note is in a program that's not drag-and-drop-capable with Microsoft software (and you'll know that's the case when you try to drag and drop and it doesn't work), you can still copy and paste the text into a note. Select the text you want to save as a note and use that program's Copy command (usually the keyboard shortcut CTRL-C works). Then, create a new note and press CTRL-V to paste the copied text.

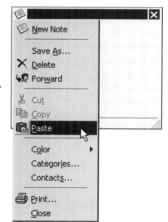

You can also paste cut or copied text by clicking the note icon in the upper-left corner of the note and then clicking Paste.

Dragging a Note into Another Item

Suppose that some months ago you created a note to save the procedure for bypassing the company's nested telephone menus. A colleague sent it to you in an e-mail, and you saved it as a note; now, another associate wants to get the procedure from you.

To send your associate the procedure quickly, open the Notes window. Drag the note's icon (*not* the open note) onto the Inbox icon in the Outlook bar—a new e-mail message is created with the contents of the note in the message. The following is a new message and the note from which it was created.

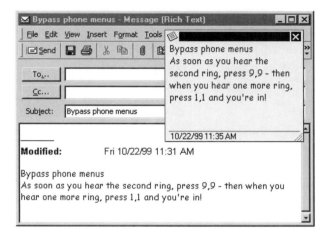

You can create any kind of Outlook item—task, appointment, Journal entry, and so forth—from a note by dragging the note to the appropriate icon in the Outlook bar.

Opening, Resizing, and Deleting Notes

If you do nothing more elaborate with your notes, you'll still need to know how to open them, resize them for easier reading, and delete them.

Opening Notes

To open an existing note, double-click the note in the Notes window. The note opens in the size it was when you closed it.

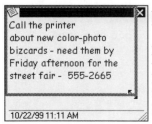

Resizing Notes

All notes are created in a default size (small, medium, or large). No matter what the default size of a note, it probably won't fit your text precisely. To resize an open note so that you can read the entire text without wasting desktop space, drag the lower-right corner of the note to a new shape and size.

If you find that all of your new notes are too small, or too big, you can change the default new note size. Click Tools | Options, and on the Preferences tab, click the Note Options button. In the Notes Options dialog box that appears, select a size in the Size list box, and then click OK twice to close both dialog boxes.

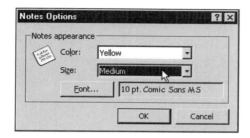

Deleting Notes

Notes are only meant to be semipermanent; that might mean a day, or it might mean three years, but eventually you'll want to delete some of your notes. All deleted notes are moved to the Deleted Items folder, where you can retrieve them until you empty the Deleted Items folder. Here are some techniques for deleting notes:

- To delete an open note, click the note icon in the upper-left corner of the note, and click Delete.

- To delete closed notes, select the notes you want to delete, right-click one of the selected notes, and click Delete. To select multiple notes, you can use the CTRL or SHIFT key, or you can "lasso" several adjacent notes by dragging across them with your mouse.

- You can also delete selected closed notes by clicking the Delete button on the toolbar.

Organizing Notes

The default view of Notes is icon view, which is what you've seen in all the illustrations earlier in this chapter. Icon view has three different arrangements: Large Icons, Small Icons, and List. You can switch

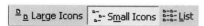

between these three arrangements by clicking the appropriate buttons on the Outlook toolbar.

Large Icons and Small Icons can be dragged around into your own custom arrangement, but the List arrangement cannot be rearranged by dragging.

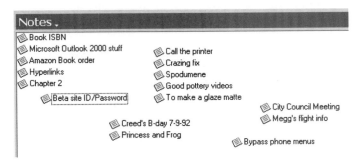

Whenever you change your Notes view or arrangement, the custom arrangement you carefully dragged your icons into may be lost, and you'll have to rearrange them by dragging again.

 *If you lose a note off the screen (for example, if you know it's there somewhere and just can't find it), change your view to icons and then click List on the toolbar—all the notes will be rearranged alphabetically into an organized list with small icons at the left side of the window.*

To keep your custom icon arrangement, but straighten it, right-click an empty area of the Notes window and click Line Up Icons.

You can switch to several other useful views of your notes by clicking View | Current View, and selecting one of the following views from the menu (all of these views are table-type views):

■ Notes List is an AutoPreview of your notes

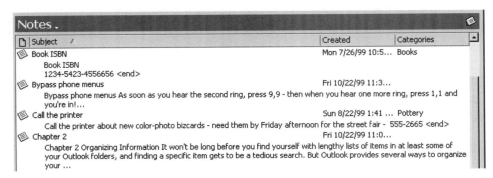

■ Last Seven Days shows the notes you created or edited during the last seven days, in AutoPreview

■ By Category and By Color both group your notes according to colors or categories that you've applied to them

Changing Note Color and Font

Note colors and fonts are not mission-critical options, but the ability to personalize your notes can make your working environment more pleasant.

If you get tired of the default yellow color of new notes, you can change the default color to blue, green, pink, or white; and you can change the colors of individual notes, too. Similarly, if you don't like Microsoft's choice of default font for your notes, you can change the note font to any font on your computer.

Changing the Color of a Single Note

You can use note colors to organize your notes visually. For example, in the Notes window shown next, my notes that pertain to pottery are colored pink, notes that pertain to the book business are yellow, and family-oriented notes are blue (it may be hard to tell the colors apart in this shades-of-gray illustration, but you get the idea). Even if the notes get mixed up when I switch views, I can tell at a glance which notes belong in which general group.

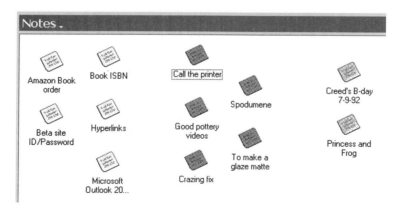

To change the color of a single note, right-click the note's icon, click Color, and then click a color.

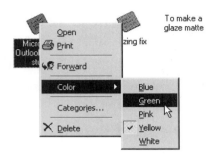

Changing the Default Note Color

Would you like all of your notes to start out in a crisp, white color? This is how you can change the default note color:

1. Click Tools | Options.

2. On the Preferences tab, click the Note Options button.

3. In the Notes Options dialog box, choose a color from the Color list box. Then, click OK twice to close both dialog boxes.

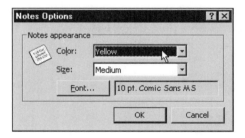

Changing the Note Font

Microsoft's choice of Comic Sans is a good, readable font for notes, but if you want to change it, here's how:

1. Click Tools | Options.

2. On the Preferences tab, click the Note Options button.

3. In the Notes Options dialog box, click the Font button. Choose a font, style, size, and color in the Font dialog box, and then click OK three times to close all the dialog boxes.

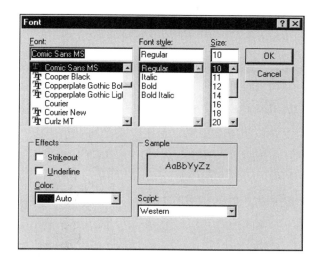

All of your notes will change to the new font (you can't change the font in single notes).

Adding Categories and Contacts to a Note

Adding Categories and Contacts to notes are two more means of organizing a large group of notes. If you categorize your notes, you'll be able to use the By Categories view to group them and locate related notes quickly.

Any time you associate an Outlook item with a specific contact (or contacts), that item appears in the specific contact's Contact dialog box Activities tab. A contact's associated items, including notes, accumulate in their Activities tab so that you have easy access to every bit of information relative to that contact from one place, as shown in Figure 8-5. Examples of notes you might want to associate with a contact are bits of information you picked up in a conversation with them, a snippet of text they sent you in an e-mail message, or information that a background investigation turned up about them—whatever is worth keeping in association with that contact.

8

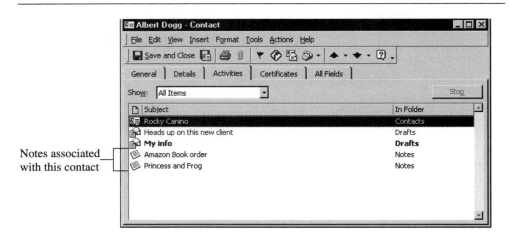

Notes associated with this contact

FIGURE 8-5 All of these Outlook items had this contact added to the item

Categorizing a Note

To add a category (or multiple categories) to a note, right-click the note and click Categories. In the Categories dialog box, click the check boxes for the categories you want to add to the note, and then click OK.

You can learn how to use Categories in greater detail in Chapter 2. After you categorize your notes, you can group them by switching to the By Category view.

 *To add the same categories to several notes at once, select all the notes, right-click any selected note, and then add the categories.*

Associating a Note with a Contact

Figure 8-5 shows a contact's Activities tab that lists several Outlook items associated with that contact. To associate a note with specific contacts, follow these steps:

1. Open the note.

2. Click the note icon in the upper-left corner of the note, and click Contacts on the menu that appears.

3. In the Contacts for Note dialog box, click the Contacts button.

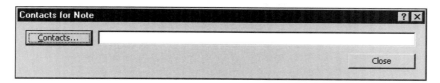

4. In the lower pane of the Select Items dialog box that appears, click the contact name(s) you want the note to be associated with. Use the SHIFT or CTRL key to select multiple names.

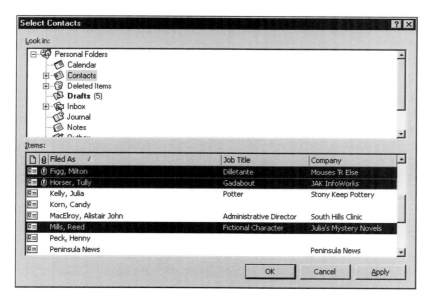

5. Click Apply, and then click OK.

6. Click Close to close the Contacts for Note dialog box.

Any associated notes appear in the contact's Activities tab; to open a note (or any other Outlook item) from the list in the contact's Activities tab, double-click the item.

This chapter showed you how to do everything with Outlook's Notes, a simple but remarkably efficient tool in your computer workplace. In the next chapter, you'll learn how to use Outlook's Calendar.

8

Chapter 9

Scheduling Everything with Outlook's Calendar

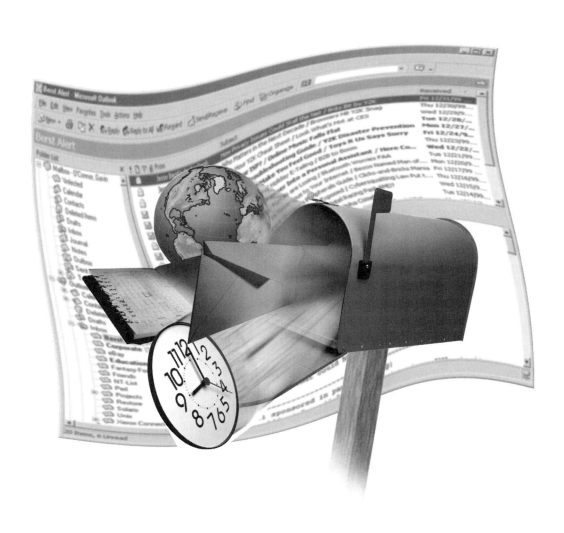

How to . . .

- Schedule appointments, events, and meetings

- Use appointment reminders

- Schedule automatically recurring appointments and events

- Use the TaskPad

- Put your Calendar on a Web page to share it with others

- Change your Calendar view

- Schedule meetings with several people

Calendars are a big business—stationery stores carry all kinds, and there's a calendar for nearly every purpose. But, if you need two or three different kinds of calendars, such as a monthly calendar, a daily calendar, and a small paper calendar to take with you away from the office, that's a lot of calendars to keep track of. Outlook has a better way: the Outlook Calendar can be switched to monthly, weekly, or daily views, with countless variations in between.

More things the Outlook Calendar can do for you are as follows:

- Differentiate all-day events from specific-time appointments

- Automatically schedule appointments and events that reoccur regularly

- Remind you, with a message or a sound, of upcoming appointments

- Show you a list of your tasks and due dates (or not—it's your choice)

- Coordinate with other Outlook folders by dragging and dropping information

- Schedule meetings for several people on a company network

You'll learn how to do all of these things in this chapter. But first, you need to understand Outlook' definitions of *appointments*, *events*, and *meetings*.

- An *appointment* is an activity that you don't officially invite other people to, such as a dental appointment or a meeting with your financial planner.

■ An *event* is an activity that lasts 24 hours or more, such as a vacation or a trade show, and is considered free time by Outlook (you can schedule appointments during an event).

■ A *meeting* is an appointment that you officially invite other people to. Invitees respond to your invitation, and their RSVPs appear in your Inbox.

Changing Your Calendar View

To start, you'll learn how to switch Calendar views, so that everything you learn in the rest of this chapter will be easier to follow. By default, Calendar appears in Day/Week/Month view, as shown in Figure 9-1.

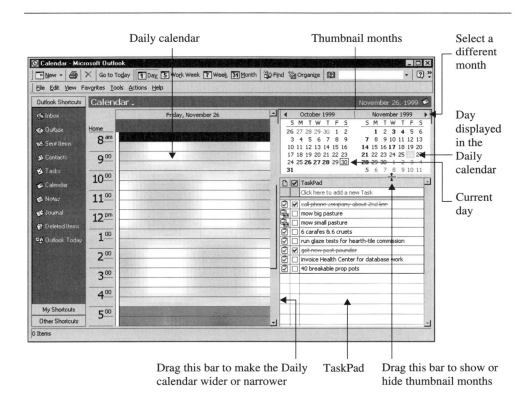

FIGURE 9-1   Calendar's Day/Week/Month view

The Calendar offers several views. To select a different view, click View | Current View and then click the name of the view you want. Most of the views are table-type lists of appointments and events. The view you'll work in most is the Day/Week/Month view.

NOTE *The Day/Week/Month With AutoPreview view is just like the Day/Week/Month view, except that the AutoPreview allows notes you type in the Appointment dialog box to appear in the Daily calendar.*

The Day/Week/Month view is most useful because it's so easy to switch between daily, weekly, monthly, several days, work week, and other calendar views. Also, Day/Week/Month view includes the TaskPad, a short list of tasks from your Tasks folder. You can hide or show the TaskPad, and change the set of tasks that are displayed.

To alter your Day/Week/Month view, use the buttons on the toolbar, shown in Figure 9-2.

Here are some tips for tweaking your Calendar view:

- To show a specific Daily calendar, click that date in the thumbnail month.

- Whatever your view, and whatever dates are displayed, you can jump to the current day by clicking the Go To Today button.

- To show two or three consecutive days in the Daily calendar, drag to select those dates in the thumbnail month.

- To show a few nonconsecutive days in the Daily calendar, hold down CTRL while you click to select those dates in the thumbnail month.

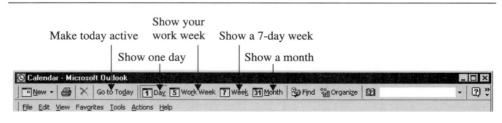

FIGURE 9-2   Change your Calendar view with toolbar buttons

- To show a different thumbnail month, click the thumbnail title bar and select a different month from the list that appears.

- To show four thumbnail months instead of two, point to the horizontal bar between the TaskPad and the thumbnail months, and when the pointer becomes a two-headed arrow, drag downward. Drag the bar upward again to make your TaskPad taller.

- To make the Daily calendar wider and show only one column of thumbnail months, point to the vertical bar between the Daily calendar and the thumbnail months, and when the pointer becomes a two-headed arrow, drag to the right. Drag the bar to the left to show more thumbnail months and a narrower Daily calendar.

- To scroll through the year in Monthly view, drag the vertical scroll bar on the right side of the Outlook window. When you drag the scroll bar, a ScreenTip appears that tells you the date in the upper-left corner of the Monthly view.

- To reset the Work Week view to show your real work week (for example, if you work ten hours a day, Wednesday through Saturday), click Tools | Options. On the Preferences tab, click the Calendar Options button. Under Calendar Work Week, mark only the check boxes for your workdays, and set your workday Start Time and End Time. Then, click OK twice to close both dialog boxes.

9

TIP *To display Saturday and Sunday in separate columns in your Monthly view, right-click in your Monthly view and click Customize Current View. Click the Other Settings button, clear the Compress Weekend Days check box, and click OK twice to close both dialog boxes.*

Changing the TaskPad

The TaskPad only appears in Daily and Weekly views. You can hide your TaskPad by dragging the bar above the TaskPad downward until you display thumbnail months all down the right side of your Calendar window. But if you hide your TaskPad (or someone else hides it for you), you'll need to drag it back upward into view. To do that, run your mouse slowly between the bottom of the Outlook window and the bottom border of the thumbnail months. When the mouse pointer becomes a two-headed arrow, drag upward above the lowest row of thumbnail months, and release the mouse button.

February 2000	March 2000
S M T W T F S	S M T W T F S
1 2 3 4 5	1 2 3 4
6 7 8 9 10 11 12	**5** 6 7 8 9 10 11
13 14 15 16 17 18 19	**12** 13 14 15 16 17 18
20 21 22 23 24 25 26	**19** 20 21 22 23 24 25
27 28 29	**26** 27 28 29 30 31 1
	2 3 4 5 6 7 8

TIP *To add a task to the TaskPad, click in the Click Here To Add A New Task box, type the task, and press* ENTER. *The task is added to both the TaskPad and your Tasks folder. To delete a TaskPad task, right-click the task and click Delete.*

The TaskPad is really handy, because your tasks shown are right there in your calendar. You can make it even handier by making a few changes:

- To filter your tasks (for example, to show only those tasks that are overdue), click View | TaskPad View, and click the set of tasks you want to display.

- To add another field to the TaskPad (for example, to show task due dates), right-click the TaskPad title bar and click Field Chooser. Drag the field button out of the Field Chooser and drop it on the TaskPad title bar (the red arrows show you where it will appear when you drop it). Click the Field Chooser's X close button to close it.

- To remove a field from the TaskPad, drag the field heading button away from the TaskPad and drop it when you see the big X.

- To sort the tasks in the TaskPad, click the heading button for the field you want to sort by. Click the heading button again to reverse the sort by that field.

Working in Multiple Time Zones

If your business requires you to make phone calls to contacts in other time zones, it's helpful to know what time it is where they are (so you know you're calling during business hours). You can show two time zones side by side in the Daily calendar, like this:

1. Click Tools | Options, and on the Preferences tab, click the Calendar Options button. The Calendar Options dialog box appears.

2. In the Calendar Options dialog box, click the Time Zone button. The Time Zone dialog box appears.

3. In the Time Zone dialog box, your own computer's time zone is displayed at the top. Type a name for your time zone (such as **Home**) so that you can identify it in your calendar.

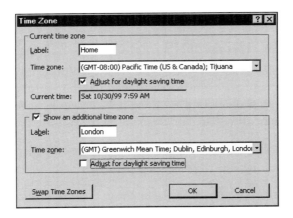

4. Mark the Show An Additional Time Zone check box, and type an identifying label. Then, choose the second time zone from the Time Zone list box. Mark or clear the Adjust For Daylight Saving Time check box depending on whether or not the second time zone switches to daylight saving.

TIP   *If you want to show just one time zone in your calendar, but want to be able to switch easily between two time zones, follow the preceding steps 1 through 3, and then clear the Show An Additional Time Zone check box in step 4. Whenever you want to switch the time zone display, open the Time Zone dialog box and click the Swap Time Zones button.*

5. Click OK three times to close all the open dialog boxes. When you have a second time zone displayed, your Daily view looks like the following example.

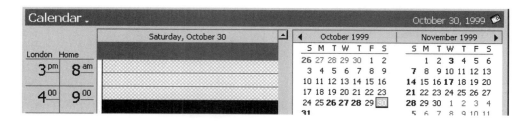

 *Outlook displays the Current Time Zone date and time based on your computer's Windows settings. To adjust the current date or time for the Current Time Zone, double-click the time on the right end of your Windows taskbar and make your changes there.*

Scheduling Appointments, Events, and Holidays

Outlook's Calendar helps you keep track of your appointments and events, and Outlook can schedule a year's worth of national and religious holidays for you. Scheduling, changing, and deleting anything recorded in your Calendar is quick, and if you need to open or delete any Calendar item, you use the same methods as in any other Outlook folder.

To open a Calendar item (for example, to check or change event details), double-click the item. To delete a Calendar item (for example, an appointment that was canceled), either click the item and click the Delete button on the toolbar or right-click the item and click Delete.

Making Appointments

As a solitary writer with no company network, I use Calendar to keep track of my life, both work and personal (and sometimes it's hard to tell the difference between the two). For example, my quarterly tax payment due dates don't slip by unnoticed, because I can schedule them and be reminded two days in advance that it's time to send the check.

If you use Outlook on a company network, Calendar can do even more for you. You can designate an appointment's time slot as "free," "busy," "tentative," or "out of office," so co-workers who have access to your calendar on the network can plan meetings to accommodate your schedule.

Appointments can occur one time only, or they can be set to recur automatically on a regular schedule (daily, weekly, the first Tuesday of every month, and so forth).

Create an Appointment

The quickest way to set an appointment, with no details, is simple: show the day for the appointment in Daily view, and drag to select a block of scheduled time.

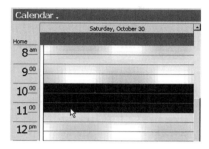

Type the name of the appointment (just start typing, and the text will appear in the time block you selected) and then press ENTER.

Each time slot in the Daily calendar represents a half hour. To select a block of, say, two hours, point to the middle area of the starting time slot, hold down your left mouse button, and drag down the "ladder" of time slots until four half-hour slots are highlighted.

But what if you need to create an appointment with more details? For example, suppose your company supports an ongoing Good Health seminar, and you're considering attending one of the seminars to see if it interests you. The seminar is given only once a month, and you don't want to miss the next one, so you schedule an appointment (with a reminder) in Calendar. To schedule the appointment, follow these steps:

1. Show the Calendar in the Outlook window (click the Calendar icon in the Outlook bar).

2. On the toolbar, click the New button.

9

> **TIP** *The New button always creates a new item for the folder that's displayed in the Outlook window. If you want to create a different type of new item, you can click the arrow next to the New button and select the type of item from the button's list.*

3. In the Appointment dialog box that appears, shown in Figure 9-3, type a name for the appointment in the Subject box, and type a location in the Location box.

4. Enter Start Time and End Time dates and times. You can click the arrows next to the date and time boxes and click to select dates and times, or you can type something like **next mon** and **noon**, and let Outlook's AutoDate feature fill in the date and time for you.

> **TIP** *You can also double-click a time slot in Daily view to create a new appointment with the Start date and time filled in.*

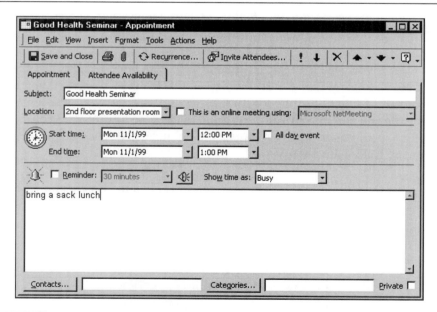

FIGURE 9-3 The Appointment dialog box

5. In the Show Time As list box, select a classification for the scheduled time.

This makes no difference if you work alone on your own computer, but if your Calendar is available on the company network, what you select here is what others see when they check whether you're available for meetings. By default, appointments are "busy" so others will know you're unavailable during those time slots.

On your Daily view, appointments are visually differentiated—the colored tabs on the left end of each appointment denote whether the appointment is "busy" (dark blue), "free" (white), "tentative" (light blue), or "out of office" (maroon).

6. If you don't want to be reminded about the appointment, clear the Reminder check box. If you want a reminder, mark the Reminder check box and then choose a suitable advance notice in the Reminder list box.

If your computer is equipped to play sounds, and you want an audible reminder, click the little speaker button. In the Reminder Sound dialog box, mark the Play This Sound check box (then click OK).

7. Type extra notes to yourself in the large box at the bottom of the Appointment dialog box. If you set your Calendar view to Day/Week/Month With AutoPreview, those notes appear in the appointment in Daily view. This is a good way to remind yourself to take with you a report, extra cash, or whatever.

8. If your Calendar is available on a network and you don't want others to know the nature of your business, mark the Private check box in the lower-right corner of the dialog box. This allows the Subject line of your appointment to appear in your own Calendar but hides the subject from others on the network who have access to your Calendar folder. If you don't work on a network, you can ignore the Private check box.

9. When you're done setting up the details, click the Save And Close button on the dialog box toolbar.

Customize Your Reminder

If you find yourself consistently setting a 30-minute reminder, you can change the default reminder to 30 minutes for every new appointment. To set a default reminder time, click Tools | Options. On the Preferences tab, under Calendar, mark the Default Reminder check box, and then select 30 Minutes in the Default Reminder list box. Click the Apply button to make the change take effect immediately, and then click OK.

If you want an audible reminder for all of your appointments, meetings, events, and tasks, you can set the sound file to play by default. Click Tools | Options, and on the Other tab, click the Advanced Options button. In the Advanced Options dialog box, click the Reminder Options button. In the Reminder Options dialog box, mark the Play Reminder Sound check box (and if you have a sound file you particularly like, click the Browse button and choose that file). Then, click OK three times to close all the dialog boxes and apply your changes immediately.

Respond to the Reminder

When you get a reminder, it will look similar to the following example.

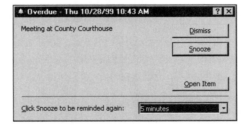

You have three options:

- To get rid of the reminder and head off to your appointment, click the Dismiss button.

- To hide the reminder and be reminded again in five minutes, click the Snooze button. (If you want to snooze for, say, ten minutes, change the Snooze time in the list box.)

■ If the appointment was rescheduled and you forgot to change your Calendar, click the Open Item button and change the appointment details.

Change an Appointment

Appointments are not written in stone—they get postponed and switched to different locations quite often, and you may be asked to bring along yet another report.

To change an appointment's details, such as the location or your notes to yourself, follow these steps:

1. Double-click the appointment to open the Appointment dialog box.

2. Make your changes by editing the appropriate fields (for example, you can change the Start date or time, enter a different Location, or add a note to bring a sack lunch).

3. Click the Save And Close button to save your changes and close the Appointment dialog box.

If you only need to change the time or date of the appointment, you can make those changes with your mouse:

■ In any view (Daily, Weekly, or Monthly), point to the left side of the appointment. When the mouse pointer becomes a four-headed arrow, drag the appointment to a new time or date.

■ You can drag an appointment to a different day in the week or month, and it appears with the same time slot on the new day.

■ In any view, you can drag an appointment to a different month by dropping it on a date in one of the thumbnail months, as shown in Figure 9-4. The appointment keeps the same time slot on the new day.

■ If you need to change the time as well as the date, switch to Daily view and drag the appointment to a new time slot after you move it.

■ To change the allotted time for an appointment (for example, you expect a meeting to run for an extra hour), show the appointment in Daily view. Point to the bottom border of the appointment, and when the mouse pointer becomes a two-headed arrow, drag the border down to fill the entire new time slot.

9

Drag an appointment from your
Daily schedule…

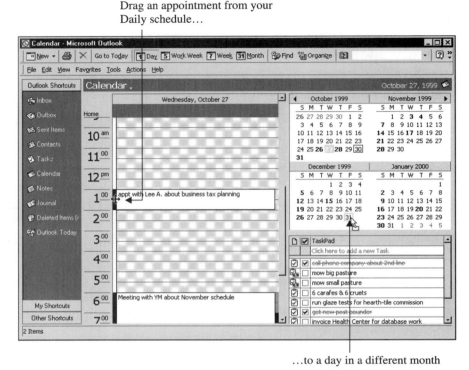

…to a day in a different month

FIGURE 9-4 Drag an appointment from a Daily schedule to a different month

Schedule a Recurring Appointment

Suppose you went to the Good Health seminar and found it vastly informative and entertaining, so you want to attend regularly. The seminars occur on the first Monday of every month, and you can create a *recurring* appointment that appears automatically on your calendar every month. Setting a recurring appointment is the same as setting a single appointment, except that you also set a recurrence pattern.

To create a new recurring appointment, open the Calendar folder and click Actions | New Recurring Appointment. A new Appointment dialog box and an Appointment Recurrence dialog box appear.

To add a recurrence pattern to an existing appointment, double-click the appointment to open it, and click the Recurrence button on the Appointment dialog box toolbar.

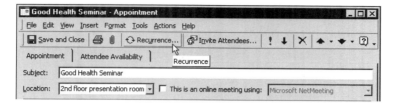

To set a recurrence pattern, follow these steps:

1. In the Appointment Recurrence dialog box, shown in Figure 9-5, enter the Start and End times.

2. Click a Recurrence Pattern option. Each option (Daily, Weekly, Monthly, Yearly) displays its own set of frequency options.

3. Set the frequency for the pattern you selected. For example, the Good Health seminar occurs on the first Monday of every month, so in Figure 9-5, I set a **Monthly** pattern and selected the **first Monday** of every **1** month.

9

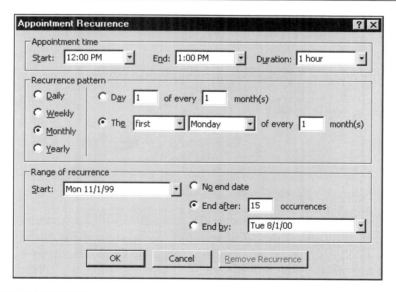

FIGURE 9-5   The Appointment Recurrence dialog box

4. Under Range Of Recurrence, you can set an ending date for the pattern of appointments. For example, if you know there are only 15 more Good Health seminars, you can click the End After option, and type **15** Occurrences. Outlook will only schedule 15 of these monthly appointments.

5. Click OK to close the Appointment Recurrence dialog box, make any changes you need to make in the Appointment dialog box, and then click Save And Close.

You can tell which appointments on your Calendar are recurring appointments because they'll have a recurrence symbol on the left, which looks like two arrows forming a circle.

CHANGE DETAILS FOR A RECURRING APPOINTMENT If you need to change any details for a recurring appointment, double-click the appointment to open it. You'll see the Open Recurring Item dialog box, asking whether you want to change the whole series or just this one appointment.

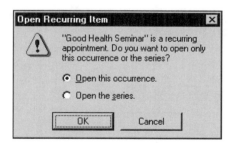

If, for example, you need to change the location of your appointment just this once, click the Open This Occurrence option; but if you need to change the location for all the remaining appointments, click the Open The Series option.

The Appointment dialog box appears; make your changes and click Save And Close.

If you need to change the recurrence pattern itself (for example, the Good Health seminar is switching to the second Wednesday of every month), open the

Appointment dialog box for the series, click the Recurrence button on the toolbar, and make the changes. Click OK and then click Save And Close to close the two dialog boxes.

DELETE A RECURRENCE PATTERN   If the Good Health seminars are canceled, or you just decide that you're healthy enough and don't want to attend any more, you can cancel the series of appointments and remove them all from your Calendar.

Open the appointment and click the Open The Series option in the Open Recurring Item dialog box. In the Appointment dialog box, click the Recurrence button. In the Recurrence Pattern dialog box, click the Remove Recurrence button, and then click Save And Close to close the Appointment dialog box.

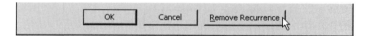

Scheduling Events

Calendar defines *events* as lasting from midnight to midnight on the day(s) you schedule. Because events are occasions, such as birthdays, trade shows, vacations, and week-long motorcycle club reunions, they don't present a conflict with appointments in your calendar (Outlook assumes that you can keep your dentist appointment during your week-long motorcycle club reunion).

An event appears as a gray *banner* that stretches across the top of the day(s) for which the event is scheduled. You can schedule multiple events on the same day, and you can set reminders for events.

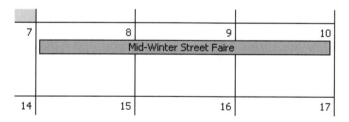

The quickest way to set a one-day event, with no details, goes like this: show the day for the event in Weekly or Monthly view, click in the day block, type the name of the event (just start typing, and your text will appear), and press ENTER. When you need to enter more details for the event, such as a location or notes to yourself, double-click the event banner to open it.

If the event spans several days, show the days in Weekly or Monthly view, and drag to select all the days. Then, type the name of the event and press ENTER.

 *To turn an appointment into an event, open the appointment, click the All Day Event check box (next to the Start and End times), and click Save And Close.*

Schedule a Detailed Single Event

The only difference between an Event dialog box and an Appointment dialog box is that an appointment has a time slot and an event does not.

Suppose you want to attend the Cayman Islands Agriculture Show, because you work in the agriculture industry and the Cayman Islands Agriculture Show gives you a good excuse to visit the islands in February. To schedule an event, follow these steps:

1. Be sure Calendar is open, and click Actions | New All Day Event. An Event dialog box opens.

2. Fill in the details for the event (subject, location, dates, and notes to yourself), and then click Save And Close.

It's a good idea to either clear the Reminder check box or set it for two days, because you probably won't be around to be reminded.

Schedule an Annual Event

So, you went to the Cayman Islands Agriculture Show and had a great time, and came back with a tan in February, and now you want to go back every year.

To schedule a recurring event, schedule a single event. With the Event dialog box open, click the Recurrence button. In the Appointment Recurrence dialog box that opens, set a yearly pattern for the event. Click OK and then click Save And Close.

You can change details for events the same way you change them for appointments: open the event, make your changes, and click Save And Close.

To delete an event, click the gray event banner in any view, and click the Delete button on the toolbar; or right-click the event banner and click Delete. Delete a recurring event the same way as a recurring appointment: double-click the event banner to open it, choose Open The Series, click the Recurrence toolbar button, click the Remove Recurrence button, and click Save And Close; then, delete the single remaining event.

Adding Holidays to Your Calendar

Do you ever find yourself wondering when National Day is in Switzerland? Or perhaps when Father's Day is in the U.S.? You can add the entire set of holidays for many countries, and all the Christian, Islamic, and Jewish holidays. Holidays appear in your Calendar as all-day events for the entire span of the holiday. To add sets of holidays to your Calendar:

1. Click Tools | Options, and on the Preferences tab, click the Calendar Options button.

2. In the Calendar Options dialog box, click the Add Holidays button.

3. In the Add Holidays To Calendar dialog box, mark check boxes for the sets of holidays you want to add.

TIP *If a check box is already marked because you installed that holiday set previously, clear the check box so you don't install a duplicate of that set.*

4. Click OK (and wait a few seconds while the holidays are installed) and then click OK twice more to close the remaining dialog boxes.

NOTE *Some sets of holidays duplicate other sets (for example, the United States and the United Kingdom have many identical holidays), so don't be surprised when duplicates appear in your Calendar. You can delete them just like any other event.*

You cannot remove holidays from the Calendar automatically, but you can remove an entire set quickly, like this:

1. Click View | Current View | Events. Your Calendar folder switches to a table-type view.

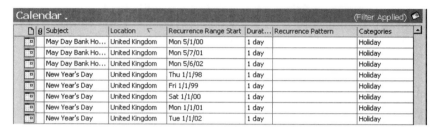

2. Click the Location header button to sort all the events by location. Each set of holidays is sorted together into a group.

3. Drag to select all the holidays in the group you want to remove, and then click the Delete button on the toolbar.

That set of holidays is removed, and you can switch your view back to the view you work most comfortably in.

Putting Your Calendar on a Web Page for Others

If you don't have a network location where you can post your calendar for your coworkers to see (or even if you do), you can share your calendar with non-network colleagues by posting your personal or team calendar on the Internet as a Web page.

If you use Outlook in the Internet Mail Only configuration, you'll need to set up a Web site where you can post your Calendar Web page. If you use Outlook in the Corporate/Workgroup configuration, with the Exchange Server, your system administrator will set up your posted Calendar location.

Sharing Free/Busy Information on the Internet

To save your Calendar as a Web page, follow these steps:

1. Open Calendar.

2. Click File | Save As Web Page.

3. In the Save As Web Page dialog box, set the Start and End dates for the amount of time you want to post.

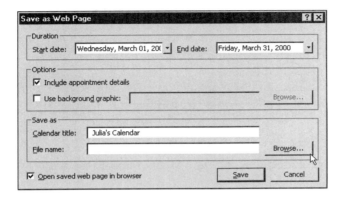

4. If you want to include your appointment notes on the Web page, leave the Include Appointment Details check box marked. If your appointments contain notes you'd rather not post for others to see, clear the Include Appointment Details check box.

5. In the Calendar Title box, give the Web page an appropriate title.

6. Click the Browse button, and in the Calendar File Name dialog box that appears, navigate to the folder where you want to save the Web page, give the Web page a File Name, and click the Select button.

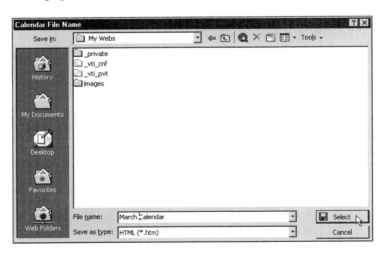

9

7. When the Save As Web Page dialog box reappears, leave the Open Saved Web Page In Browser check box marked (so you can see the Calendar Web page you've created), and click the Save button.

The Web page is saved, and your browser opens to the Web page, as shown in Figure 9-6. On the right side of the Web page are the details and notes from individual Appointment dialog boxes.

You'll need to post the Web page on your Web site so that your colleagues can visit the Web site and see when you're available for meetings.

Updating Your Web Calendar

When you change your calendar, you'll want to update the posted Web page to keep your colleagues current.

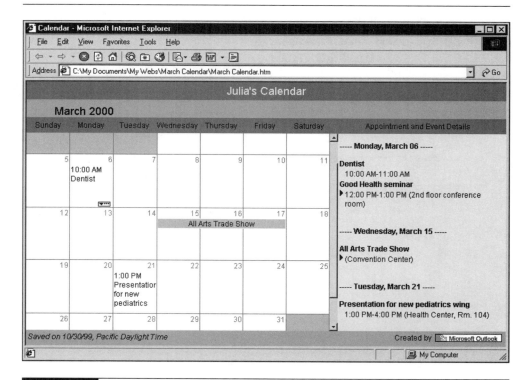

FIGURE 9-6   A month of Calendar saved as a Web page

To update the Web page calendar, find and delete the folder that bears the name of your current Web page and contains all the .htm pages and .gif images that are part of your current Calendar Web page. Delete the entire folder, so that nothing of your previous Web page remains.

Then, create a new Calendar Web page by following the steps in the preceding section.

Using the Calendar in a Workgroup

If you use Outlook on a company network, you can use the Meeting Planner to schedule and coordinate meetings with your coworkers. If you aren't using Outlook in a network environment, you can still schedule meetings by sending meeting invitations as regular e-mail messages.

If you work in a network environment, your network administrator will configure your company system so that calendar information is shared on the network in folders that others in your company have access to. Having access to coworkers' calendar information makes meeting planning a lot simpler.

9

Using the Meeting Planner

When an upcoming meeting is your responsibility, you can always use the old tried-and-true method of picking a meeting date, hoping everyone is free, and sending e-mails to let everyone know there's a meeting. But, Outlook has a feature that can make meeting planning go more smoothly, especially in a Corporate/Workgroup environment where everyone's schedules are available on the network.

Plan a Meeting

To plan a meeting using Outlook's Meeting Planner, follow these steps:

1. Open Calendar.

2. Click Actions | Plan A Meeting. The Plan A Meeting dialog box appears, shown in Figure 9-7.

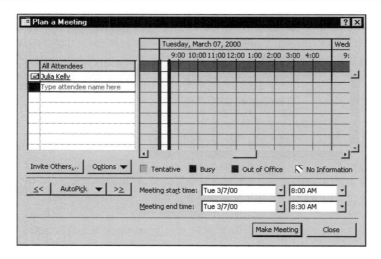

FIGURE 9-7   The Meeting Planner

3. Click the Invite Others button. The Select Attendees and Resources dialog box appears.

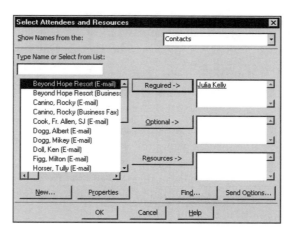

4. Double-click names of people who are required to attend your meeting; those names appear in the Required list. To add a name to the Optional list, click the name and then click the Optional button. Then, click OK to close the Select Attendees and Resources dialog box.

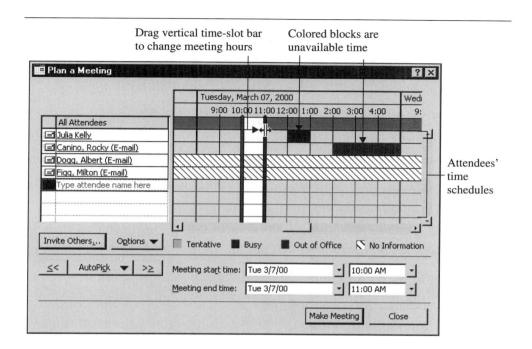

Drag vertical time-slot bar
to change meeting hours

Colored blocks are
unavailable time

Attendees'
time
schedules

FIGURE 9-8   Plan a meeting time

5. The Plan A Meeting dialog box, shown in Figure 9-8, lists all the attendees' names. The Meeting Planner checks your invitees' Free/Busy files for availability (each individual must keep their Free/Busy time updated—see the upcoming section, "How To Publish and Find Free/Busy Time").

6. Pick a meeting time. You can click the AutoPick button, and on the list that drops down, click the group that the meeting should be scheduled to accommodate, and let Outlook find the next time that's available for the whole group. You can also drag the vertical time-slot bar to a meeting time when all your attendees appear to be available (drag the time-slot borders to change the duration of the meeting).

7. Click the Make Meeting button. An e-mail meeting invitation appears. Type a Subject and a Location, and any notes that invitees should be aware of (in the large box at the bottom).

8. Click the Send button (and send the invitations like normal e-mail).

9. Click Close to close the Plan A Meeting dialog box.

After you send out invitations, the meeting appears in your invitees' Calendars.

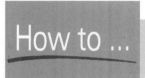

Turn an Appointment into a Meeting

Suppose you have an appointment to meet with your boss about a current project, and you and your boss decide that others should be contributing input on the project. You can turn your appointment into a meeting, like this:

1. Double-click the appointment to open it.

2. Click the Attendee Availability tab.

3. Click the Invite Others button, and invite everyone.

How to ... **Publish and Find Free/Busy Time**

To publish your Free/Busy time so others can plan meetings that include you, click Tools | Options, and on the Preferences tab, click the Calendar Options button. In the Calendar Options dialog box, click the Free/Busy Options button. In the Free/Busy Options dialog box, mark the Publish My Free/Busy Information check box, and type the server path where your Free/Busy schedule is stored.

To tell Outlook where to find your colleagues' Free/Busy time so that you can set up meetings, open each colleague's Contact dialog box. On the Details tab, under Internet Free/Busy, in the Address box, type the URL, FTP, or server path name to their Free/Busy file.

4. Set a meeting time.

5. Click the Send button, and send the invitation out with your e-mail.

Respond to a Meeting Request You Receive

When you receive an e-mail meeting request, it looks like the following example.

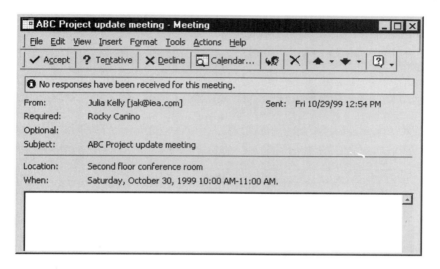

First, click the Calendar button in the meeting request to check that date in your Calendar, and see if the meeting fits in with your current schedule. The meeting appears on your Calendar.

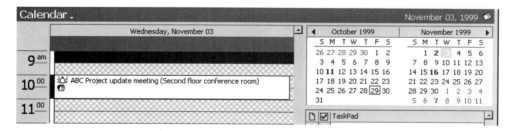

Next, click the Accept, Tentative, or Decline button in the meeting request to send an e-mail response to the invitation, and send the response out with your normal e-mail.

Check Responses to Your Meeting Invitation

Your colleagues' responses to your meeting invitation are recorded in the Attendee Availability tab of the Meeting dialog box. To check the status of your attendees, follow these steps:

1. In your Calendar, double-click the meeting to open it.

2. Click the Attendee Availability tab.

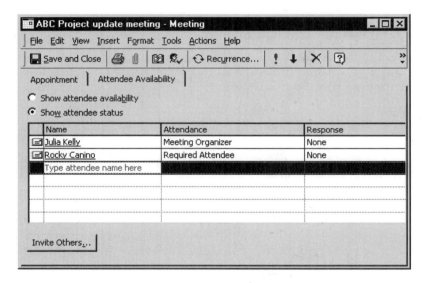

3. When meeting responses are returned via e-mail to your computer, Outlook automatically records the responses in the Response column.

Cancel a Meeting

If there's been a catastrophe and your meeting must be canceled, it's a quick procedure. Double-click the meeting in your Calendar to open it, and click the Cancel Invitations button on the meeting's toolbar.

An e-mail is sent to all the attendees to inform them that the meeting has been canceled. If you like, you can explain why the meeting was canceled, and you can send another invitation to a rescheduled meeting.

That's it for the Calendar. In the next chapter, you'll learn how to use your Tasks folder to help you work more efficiently (and not overlook important tasks).

Chapter 10

Keeping Tabs on Tasks

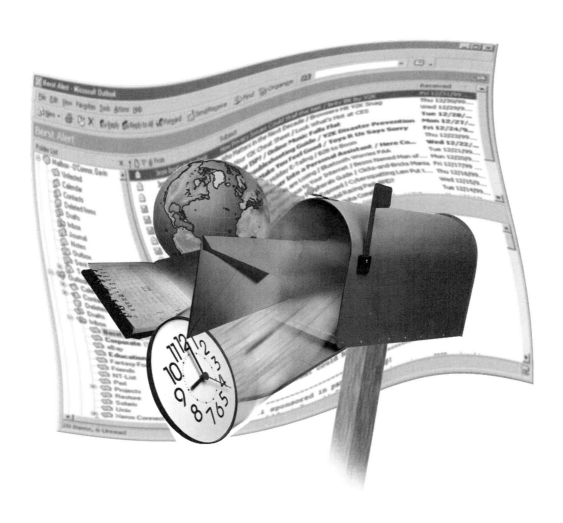

How to . . .

■ Create tasks quickly

■ Create tasks with lots of detail

■ Edit tasks

■ Skip an occurrence of a recurring task

■ Stop a recurring task

■ Mark a task as complete

■ Delete tasks

■ Sort and reorganize your task list

■ Assign a task to others

■ Accept or decline an assigned task

A *task* is something that needs to be done. In this day and age, our lives are so full of tasks, both work-related and personal, that without a to-do list, it's easy to inadvertently overlook something important. Outlook's Tasks folder was created to help prevent crises such as an overlooked important task.

A task might be any of the following:

■ A one-time errand, such as buying a new color printer

■ A *recurring* task that needs to be done at regular intervals, such as creating a monthly departmental expense report

■ A *regenerating* task that reassigns itself when you complete it, such as ordering more printer toner three months after the last order was placed

■ A project you assign to someone else (and you need to keep tabs on its progress)

■ A work project for which you need to keep accurate time and billing records

To open the Tasks folder, click the Tasks icon in your Outlook bar. The Tasks window, shown in Figure 10-1, lists all of your tasks, along with any Status, Due Date,

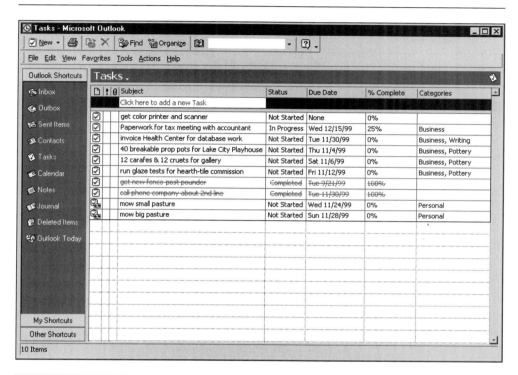

FIGURE 10-1   The Tasks window

% Complete, and Categories you might assign to each task (the fields displayed depend on the view you select).

All the tasks in your Tasks folder are also visible in the TaskPad, a minilist of tasks, in the Calendar window.

If you don't see the same list in the Tasks window and in the TaskPad, you have differently filtered views displayed. To show all of your tasks in both lists, click View | Current View | Simple List in the Tasks folder, and click View | TaskPad View | All Tasks in the Calendar folder.

Creating Tasks Quickly

When you create a task, the minimum required information is a subject or title for the task. Simply click in the Click Here To Add New Task box at the top of the task list, type a subject, press ENTER, and you're done. The task remains on your list until you delete it.

Creating Tasks with More Details

Outlook's Tasks has a lot more to offer than a simple listing of task subjects, and with a little detailed input in the Task dialog box, you can take advantage of these task features.

To open a new Task dialog box, do one of these things:

■ Double-click in an empty part of the Tasks window

■ With the Tasks window open, click the New button on the left end of the toolbar

■ From any other Outlook window, click File | New | Task

■ From any other Outlook window, click the arrow next to the New button and click Task

■ With the Tasks window open, press CTRL-N

■ From any other Outlook window, press CTRL-SHIFT-K. The Task dialog box appears (shown in Figure 10-2).

To fill in details for a task, follow these steps:

1. Type a subject, such as **tax paperwork to accountant**, in the Subject box on the Task tab.

2. Determine whether a due date exists for the task.

   ■ If your task is something like "buy a cordless keyboard and mouse" and you have no time limit, leave None selected in the Due Date list box.

   ■ If your task has a due date for completion, and/or a start date, set those dates in the Due Date and Start Date list boxes.

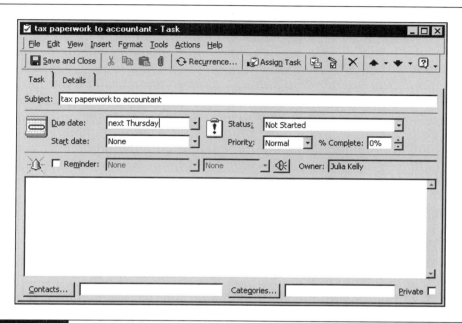

FIGURE 10-2   A Task dialog box

10

> **TIP**   *Remember AutoDate? You can type your Due Date and Start Date in words, such as **week from tomorrow**, and let Outlook figure out the date; or you can click the down arrow on each list box and click a date in the date navigator (the thumbnail month) that appears.*

3. If you want the task to appear in your list on a recurring basis (for example, the second Tuesday of each month), click the Recurrence button on the dialog box toolbar. A Task Recurrence dialog box appears. It's exactly like the Appointment Recurrence dialog box in Calendar. Recurring tasks appear on your list one at a time—when you mark one as complete, the next one pops up.

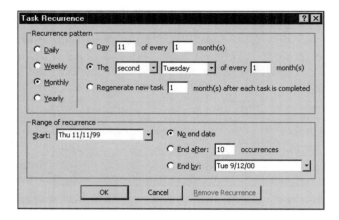

Suppose you prepare a project status report for delivery every month, and you want to complete it by the second Tuesday of each month. To make the task reappear with the next due date every time you complete the existing task, click the Monthly option, and then select The Second Tuesday Of Every 1 Month, and click OK.

4. If, instead, you want the task to reappear a specific amount of time after you complete it (but not regularly every third Monday, for example), then you want to create a *regenerating* task.

An example of a regenerating task might be changing the oil in your car every three months. If you happen to wait four months to change the oil, you'll want the task to reappear with a due date three months after you actually changed the oil, not every three months on the calendar. In the next illustration, ordering a new supply of printer toner two months after the last order is a regenerating task.

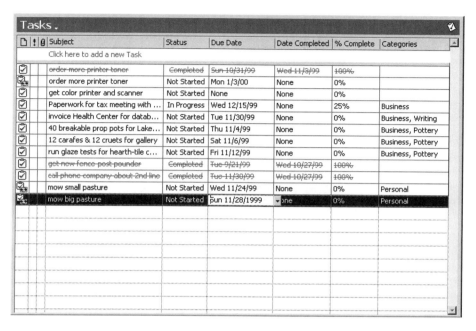

To make a task regenerate rather than recur, click the Regenerate New Task option in the Task Recurrence dialog box, and set a regeneration time period.

5. If you set a schedule for recurrence or regeneration, click OK to close the Task Recurrence dialog box and continue filling in the Task dialog box.

6. If you want to be reminded about a task before it's due, click the Reminder check box and set a date and time to be reminded. Task reminders are identical to Calendar reminders.

7. If you work on a corporate network and want to keep your task subject invisible to others on the network, click the Private check box in the lower-right corner.

10

8. If the task is of especially high or low priority, set a priority level in the Priority list box. Setting a priority level allows you to sort your tasks by priority and reduces the odds of overlooking a high-priority task.

9. When you're finished filling in details, click the Save And Close button.

The task appears in your task list, and if you set a reminder, a reminder message pops up on your screen on the morning of the due date.

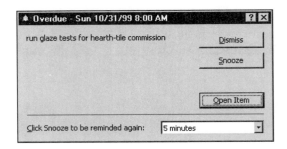

Here are a few more tips for tasks:

■ If you can't begin a project until supplies are delivered, but the due date remains the same regardless of when the project began, you may need to reset the Start Date. But changing the Start Date resets the Due Date, because Outlook assumes the project still needs the original amount of time you allowed it. To reset the Start Date without changing the Due Date, set the Start Date to None, and then set a new Start Date.

■ You can change the default reminder time from 8:00 A.M. to any time of day that suits you. Click Tools | Options, and on the Preferences tab, under Tasks, select a new time in the Reminder Time list box.

Editing Tasks

If you need to change anything about a task (for example, the due date, recurrence frequency, or reminder time), follow these steps to make changes in the Task dialog box:

1. Double-click the task to open it.

2. Make the necessary changes in the dialog box. If you need to change the task's recurrence or regeneration pattern, click the Recurrence button, make your changes, and click OK.

3. Click the Save And Close button to save your changes.

Skipping an Occurrence of a Recurring Task

If your every-third-Friday division report was scheduled for tomorrow but has been canceled (just this once), you can cancel that one occurrence without canceling the entire series. Double-click the task to open it, click Actions | Skip Occurrence, and then click Save And Close.

Stopping a Recurring Task

If your every-third-Friday division report is no longer necessary because your division has been reorganized and the new supervisor doesn't want the report, you can cancel the series of recurring tasks. Double-click the task to open it, and on the task toolbar, click the Recurrence button. In the Task Recurrence dialog box, click the Remove Recurrence button, and then click Save And Close. The single scheduled task remains in your list, but it won't be rescheduled.

10

Marking Tasks As Completed

When you finish a task, you can either delete it or leave it in your list and mark it as complete. Marking the task as complete gives you something to point to when you're asked, "What have you been doing all day?" Besides giving you a sense of accomplishment, if the task was assigned to you by someone else, your completion is reported automatically to the person who assigned it to you (you'll learn more about assigning and accepting tasks later in this chapter).

To mark a task as complete, either click the check box in the Complete field in the task list or right-click the task and click Mark Complete. The task remains in your list, but changes color and is crossed out.

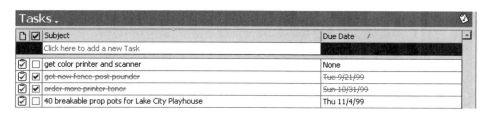

 *The Complete field, with the check boxes, appears in the Simple List view, and you can add it to other views. See Chapter 2 to learn how to add fields to a view.*

Deleting Tasks

To delete tasks, select the task(s) you want to delete. (Use the CTRL or SHIFT key to select multiple tasks.) Delete the selected task(s) by clicking the Delete button on the toolbar, or by right-clicking one of the selected tasks and clicking Delete, or by pressing the DELETE key.

If you're deleting a recurring task, you'll see a dialog box that asks whether you want to Delete All or Delete This One. Click the option you want and click OK.

Sorting and Reorganizing Tasks

To change your view of your tasks, click View | Current View, and select a different view.

The Simple List and Detailed List views show all of your tasks, and most of the other views are filtered table-type views. Like all table-type views, you can add fields (right-click any header button, click Field Chooser, and drag field buttons into the header row), delete fields (drag the header button away from the header row and drop it), and sort by any field (click the field header button).

You can also group your tasks by any field: right-click the field header row, click Group By Box, and then drag the field header button into the Group By box.

The Timeline view shows tasks on a timeline according to their due dates, and can show you when your workload is going to be heavy. You can switch between Daily, Weekly, and Monthly timelines by clicking the appropriately named toolbar buttons.

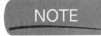 *See Chapter 2 to learn more about how to organize table views.*

Recording Billing, Mileage, Contact, and Company Information for a Task

The Details tab of a Task dialog box is a good place to store all the job details for a specific project. Also on the Task tab, you can record all the contacts who are associated with that task.

To record these details for a task, double-click the task to open it. Here are some hints for filling in the task fields:

■ On the Task tab, click the Contacts button and then double-click names of associated contacts in the Select Names dialog box. Those contact names will appear in this task, and this task will appear in the Activities tabs for those contacts.

■ On the Details tab, type information such as hourly fee or account name/number in the Billing Information box.

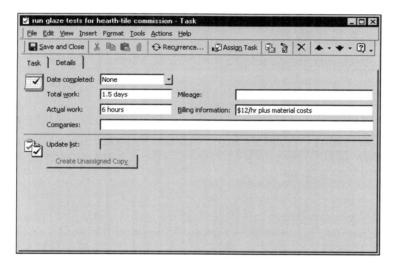

■ Record the mileage you travel for the task in the Mileage box. The Mileage field doesn't do any arithmetic, so here are some ideas for recording cumulative mileage: you can add it up and type a new number after each trip, or enter each trip's mileage separately (separate the trips, as in **100 + 100 + 150**) and add them up later.

■ Type the names of other companies associated with the task in the Companies box.

■ Record an estimate of the number of hours required for the task in the Total Work box (the hours are automatically converted into days or weeks).

■ Record the number of actual hours spent on the task in the Actual Work box (the hours are automatically converted into days or weeks).

To change the hours/day used by Outlook to convert your work hours into days and weeks, click Tools | Options and click the Other tab. Click the Advanced Options button, and in the Advanced Options dialog box, type new numbers into the Task Working Hours Per Day and Task Working Hours Per Week boxes.

Keeping Track of Work Others Do by Assigning Tasks

Task assignments enable you to delegate work to others and keep track of their progress. You assign a task to someone by sending them a *task request*, which is a polite electronic way to say "Here, you do this."

You can assign tasks to anyone who uses any version of Outlook, whether or not they're on your company network. Non-Outlook users will get e-mail messages with the task information, but without the Accept and Decline buttons.

When you send someone a task request, you give up ownership of that task. You can keep an updated copy of the task in your task list and receive status reports, but once someone else has accepted the task, you cannot change task information such as the due date or percentage complete. Only the owner of the task can make changes to the task.

Not only can you assign tasks to others, they can assign tasks to you. When someone assigns you a task, you have three options:

■ When you receive the task, you become the temporary owner of the task. You can accept it, decline it, or assign it to someone else.

■ When you accept a task, you become the permanent owner and are the only one who can make changes to it.

■ If you decline the task, it's returned to the person who sent it to you.

A task request (shown in Figure 10-3) is similar to a task, except that it has a To box, a Send button, and a couple of progress-notification check boxes.

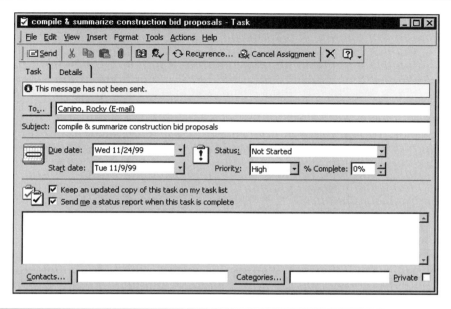

FIGURE 10-3   A task request

To assign a task to someone else, follow these steps:

1. Right-click the task list and click New Task Request. You can also click File | New | Task Request, or open an existing task that you want to assign and click the Assign Task button on the task toolbar.

2. In the Task dialog box, click the To button. In the Select Task Recipient dialog box that appears, double-click the name of the contact you're assigning the task to, and then click OK.

3. Fill in the remainder of the dialog box in the same way as a normal task.

4. To have your copy of the task automatically updated whenever the task's owner makes changes, mark the Keep An Updated Copy Of This Task On My Task List check box. (This works only if the task's owner is on your network.)

> TIP
>
> *You can receive updates about a task from only one person. If you need to assign the task to several people and receive updates from all of them, create a separate task request for each person.*

5. To be notified when the task is marked Complete, mark the Send Me A Status Report When This Task Is Complete check box. (This works only if the task's owner is on your network.)

6. Click the Send button. The task is sent via e-mail to the lucky recipient.

If the contact to whom you assigned the task is using any version of Outlook, they'll receive a message about the task that has an Accept button, a Decline button, and an Assign Task button on the message toolbar. If the task recipient is not using Outlook, they'll receive a normal e-mail message and can reply with a normal e-mail message.

Accepting, Declining, and Assigning Tasks

When someone sends you a task request, you'll receive an e-mail message that's labeled Task Request. When you open it, you can accept, decline, or reassign the task.

If you click the Accept button, the task is automatically added to your task list and you become the owner of the task. A message indicating your acceptance is sent to the person who assigned you the task.

If you click the Decline button, a message indicating your "No, thanks" response is sent to the person who assigned you the task.

When you click the Send button to send your response, you'll have the opportunity to add your own message. To explain why you must decline, or to tell them how delighted you are to be selected for the task, click the Edit Response Before Sending option in the dialog box that appears, and click OK.

NOTE   *If circumstances change after you accept a task and you no longer can complete the task, you can decline it. Open the task and click Actions | Decline Task.*

To assign a task you receive to someone else (for example, if your boss assigns you a task, but it's really a task for your assistant), you must first accept the assigned task and become the task's owner. Then, you can click the Assign Task button on the task's toolbar and assign the task to a third party (your assistant) by following the procedure described earlier, in the section "Keeping Track of Work Others Do by Assigning Tasks."

Updating Task Status

If someone assigns you a task, you can keep them apprised of your progress by sending a status report.

Open the task, and in the Task dialog box, on the Task tab, select an entry in the Status list box, and use the % Complete spin box to record an approximate state of progress. On the Details tab, update your Actual Work hours and Mileage, and any other details that change.

When you're ready to send the updated status, click Actions | Send Status Report. In the To and Cc boxes, enter the names of contacts who should get copies of the report. The names of everyone associated with the task request are added to the list of report recipients automatically.

> NOTE
>
> *Outlook periodically checks your Inbox for task update messages. When you assign a task to someone else and receive a task update message, the task is updated in your task list and the message in your Inbox is deleted.*

Now that you know how to keep track of your upcoming and in-progress tasks, you'll learn in Chapter 11 how to use Outlook's Journal to record your activities.

10

Chapter 11

Keeping a Work Diary with the Journal

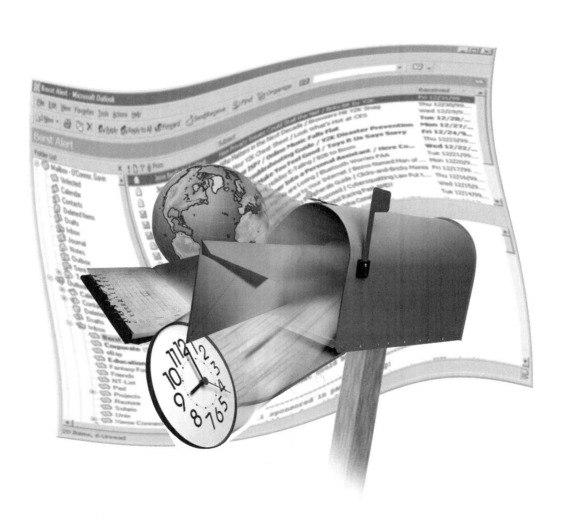

How to . . .

■ Record activities manually

■ Record activities automatically

■ Change Journal entries

■ Connect Journal activities to specific contacts

■ Change your view of the Journal

■ Delete Journal items

Outlook's Journal is an electronic diary. Everything that you normally write in your calendar or day planner (what you did, when you did it, and all the details you want to remember) you can record in the Journal. But Journal is better than a paper diary, because it can automatically record activities such as e-mail messages you send to your boss and Access databases you work on.

Some activities, such as a conversation in a trade show parking lot or a shopping excursion to find a new printer, can't be recorded automatically, but you can record anything manually. For example, you can record a phone call (not the voices, just the activity) and use Journal's timer to record the duration of the phone call in your Journal entry.

To open the Journal window, click the Journal icon in the Outlook bar. If you're new to Outlook, you'll probably find a few entries in your Journal already, because, by default, Journal records some items automatically. Figure 11-1 shows what a Journal window looks like after you've been using it for a while with lots of entries recorded automatically.

Recording Activities Automatically

Items you can have automatically entered in Journal include e-mail messages you send and receive, meeting and task requests and responses, and files you create or open in Microsoft Access, Excel, Word, and PowerPoint.

Recording E-Mail Automatically

Recording e-mail to and from your colleagues in Journal is yet another way to keep track of your discussions and decisions concerning a project. If you

Show current day   Switch timeline to Day, Week, or Month

Click here to display
Date Navigator

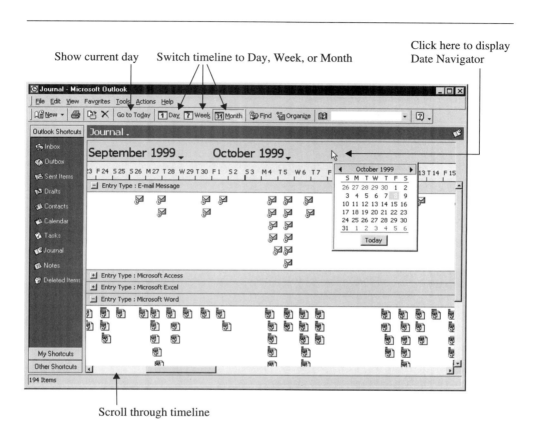

Scroll through timeline

FIGURE 11-1   Journal records items automatically while you work

automatically record all the e-mail messages to and from all of your contacts on
a particular project, it's easy to locate those messages later.

This is how to record e-mail you have sent to and received from specific contacts:

1. Click Tools | Options.

2. In the Options dialog box, on the Preferences tab, click the Journal Options
   button (under Contacts Preferences). The Journal Options dialog box,
   shown in Figure 11-2, appears.

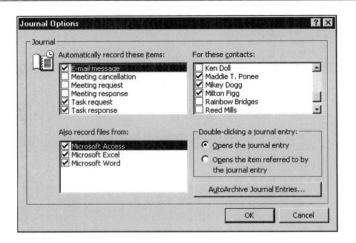

FIGURE 11-2   Set automatic recording in the Journal Options dialog box

3. In the Automatically Record These Items list box, mark check boxes for the items you want to keep a record of.

4. In the For These Contacts list box, mark check boxes for the contacts whose e-mail you want to record. In Figure 11-2, my Journal is set to record all the e-mail messages, task requests, and task responses that are sent and received between me and all the check-marked contacts.

Journal records each e-mail item when it's sent or received, not when you create it.

5. Click OK twice to close both dialog boxes.

Recording Documents Automatically

Suppose you create and maintain custom Excel spreadsheets for the different divisions in your corporate enterprise. In the course of a busy day, it's easy to forget to write down whose file you worked on and for how long. There's a better way than paper: you can have Journal automatically record every Excel file you open, and have it record when and how long you had each file open.

Here's how to automatically record files you create or open:

1. Click Tools | Options.

2. In the Options dialog box, on the Preferences tab, click the Journal Options button. The lower half of the Journal Options dialog box is shown here.

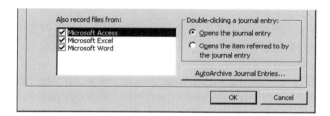

3. In the Also Record Files From list box, mark check boxes for the programs you want to record your work in. All the files in each program you mark will be recorded. (If you don't want a record of a particular file, you can delete it later.)

Journal can automatically record work only in the Microsoft Office programs Access, Excel, Word, PowerPoint, and Office Binder, but you can enter your work in other programs manually.

NOTE *If you don't have a particular Microsoft Office program installed (such as Access or PowerPoint), you won't see the option to record it automatically.*

4. By default, double-clicking an icon in the Journal timeline opens the Journal entry. If you'd rather have the associated file open when you double-click the icon, click the Opens The Item Referred To By The Journal Entry option.

11

Regardless of which option you choose to be the default of the Journal Options dialog box, you can always right-click an icon from the Journal timeline and then choose either Open Journal Entry or Open Item Referred To.

5. Click OK twice to close both dialog boxes.

Recording Activities Yourself

Automatic recording can save you from frustrating situations. For example, suppose it's the end of the month and you need to remember how many hours you worked on the Renaissance Festival Association newsletter, so that you can invoice them properly. If your work on the newsletter was done in Word files, automatic recording of all Word files would have recorded your hours on that file, and it's no big deal to add them up. But, what if the newsletter is done in WordPerfect? You can't record WordPerfect files automatically in Journal, but you can record them manually (and at the end of the month, you'll be glad you did). Or, what if you don't want to record your work in *every* Word file, just in specific files? Instead of turning on automatic recording for all Word files, you can record your work in just those specific files.

Recording Work in a File Manually

To keep a record of when and how long you worked in a file (along with any extraneous notes to yourself), follow these steps:

1. Locate the file you want to work in. You can navigate to the folder that contains the file using any technique you like (the My Computer window is my favorite).

2. Drag the file icon in the folder window to the Journal icon in the Outlook bar. It's easiest to drag and drop the file if you resize both Outlook and the folder window, as shown in Figure 11-3.

Drag from here...   ...to here.

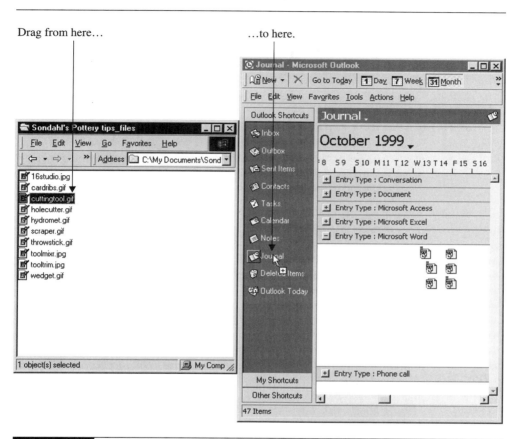

FIGURE 11-3   Drag the file to the Journal icon in the Outlook bar

A new Journal Entry dialog box opens, with a shortcut to your file (shown in Figure 11-4), and the current date and time are filled in.

3. Click the Start Timer button to begin recording your working hours, and then double-click the file shortcut icon to open the file. At any time, you can enter notes to yourself in the box where the shortcut icon is located.

4. When you finish working in the file, remember to stop the Journal timer by clicking the Save And Close button in the Journal Entry dialog box.

11

File shortcut   Start Timer button

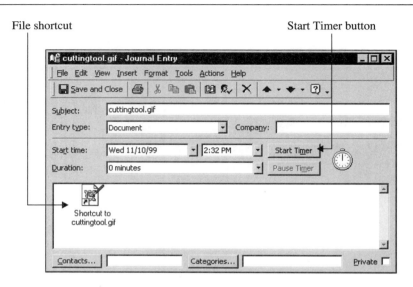

The Journal Entry dialog box contains a shortcut to the file

If you need to take a temporary break in your work, like to go eat lunch, click the Pause Timer button. When you return to work on the file, click the Start Timer button to continue recording your working hours.

Recording Outlook Items Manually

If you've got an Outlook item, such as a task, that you want to record in Journal, it's even easier than recording a file.

Open the Outlook window where the item is listed (for example, I want to record how much time I spend on my task to clean out my filing cabinets). Drag the item's icon from its own window and drop it on the Journal icon in the Outlook bar (shown in Figure 11-5).

A new Journal Entry dialog box opens, with an icon for the task or other Outlook item. Click the Start Timer button and carry out the task. You can fill in details about accomplishing the task by double-clicking the icon in the Journal entry.

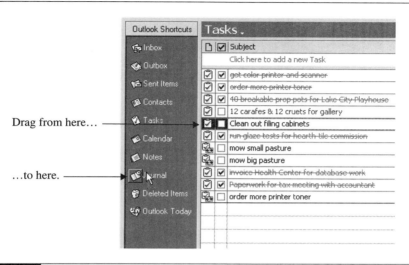

Drag from here...

...to here.

FIGURE 11-5   Record a task in Journal

NOTE   *If you see a virus warning when you double-click the Outlook item's icon to open it, you can safely ignore the warning and click Yes, because you're opening your own file and it's not likely to be infected. But, if you see this warning before you open a file that came into your computer from outside, think twice about whether it might be virus-infected. You can always run your computer's virus scanner program on the file before you open it, if you want to be sure.*

Click the Save And Close button when you're finished, and you'll have a Journal record of when you did the task and how long it took.

Recording Other Activities Manually

Any activity you want to record can be entered in Journal—phone calls, conversations, meetings, anything. For example, time you spend on the Internet (and that can be considerable) can be recorded, along with any Web page addresses you want to save and other notes you feel like jotting down.

Suppose your boss wants to build a living bamboo fence around your office building, and you're in charge of finding bamboo resources and information. Because you're doing this project on work time, you'll want to record the time you spend on it as well as hyperlinks to any good Web sites you come up with. You can do all of these things in Journal, and this is how:

1. Double-click a blank area in your Journal window. A new Journal Entry dialog box opens.

2. In the Subject box, type a description of your activity.

3. In the Entry Type list box, select an appropriate entry type for your activity. You can't create your own entry type, but several different entry types are available. In this example, I'm doing an Internet search, so I'll select Remote Session. Type any notes, including hyperlinks, in the large box.

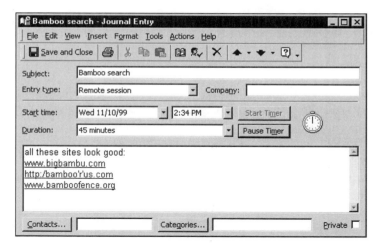

4. Click the Start Timer button to begin recording your activity.

5. While you're working, type any notes about your activity in the large box. In your Internet search, you may come up with several bamboo resources, and you can enter their hyperlinks in the large box so that you have quick access to them later. To enter Web addresses, type **http:/** or **www.** followed by the rest of the Web address, and Outlook turns them into blue, underlined hyperlinks automatically.

6. When you're finished with your activity, click the Save And Close button to stop the timer and close the Journal entry.

Changing Journal Entries

Journal entries are not set in concrete. You can change any details of an entry, add more notes to yourself, add associated contacts' names or categories, and change the duration of your activity. You can also move the entry to a different position in the Journal timeline, if somehow you entered the wrong start date or time when you began recording the activity.

Modify Entries

Suppose that in the middle of your boring department budget meeting, you realize that you didn't set the Journal timer while you were working on a spreadsheet. You know that you worked on it for about three hours, however, so you can change the Journal entry to reflect your work time. To change the duration of an existing Journal entry, follow these steps:

1. Open Journal, and double-click the entry to open it.

2. In the Duration box, select the 0 Minutes entry, type **3 hrs** to replace it, and press ENTER.

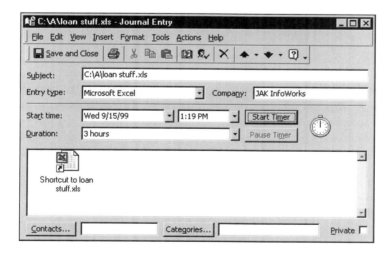

3. Click the Save And Close button. The entry's icon in the Journal timeline reflects the three-hour duration of your work.

Move Entries

What if you belatedly entered a phone call you made yesterday, and when you entered the Start date, you inadvertently entered the wrong date? When you later notice that the Journal entry is in the wrong spot on the timeline, you can move the entry to the correct date, like this:

1. Double-click the entry to open it.

2. Click the arrow next to the Start Time date list box, and select the correct date.

3. Click the Save And Close button.

Delete Entries

Deleting a single entry in your timeline is quick: either click the entry's icon and press DELETE, or right-click the entry's icon and click Delete.

But, what if you've been automatically recording your work in Excel workbooks, and you've been experimenting with Excel, creating lots of test workbooks that you don't want to save or keep a record of. Now you've got lots of useless entries cluttering up your Journal window. You can delete them one at a time, but it's faster to switch to a table-type view of your entries, sort them so that all the useless entries are in one place, and delete them all at once. This is how you do it:

1. In the Journal window, click View | Current View | Entry List. Your view switches to a table-type view of all your Journal entries, shown in Figure 11-6.

2. To sort all the Excel files together, click the Entry Type column header. To sort specific Excel files together within the group of Excel files (see Figure 11-6), hold down the SHIFT key while you click the Subject column header.

TIP
You can sort by up to four categories using this SHIFT-and-click technique.

3. To select and delete several Journal entries, press SHIFT or CTRL to select the entries you want to delete, and then click the Delete button on the toolbar. (You can also press the DELETE key, or right-click any of the selected entries and click Delete.)

Click header buttons to sort the table

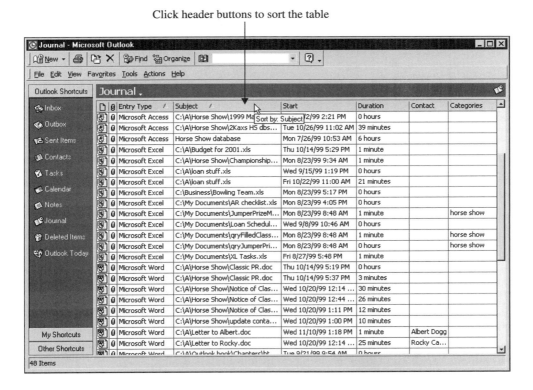

FIGURE 11-6   The Entry List view of Journal makes it easier to locate several similar entries

4. When you finish deleting the Journal entries that you don't want, click View | Current View | By Type to switch back to the default timeline view.

Connect Journal Activities to Individual Contacts

If you work on a project in coordination with specific contacts, you can associate your Journal entries for that project with the contacts with whom you share the project. All of your Journal entries that are associated with a contact will appear in that contact's Activities tab.

For example, the following window shows a Journal entry for a Word letter to my associate Albert. To connect this Journal entry and document to the Contacts entry for Albert, I clicked the Contacts button at the bottom of the Journal Entry dialog box.

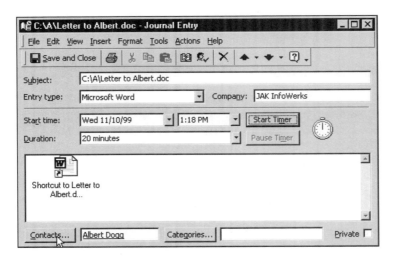

In the Select Contacts dialog box that appears, click the Contact names that this Journal entry is associated with (use the SHIFT and CTRL keys to select multiple names), and then click OK. The selected names appear in the Contacts box at the bottom of the Journal Entry dialog box.

So what does this do for you? When you open the Contact dialog box for an associated contact, and click the Activities tab, you'll see a list like the following window. The Activities tab lists every Outlook item associated with a contact, and you can open any listed item by double-clicking it. It's one more way in which Outlook keeps all of your information interconnected.

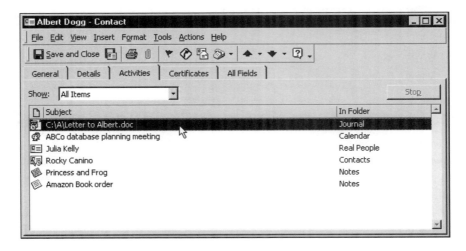

Changing Your View

When you look at the Journal in a monthly timeline view, you get a good overall picture of your recorded activities, but you have to point to an individual icon to discover what the activity was (when you point to the icon, the Subject label appears). You can make a few changes to your Journal timeline views so that the Subject labels for icons are always visible in the monthly view, and the labels are the length you find most useful. You can also show week numbers in the timeline heading, which is useful for planning in some industries.

Displaying Item Labels in the Monthly Timeline

To display item labels in the monthly timeline, follow these steps:

1. Right-click in an empty area of the Journal window, and click Other Settings on the shortcut menu.

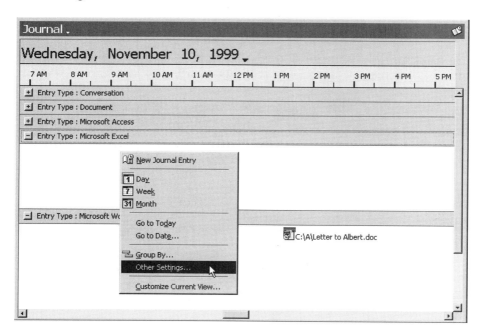

2. In the Format Timeline View dialog box that appears, mark the Show Label When Viewing By Month check box.

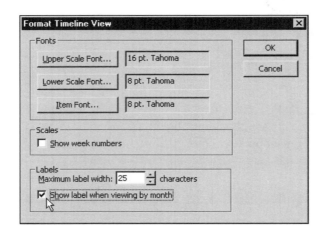

TIP *By default, the label width is 25 characters wide, but if you find that your labels are too short or too long, return to this dialog box and change the number in the Maximum Label Width box. The label width applies to the labels in the Day and Week timelines as well as the Month timeline.*

3. Click OK to close the dialog box. The following illustration shows a Month timeline view with 25-character labels displayed.

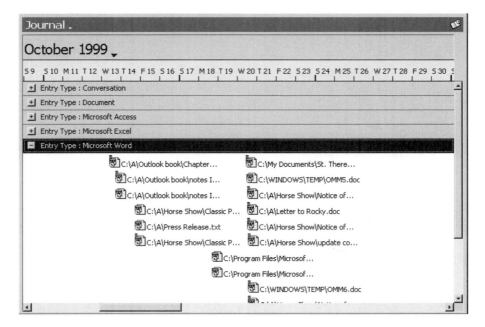

Showing Week Numbers

In some industries, it's important to know what week of the year it is. You can show week numbers in your timeline view like this:

1. Right-click in an empty area of the Journal window, and click Other Settings on the shortcut menu.

2. In the Format Timeline View dialog box that appears, mark the Show Week Numbers check box.

3. Click OK to close the dialog box. In the monthly timeline, week numbers replace the dates, but in the Week and Day views, both the week number and date are displayed in the timeline header.

That's it for Journal. If you set up Journal to record messages and files automatically while you work, you may find it remarkably helpful when you try to figure out when you last worked on a file, or how much time you spent on a project two months ago.

In the next chapter, you'll learn how to use Outlook to manage all the files on your hard drive.

11

Chapter 12

Managing Other Files from Outlook

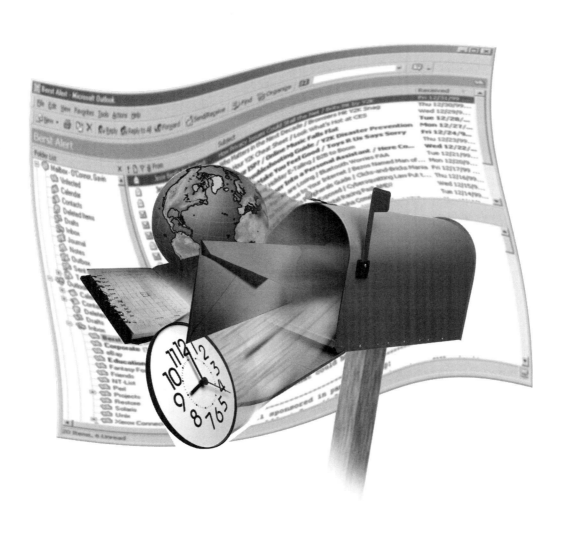

How to . . .

- Use Outlook to find folders and files on your hard drive

- Change file properties without opening the files

- Open files from within Outlook

- Use Outlook to move, copy, and print files

- Change your file-window view

- Connect to a network drive

Outlook is an information manager, and in the time-honored managerial tradition, Outlook wants to manage everything—your schedule, your to-do lists, your lists of contacts, and all the files on your computer. In fact, when it comes to managing the files on your hard drive, Outlook has a lot more to offer than Windows Explorer. You'll learn how to manage your files more efficiently with Outlook in this chapter.

You can open and view any file on your hard drive or network from within Outlook. The My Computer shortcut icon in your Outlook bar is a shortcut to the My Computer icon on your Windows desktop. Both icons open the My Computer window, which gives you access to all the files on your hard drive or network. You can use Outlook's file windows to move and copy files from one hard drive folder to another, print files, preview files, and view and change file properties without opening the files.

If you're already familiar with Windows 95/98, much of what you'll learn in this chapter will be familiar, but you'll learn how to do much more than just carry out familiar Windows file procedures from within Outlook.

Viewing Hard Drive Files in Outlook

One big advantage that Outlook has over your Windows file windows is that in Outlook, you can display each file's properties (author, keywords, title, categories, the template a file is based on, and lots more).

Name	Author	Type	Size	Modified	Keywords
Fidelity II performance...		Text Document	212 B	Fri 7/31/98 11:36 AM	
Shippers.xls	Julia Kelly	Microsoft Excel Work...	14 KB	Fri 7/31/98 3:23 PM	
Tig-6273.xls	Julia Kelly	Microsoft Excel Work...	21 KB	Fri 7/31/98 3:32 PM	invoice
Hav-5652.xls	Julia Kelly	Microsoft Excel Work...	21 KB	Fri 7/31/98 3:32 PM	invoice
Hav-5591.xls	Julia Kelly	Microsoft Excel Work...	21 KB	Fri 7/31/98 3:32 PM	invoice
And-6253.xls	Julia Kelly	Microsoft Excel Work...	21 KB	Fri 7/31/98 3:32 PM	invoice
And-5837.xls	Julia Kelly	Microsoft Excel Work...	21 KB	Fri 7/31/98 3:33 PM	invoice
And-5052.xls	Julia Kelly	Microsoft Excel Work...	21 KB	Fri 7/31/98 3:33 PM	invoice
Grade Sheets.xls	Julia Kelly	Microsoft Excel Work...	18 KB	Fri 8/7/98 5:11 PM	
Capital Improvements.xls	Julia Kelly	Microsoft Excel Work...	18 KB	Sat 8/8/98 12:19 PM	
Charts.xls	Julia Kelly	Microsoft Excel Work...	93 KB	Mon 8/31/98 2:24 PM	
marker2.bmp		Bitmap Image	34 KB	Mon 8/31/98 5:47 PM	
SKP Invoice1.xls	Village Software	Microsoft Excel Work...	292 KB	Wed 9/9/98 1:14 PM	
Graphics.xls	Julia Kelly	Microsoft Excel Work...	18 KB	Wed 9/9/98 1:57 PM	
Commissions Report.doc	Julia Kelly	Microsoft Word Docu...	24 KB	Thu 9/24/98 2:16 PM	
Donations.xls		Microsoft Excel Work...	41 KB	Thu 9/24/98 2:35 PM	
Formats.xls	Julia Kelly	Microsoft Excel Work...	48 KB	Fri 11/6/98 10:51 AM	
Theatre Seating.xls	Julia Kelly	Microsoft Excel Work...	340 KB	Fri 11/6/98 2:05 PM	
Creative Charts.xls	Julia Kelly	Microsoft Excel Work...	39 KB	Fri 11/6/98 2:10 PM	
Summarize.xls	Julia Kelly	Microsoft Excel Work...	99 KB	Fri 11/6/98 3:24 PM	
Pivot Analyses.xls	Julia Kelly	Microsoft Excel Work...	32 KB	Fri 11/6/98 4:43 PM	
Chart Formats.xls	Julia Kelly	Microsoft Excel Work...	94 KB	Fri 11/6/98 5:33 PM	
Payments.xls		Microsoft Excel Work...	38 KB	Sat 11/7/98 3:23 PM	

From the My Computer window in Outlook, you can view and open any of your computer files, such as word processing documents, spreadsheet and database files, and whatever else is lurking on your hard drive. You can copy, move, print, and delete files from Outlook's file windows, and you can create shortcuts to specific folders so that you can open them quickly without navigating through your hard drive's file tree.

Navigating to Files in Outlook

The first thing you'll need for folder and file navigation is Outlook's Advanced toolbar. To display it, right-click Outlook's toolbar or menu bar, and click Advanced.

Next, follow these steps to open your My Computer window in Outlook:

1. In the Outlook bar, click the Other Shortcuts button. The Other Shortcuts group opens, and the My Computer icon appears in your Outlook bar.

12

 *If you've lost or can't find the Other Shortcuts button in your Outlook bar, see Chapter 15 to learn how to create an Outlook bar group and put shortcut icons into it.*

2. Click the My Computer icon in the Outlook bar. The Outlook window switches to a My Computer window, as shown in Figure 12-1.

The My Computer file window shows the drives available for you to explore or navigate through, including your floppy-disk and CD-ROM drives, and any network drives your computer is aware of. (You'll learn how to map network drives in Outlook later in this chapter.)

To navigate to a specific folder and file, follow these steps:

1. In the file window, double-click the icon for the drive where the folder and file are stored. The contents of the drive appear in the file window, as shown in Figure 12-2.

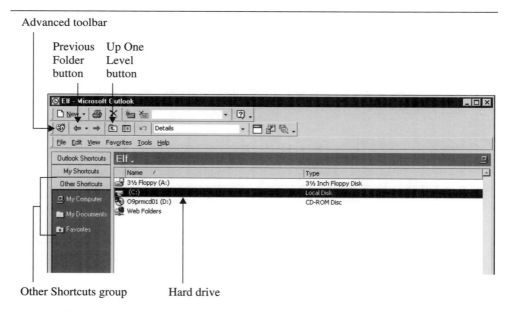

Advanced toolbar

Previous   Up One
Folder   Level
button   button

Other Shortcuts group   Hard drive

FIGURE 12-1   The My Computer window in Outlook

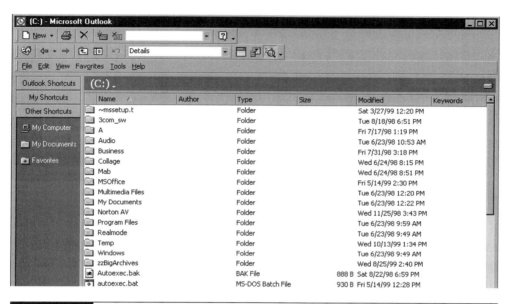

FIGURE 12-2   My hard drive file tree

2. Double-click your way through folder after folder until you arrive at the folder where your file is stored. Here are some tips for folder and file navigation:

- The Folder banner shows the name of the folder that's displayed in the file window.

- To back up to the previous folder you had open, click the Previous Folder button on the Advanced toolbar.

- To back up one level in the file tree, click the Up One Level button on the Advanced toolbar.

- To open a folder you previously had open, without clicking through each intermediate folder, click the arrow next to the Previous Folder button, and select the folder you want to open. The Next Folder button works the same way, jumping forward to folders you've already opened.

12

Previewing Files in Outlook

Sometimes, it's difficult to remember which file is exactly the one you need, and opening each one can be annoyingly time-consuming when you're in a hurry. A faster way to look at different files is to use Quick View, like this:

1. Right-click the file you want to take a look at.

2. Click Quick View on the shortcut menu. A Quick View window opens; you can scroll through the entire document, but you can't edit it (Quick View is just for looking).

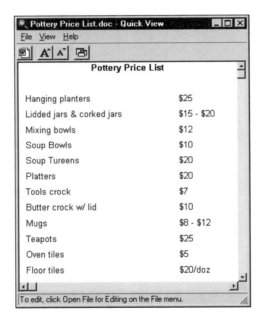

 *Not every file can be opened in Quick View (for example, Publisher files can't be opened in Quick View). Also, if you're using Windows 98, you can open all Office files in Quick View, but if you're using Windows 95, you can only open files that are saved as Office 95 or earlier file types.*

3. To glance at several different files in rapid succession, resize the Outlook window to make it smaller, and position the Outlook and Quick View windows side by side or overlapping, so that you can see both at the same time (as shown in Figure 12-3).

Drag and drop the file icon
into Quick View window

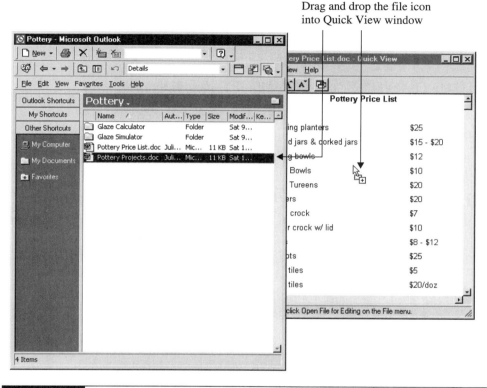

FIGURE 12-3   Position the Outlook and Quick View windows so that you can see both

Drag the icon for the next file you want to view into the Quick View window. The new file replaces the previous file in the Quick View window.

The Replace Window button on the Quick View toolbar is supposed to switch between viewing each file in the same window and viewing different files in separate windows, but it has never (in my recollection) functioned at all, so you can ignore it.

What if you prefer to work with Outlook maximized on your screen? Every time you click an icon in the Outlook window, the Quick View window disappears behind the Outlook window. Try this: drag the file icon down to the Quick View window's button on your taskbar, hold it over the button for a moment (don't release your mouse button yet), and when the Quick View window reappears, drag the icon up and drop it in the Quick View window.

4. When you locate the file you want, you can open it for editing by clicking the Open File for Editing button on the Quick View toolbar, or close the Quick View window and continue with your task.

Opening, Moving, Copying, Printing, and Deleting Files from Outlook

Everything you can do with your hard drive files from your Windows desktop or Windows Explorer, you can do from Outlook.

Opening Files from Outlook

To open a file, double-click its icon. The program that runs the file starts, and the file opens in the program. At that point, you're working in the program (Excel, Publisher, whatever) and Outlook retires to the background.

Moving or Copying Files to Another Folder

You can move or copy files from one folder to another by dragging them, like this:

1. On Outlook's Advanced toolbar, click the Folder List button. (You can also click the folder-name button in the Folder banner, and then click the pushpin icon in the Folder list to keep the list open.) The Folder list appears next to the file window, as shown in Figure 12-4.

2. In the Folder list, locate the folder into which you want to move or copy a file. Click the small plus symbols to show subfolders.

3. In the file window, navigate to the file you want to move or copy.

When moving or copying files, the trick is to first display the folder or subfolder destination you want in the Folder list, and then display the file in the file window.

4. Drag the file you want to move or copy from the file window to the destination folder icon in the Folder list. To move the file, drag and drop it on the folder icon. To copy the file, press the CTRL key while you release the mouse button to drop the file on the folder icon.

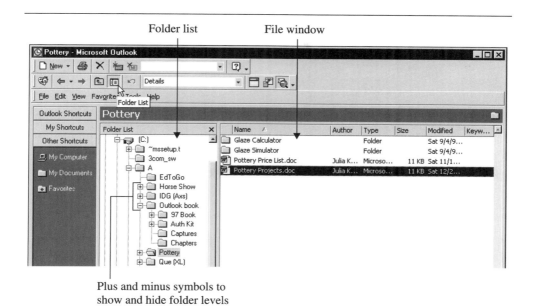

Folder list   File window

Plus and minus symbols to
show and hide folder levels

FIGURE 12-4 The Folder list and file window

Copying a File to a Floppy Disk

To copy a file to a disk in your floppy disk drive, do this:

1. Make sure there's a disk in your disk drive.

2. In Outlook's file window, right-click the file you want to copy, point to Send To, and click the name of your floppy disk drive.

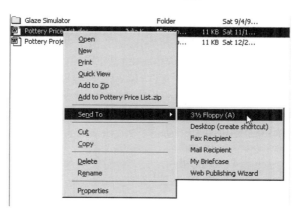

 *When you make changes to files, such as renaming, copying, deleting, or moving, the changes may not be immediately visible in the Outlook window. To refresh the window, click View | Refresh. To refresh a window even faster, press F5.*

Printing a File

Suppose you've completed the quarterly report and printed copies for your division meeting, and at the last minute, a coworker asks you to bring an extra copy for a visitor. You can print it quickly, without the extra time spent opening the program and opening the file. To print a file from Outlook's file window, follow these steps:

1. In Outlook's file window, right-click the file you want to print.

2. Click Print on the shortcut menu and you'll see the program and first page flash briefly on the computer screen; the file is sent to the printer, and the file and program close.

Deleting a File

To delete a file from Outlook's file window, right-click the file and click Delete. The file is sent to your Windows Recycle Bin, where it takes up hard drive space until you empty the Recycle Bin.

Creating New Hard Drive Folders

When you accumulate lots of files in a single folder (for example, if you allow your Microsoft programs to save every file to the default My Documents folder), soon you'll have a very long list in which it's difficult to locate files quickly. Creating subfolders and moving files into those subfolders can help you get your files organized. To create new subfolders from Outlook, follow these steps:

1. In Outlook's file window, open the folder in which you want to create a new subfolder. (For this example, open the folder that contains the really long list of files.)

2. Click File | New | Folder. A Create New Folder dialog box appears.

3. Type a name for the new folder, and click OK.

Now, you can follow the procedure in the previous section, "Moving or Copying Files to Another Folder," to segregate and organize your files. If you don't see your new subfolder in the Folder list, press F5 to refresh the Outlook window.

Using File Properties in Outlook

The Outlook file window shows you several file properties, such as keywords and author, and you can display more properties, such as title and subject. You can change those properties from within Outlook's file window, and you can organize your list of files by sorting and grouping, using the same procedures as you'd use to sort or group Outlook items, such as e-mail messages.

Displaying File Properties

Do you want to see file titles (the first few words of each document)? Or the templates each file was based on? To display more file properties, use the Field Chooser to display those fields, like this:

1. Right-click the file window's heading row and click Field Chooser.

2. In the list box at the top of the Field Chooser, select All File Fields.

3. Drag field buttons for the fields (file properties) you want to display, and drop them in position in the file window's heading row.

4. Close the Field Chooser by clicking its X close button.

To remove a file property from the window, drag that field's heading button away from the heading row and drop it.

 *To sort files, click the heading button for the field you want to sort on. See Chapter 2 to learn how to use sorting, grouping, and other organizing techniques.*

Changing File Properties

Suppose you notice that some of your files have "Valued Customer" as their author instead of your name, or suppose you want to add the keyword "invoice" to all of your invoice files so that you can search for the whole group at accounting time. You can change a file's properties from the Outlook file window without opening the file, like this:

1. Right-click the file whose properties you want to change.

2. Click Properties. The Properties dialog box appears.

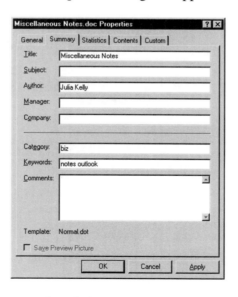

3. Click the Summary tab and change any properties that need changing. For example, change the author name if it's wrong, and add keywords to use in searches.

4. Click OK. Any properties you added or changed appear in the property fields when you have them displayed in the file window.

Changing Your File View

Here's another advantage Outlook's file window has over your Windows file windows: you can display your files in all the same ways that you can display Outlook items. You can display a folder's files in a timeline according to when you worked on them, or grouped by author or file type, or as icons without all the file property details.

To change your file view, click View | Current View and click the name of the view you want. Here are some more tips for changing your view in an Outlook file window:

■ Any view you select only applies to the displayed folder window; all folder windows retain whatever view you select until you change it.

■ You can display and change file properties in any view.

■ You can most easily sort by file properties in Details view.

■ In Document Timeline view, you can switch between Day, Week, and Month timelines by clicking the appropriate toolbar buttons.

■ From any view, you can insert a file into an e-mail message by dragging the file's icon to the Inbox icon in the Outlook bar. A new message is created that contains the attached file.

Creating an Outlook Bar Shortcut to a File or Folder

Is there a file you work on so often that it would be really convenient to have a shortcut to that file on your Outlook bar? Or, do you have a folder that you open so many times a day that an Outlook bar shortcut icon would be a time-saver? Here's how you can create those Outlook bar shortcuts:

1. Open the file window where the folder or file you want a shortcut to is stored.

2. Open the Outlook bar group where you want to create a shortcut (the Other Shortcuts group, the My Shortcuts group, or a new custom group—perhaps named My Files).

12

3. Drag the file or folder icon into the Outlook bar and drop it, as shown in the following illustration. I've created a shortcut to my Chapters folder, and I'm creating a shortcut to my Chapter 12 file so that I can open it quickly during the week that I'm working on it.

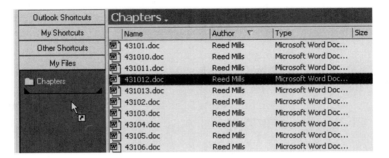

When you don't need an Outlook bar shortcut any more, right-click the shortcut and click Remove From Outlook Bar. When you're asked if you're sure, click Yes. These are just shortcuts that point to the files and folders, and removing them won't affect the actual files or folders.

Connecting to a Network Drive

If you're using Outlook on a network, you can *map* (create access to) network drives on other computers so that you can open file windows to files other than those on your local hard drive. It doesn't matter whether you use Outlook in the Internet Mail Only configuration or the Corporate/Workgroup configuration, as long as the drive in the other computer that you want to map has Sharing allowed.

NOTE *To share a drive with other computers, open Windows Explorer. Right-click the drive you want to share (so other computers can map it), and click Sharing. In the Properties dialog box, on the Shared tab, click the Shared As option, click an Access Type option, and then click OK. See your Windows documentation to learn more about sharing network drives.*

This is how you map other (shared) network drives in Outlook:

1. Open any file window.

2. Click Tools | Map Network Drive. The Map Network Drive dialog box appears.

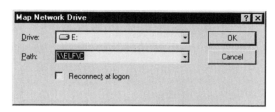

3. In the Path box, type the name of the computer and drive in this format: **\\computername\drive**.

 *If you mark the Reconnect At Logon check box, your computer will open the connection to the network drive every time you start up. This takes extra startup time, so you might want to leave the check box unmarked, and map the drive only when you need to use it.*

4. Click OK. The drive for that computer appears in Outlook's My Computer folder (I'm mapping the hard drive of my laptop computer named "Elf" in the following example), and you can open it just like any drive or folder on your local hard drive. You can also create an Outlook bar shortcut to the mapped drive.

12

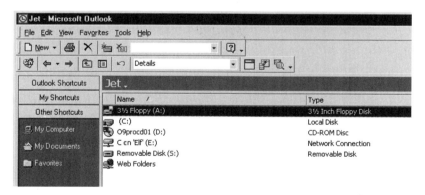

That's it for using Outlook to manage all the other files on your computer (and your network). In the next chapter, you'll learn how to print Outlook items, such as your Calendar and e-mail messages, in every possible way (and there are more ways to print Outlook items than you'd think).

Chapter 13 Printing Everything

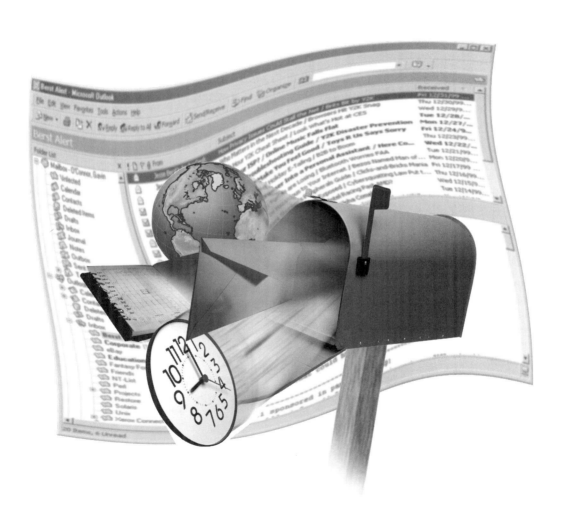

How to . . .

- ■ Print individual Outlook items
- ■ Print lists of Outlook items
- ■ Set up printed pages
- ■ Preview pages before printing
- ■ Print your calendar in several different styles

The paperless office is a myth. Even in the most computerized corporate arenas, data is backed up on paper as well as electronically, and there are many occasions when paper is simply more practical (such as when you're in a committee meeting, working out dates for activities on your calendar, or when you need a pocket-sized list of contacts' addresses and phone numbers).

Outlook can print anything, and in a wide variety of ways. From any Outlook folder, you can print individual items, such as the details of a single Calendar appointment, or a view of all the items in the folder (everything you see on the screen when you open an Outlook folder). Even better, you can print Outlook items in many different styles, so your printed output may not look anything like what you see on your screen.

Deciding What to Print

You can print detailed individual items (for example, a message or contact), or you can print a view (for example, a table listing all the tasks in your task list).

Printing Open Items

Sometimes, I want to print an e-mail message so that I can read it over lunch or share it with someone away from my desk. The fastest way to print any Outlook item is to send the item to the printer while the item is open.

To print an open item, click the Print button on the item's toolbar, and the item is sent immediately to the printer and printed in full detail, using the default print settings.

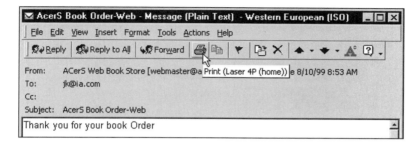

If you want to change any of the default print settings (for example, to print more than one copy, or to print attached files along with an e-mail message), click File | Print in the item's menu bar. Change the settings in the Print dialog box and then click Print.

Printing Individual Items

Suppose you want to print the details for five of the items in your task list, but you don't want to open and print each one. Fortunately, Outlook provides a more efficient way to print several individual items in full detail:

1. Select the items you want to print. Use the SHIFT or CTRL key to select multiple items.

2. Click File | Print. The Print dialog box appears, shown in Figure 13-1.

3. Under Print Style, click the Memo Style icon. Memo Style prints each individual item in full detail. The other styles (Table, Card, Booklet, Phone Directory, and so on) vary depending on which Outlook folder you're printing from.

13

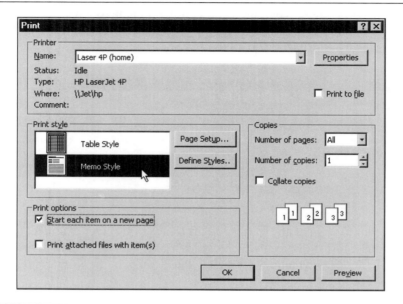

FIGURE 13-1   The Print dialog box set up to print individual items

Printing a View

Sometimes, you need a list of all the items in an Outlook folder (for example, a to-do list of tasks) rather than detailed information on individual items. You can print any table-type view, and what you see on the screen is what gets printed. To print a list of items in a folder:

1. Open the Outlook folder or subfolder that contains the items you want to print.

2. Select the view you want to print (click View | Current View, and click the name of the view you want).

   ■ Rearrange the view by moving or deleting columns until it looks like what you want to print.

   ■ If you want to print only a selected set of the items displayed on the screen, use the CTRL or SHIFT key to select them.

   ■ Sort, group, or filter a table-type view of items before you print it, so that your printout will be organized in the most efficient way for your purpose.

TIP

To print all the long entries in a column completely, right-click the column's header button and click Best Fit. The column is resized to fit its longest entries, and none of the information is truncated in the printout.

3. Click File | Print.

4. Under Print Style, shown in Figure 13-2, click the print style you want to print.

The Print Styles you can select from depend on the view you have displayed on the screen. For example, in Contacts, if you have a card view displayed, you have many more printing options than if you have the Phone List view displayed.

TIP

Memo Style always prints the individual selected item(s) in full detail.

5. If you want to print only the selected set of items displayed on the screen, click the Only Selected Rows option under Print Range.

6. Click OK to print the pages.

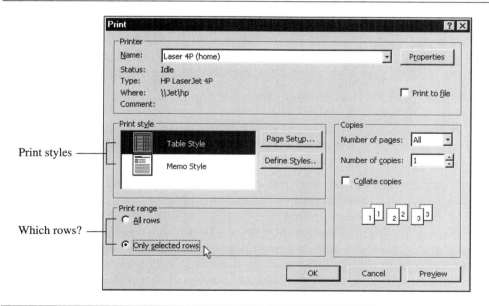

Print styles

Which rows?

FIGURE 13-2   The Print dialog box set up to print selected rows in a table view

Previewing the Printed Page

To preview the pages before you print them (which is always a good idea), click
the Preview button in the Print dialog box before you click OK. If the preview
pages (shown in Figure 13-3) aren't quite what you want, you can change the page
setup. Changing the page setup won't change what you see on the screen—it only
affects the printed pages.

Display multiple pages   Open the Print dialog box

Page Setup   Close the Print Preview

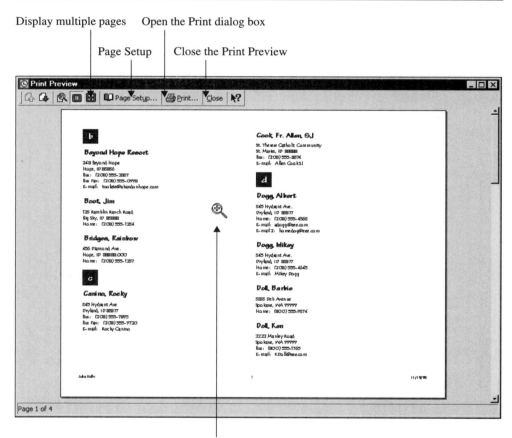

Click the magnifying-glass pointer on the page to zoom in and out

FIGURE 13-3   A print preview of Contacts in Card Style

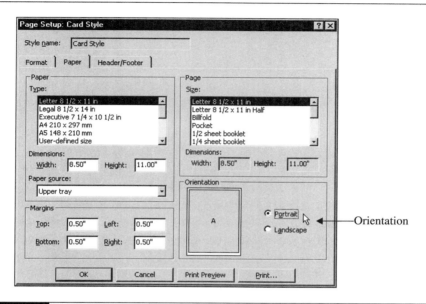

Orientation

FIGURE 13-4   Select a Portrait page orientation

For example, to change the printed page from a Landscape to a Portrait orientation, click the Page Setup button on the Preview toolbar. In the Page Setup dialog box, shown in Figure 13-4, click the Paper tab, click the Portrait Orientation option, and click OK. Print Preview shows the changes to your printed pages.

If the Print Preview looks right, click the Print button on the Preview toolbar. The Print dialog box appears. Click OK to print the pages.

Here are some of the details you can change in the Page Setup dialog box:

■ On the Format tab, you can change fonts and font sizes, and choose between using gray shading in the printed pages or making them black and white. Other options depend on the Outlook folder and print style you're setting up. Right-click an option to see a brief explanation of what the option does.

■ On the Paper tab, you can change the margins, paper size or type, printed page size or type (some printed pages will fit two or four pages on a single sheet of paper), and page orientation.

■ On the Header/Footer tab, you can change printed page headers and footers to print automated information (such as page numbers and total pages, printing date, and printing time), or delete the default automated footer information. Also, you can type and format any custom header or footer you want.

Printing Different Types of Outlook Items

Each Outlook folder has its own printing options and idiosyncrasies. In each folder, if you often find that you set up and print with a particular print style, you can save that custom print style so that you don't have to set it up repeatedly (you'll learn how to save your own print style in the section "Save a Custom Print Style," at the end of this chapter).

In any Outlook folder, if you want to print a specific set of items (such as all contacts in a particular category), filter the view so that only the items in that category (or meeting other filter criteria you set) are displayed, and then choose the All Items option in the Print dialog box. See Chapter 2 to learn how to filter a table-type view of Outlook items.

Printing Your Tasks

The tasks that are displayed in your Tasks window view will be shown in the printed list, so select the view first (perhaps Simple List, Active Tasks, or Overdue Tasks) and then set up your printed page.

Printing Your Notes

You cannot print a view of Notes when they're displayed in an icon view, although you can print individual selected Notes (in Memo Style) when an icon view is displayed. If you want to print all of your Notes as a table, click View | Current View and select a different view, such as Notes List. To print a list of notes that includes the first few lines of each note, click View | AutoPreview to display the first three lines in each note.

Printing the Journal

Journal items can only be printed as individual items in Memo Style, but you can print the attached files along with the Journal entry details. To print the attached files, in the Print dialog box, mark the Print Attached Files With Item(s) check box.

Printing Your Contacts

When you print a Contacts view, you can choose from Card Style and three Booklet Styles, as well as Phone Directory Style. If you choose Card Style or one of the Booklet Styles, you'll get two blank forms on the last page (so you can write down new contact information in your Contacts printout, instead of writing it on a scrap of paper and then losing it).

Whether you think the blank forms are a waste of paper or think they're great and want several pages of them, you can change the number of blank forms that are printed. In the Print dialog box, select Card Style or a Booklet Style and then click the Page Setup button. On the Format tab, under Options, change the number in the Blank Forms At End list box.

Printing a Calendar

Because Outlook's Calendar offers the most interesting and functional printed output, I'll show you how to print your calendar in detail. Everything you learn about printing your calendar can be applied to printing items and lists in the other Outlook folders.

You can print your calendar in just about any format you can think of: a single day, a specific week or month, or a whole set of months. You can also print your calendar in a commercial format that fits into your Day-Timer, Day Runner, or Franklin Day Planner.

Your printed calendar contains all the appointments and events you've entered in your Calendar folder, and blank calendar pages for all the days when you don't have anything scheduled.

Setting Up a Printed Calendar

There are five built-in Calendar printing styles: Daily, Weekly, Monthly, Tri-Fold, and Calendar Details. You can quickly print a Daily, Weekly, or Monthly style

13

page by switching to that view and clicking the Print button on the Calendar toolbar.

 *To see what the calendar page will look like before you print it, click File | Print Preview. If you like what you see, click the Print button on the Print Preview toolbar, and then click OK in the Print dialog box that appears.*

To see what the Tri-Fold and Calendar Details styles look like, click File | Print and, in the Print dialog box, choose a style under Print Style.

Then, click the Preview button in the lower-right corner of the Print dialog box.

Customizing Your Printed Calendar

What if you want to print three months of your calendar? Or a weekly calendar that spreads your week across two facing pages instead compressing it onto a single page? You start by customizing a print style, and then finish by choosing options in the Print dialog box. You have lots of options to choose from, and the best way to learn about them is to try different options and look at the results in Print Preview.

 *To print a completely empty calendar to distribute to others in your group, create a new calendar subfolder and print that new calendar without creating any appointments or events in it.*

CREATE A CUSTOM PRINT STYLE   To demonstrate, I'll create the printed calendar shown in Figure 13-5. It spreads each week across two facing pages (so I can

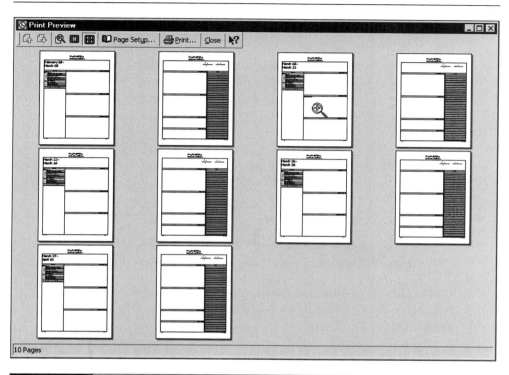

FIGURE 13-5   A custom printed calendar

13

punch holes in it and put it in a binder). I'm also going to add a custom header to each page, and each week will show my task list and an area for writing notes. I'll print a month's worth of these weekly calendars.

To do this, follow these steps:

1. Open your Calendar and select File | Page Setup | Weekly Style. The Page Setup: Weekly Style dialog box appears.

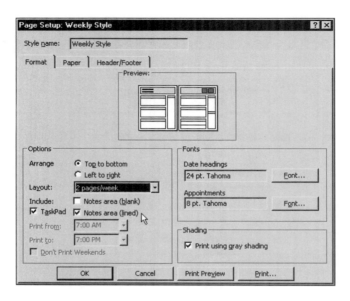

2. On the Format tab, under Options, select 2 Pages/Week in the Layout list box. Mark the TaskPad check box and the Notes Area (Lined) check box. Then click the Paper tab.

3. On the Paper tab, leave all the default settings (but play with them if you're curious about what the options do). For example, if you want to print pages for your commercial calendar binder, choose the commercial calendar type under Page, in the Size list.

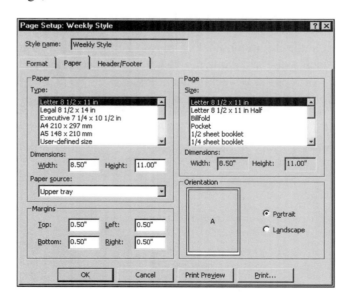

4. Click the Header/Footer tab, click in the central Header box, and type a header to appear in the center at the top of each page. Then, click the Font button to select font and font formatting for the Header entry. Enter custom Footer entries if you want them. You can delete any of the automatic entries, such as [User Name] or [Page #], if you don't want them.

Page Setup: Weekly Style   [? X]

Style name: [Weekly Style]

| Format | Paper | Header/Footer |

Header:

[14 pt. Tempus Sans ITC]   [Font...]

| | Stony Keep Pottery
Production Calendar | |

Footer:

[8 pt. Tahoma]   [Font...]

| [User Name] | [Page #] | [Date Printed] |

☑ Reverse on even pages

[OK]   [Cancel]   [Print Preview]   [Print...]

5. Click the Print button (at the bottom of the Page Setup dialog box) to open the Print dialog box. Under Print Range, select Start and End dates for your printed calendar.

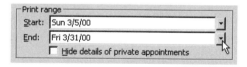

Print range
Start: [Sun 3/5/00]
End: [Fri 3/31/00]
☐ Hide details of private appointments

6. Click the Preview button for one last look, and on the Print Preview toolbar, click the Multiple Pages button to preview all the pages that you'll print. Then, on the Print Preview toolbar, click the Print button to return to the Print dialog box.

7. In the Print dialog box, click OK.

13

SAVE A CUSTOM PRINT STYLE   If you want to save a custom style so that you can use it again, follow these steps *before* you begin to customize the style:

1. Open the Print dialog box, and under Print Style, click the Define Styles button.

2. In the Define Print Styles dialog box that appears, choose the style you're going to customize, and then click the Copy button.

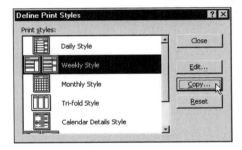

3. In the Page Setup dialog box that appears, type an identifying name for the custom style in the Style Name box. Then, set up your style in the Page Setup dialog box.

4. When you finish setting up your custom style, click OK. Your custom style appears in the Define Print Styles dialog box.

   *You can choose your new custom style in the future by clicking File | Page Setup | your custom style.*

5. Close the Define Print Styles dialog box, set Start and End dates in the Print dialog box, and click OK to print the custom calendar.

There's quite a bit you can do to customize your printed Outlook data, so it's worth your time to experiment with print styles and page setups. In the next chapter you'll learn how to use Outlook on the Web.

Chapter 14

Using Outlook on the Internet

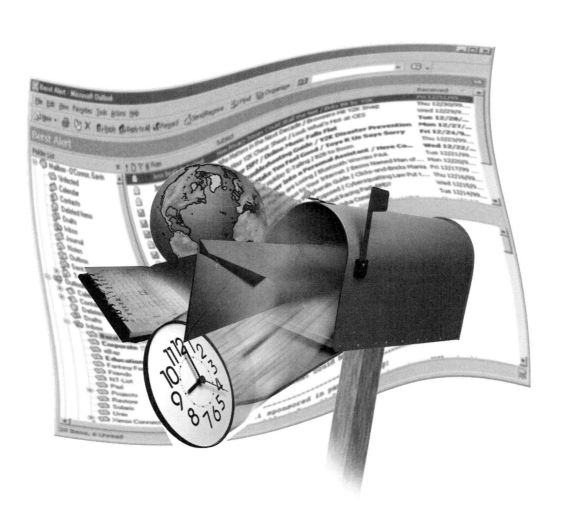

How to . . .

- Use Outlook's Web toolbar to navigate Web sites in Outlook

- Create an Outlook bar shortcut to a Web page

- Use your Favorites menu to visit Web pages

- Add Web pages to your Favorites menu

- Use Outlook to read and post messages to newsgroups

- Switch from Outlook to your browser to view an open Web page

Outlook's Web toolbar, shown in Figure 14-1, has buttons you'll recognize if you're familiar with the Internet Explorer Web browser. To display the Web toolbar, right-click in the menu bar or toolbar, and click Web.

TIP *Your Web toolbar may be on the same row as your Standard toolbar, which means several buttons will be hidden. To display the Web toolbar on its own row with no hidden buttons, point to the vertical bar at the left end of the Web toolbar. When your pointer becomes a four-headed arrow, drag the left end of the toolbar down onto its own row. Drag it around to get it where you want it.*

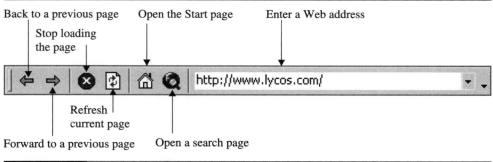

FIGURE 14-1 Outlook's Web toolbar

There are three ways to head out onto the Web from Outlook:

- Click the Search button on the Web toolbar, which opens a collection of Web search pages.

- Enter a Web address, or URL, in the toolbar's Address box and press ENTER.

- Click Outlook's Favorites menu and select a Web page name on the list.

Whichever technique you choose (and they all come in handy, depending on the situation), Outlook goes online and the Web page appears in the Outlook window.

Finding a Web Page from Within Outlook

When you open a Web page in Outlook, Outlook acts like your browser. The big difference between your browser and Outlook is that in Outlook, you can easily jump from a Web page to your Inbox, to your Calendar, to a folder on your hard drive, and so forth, all in a single program window.

Use the Web Toolbar

To find a particular Web page for the first time, you can use the Search button on the Web toolbar and then search for topics; or, you can type a Web address into the Address box on the Web toolbar.

To search for a Web page, click the Search button on the Web toolbar. Outlook dials your Internet connection, and a Web page, perhaps like the one shown in Figure 14-2, appears (the search page you see depends on your Internet setup and configuration).

On this search page, to find Web pages with contents such as shopping sites, informational sites, and so forth, click one of the search engines listed under Premier Providers. Each search engine is a little different, and if you're conducting a really thorough search for a topic, it's worth using at least a couple of different search engines. Each search engine provides search help and tips on the search engine's home page.

If you want to find a person or a business, use one of the directories listed under People and Businesses (other search pages will have similar links). Try

14

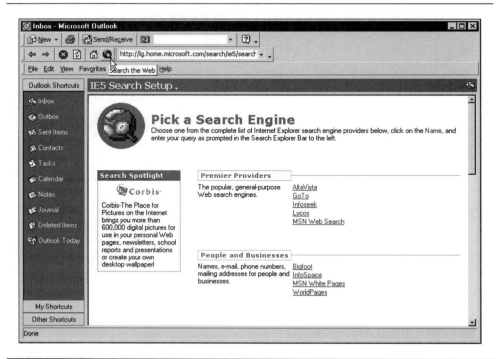

FIGURE 14-2   Click the Search button, and then click a search engine

searching for your own name—you'll find that the data isn't always completely up-to-date, but this process is faster than a trip to the local library.

If you know the Web address for a site (it seems like every television and magazine ad includes a Web address these days), type the address in the Address box.

> webmd.com

Press ENTER, and Outlook opens the Web page.

When you've been bouncing around from page to page on the Web, you'll probably find that you want to return to a page you previously had open. To back up to the previous page, click the Back button on the Web toolbar. When you back up a page, the Forward button becomes active, so you can return in the other direction to the page you last had open without having to remember which link you clicked to get there.

If you've set a particular Web page as your *start page* (the page that opens when you first launch your Internet Explorer browser), you can open that page by clicking the Start Page button on Outlook's Web toolbar. The start page doesn't have to be the Microsoft page that your browser opens by default; you can change the start page to one that you choose (perhaps your favorite search page), and whether you launch Internet Explorer without Outlook or click the Start Page button in either Outlook or Internet Explorer, your chosen start page opens.

To set your own start page, open Internet Explorer and click Tools | Internet Options. On the General page, type the address for your chosen start page in the Address box under Home Page, and then click OK.

Add a Web Page Shortcut to Your Outlook Bar

Not only are your favorite Web pages instantly accessible when you add them to your Favorites list, you can also keep a Web page close at hand by creating a shortcut to it from your Outlook bar. Use this judiciously, though—too many shortcuts in your Outlook bar will make it overcrowded and inefficient.

To add a Web page shortcut to your Outlook bar, open the Web page you want to add (open it in Outlook). Then, on Outlook's File menu, point to New and click Outlook Bar Shortcut To Web Page. Your new shortcut icon shows up in the My Shortcuts group.

Send a Web Page in a Message

Suppose you've got a terrific Web page open in Outlook, and you want to send the page to some colleagues. You can send a hyperlink to the page (which you learned how to do in Chapter 6), but you can also send a shortcut to the Web page, like this:

1. With the Web page open in your Outlook window, click Actions | Send Web Page by E-Mail. Outlook creates a new e-mail message with a shortcut icon.

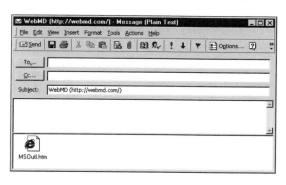

2. Address the message in the To box, and click the message's Send button.

When your colleagues receive your message, they can either double-click the icon to open the page in their browser, or drag the icon out of the message and save it on their Windows desktop or in a Windows folder, to open it in their browser later.

Using Your Favorites

If you're familiar with Microsoft's Internet Explorer, then you already know what the Favorites menu does: initially, it lists several Web sites that Microsoft hopes you'll find interesting; later, it lists any Web sites you've added yourself, so that you can open them quickly and easily. You can add your own Web pages, organize them, and delete any that you don't want.

 *You can also visit, delete, and organize Favorites Web pages by opening the Favorites folder in the Outlook window (in the Outlook bar's Other Shortcuts group, click the Favorites icon).*

Visit a Favorite Web Page

Your list of Favorites is the same whether you open it from the Windows Start menu, the Favorites menu in Internet Explorer, or the Favorites menu in Outlook, because they all get their lists from the Favorites folder on your hard drive, probably at C:/Windows/Favorites. If you're working in Outlook, there's no point in opening a separate program to get to a Web page when you can do it from within Outlook.

To visit a Favorites Web page in Outlook, click Favorites, and click the name of the Web page. To visit one of the Web pages in the folders at the top of the Favorites list, point to the folder to open it, and then click the name of a Web page.

Add a Web Page to Your Favorites List

When you've searched through endless dead-ends and have finally found the one Web page that really has the information you need, you can save it as a Favorite. This provides a single-step return to the site each time you visit it in the future.

To add a Web page to your Favorites menu:

1. Open the Web page that you want to add.

2. On Outlook's menu bar, click Favorites | Add To Favorites.

3. In the Add To Favorites dialog box, shown in Figure 14-3, either edit the name (if the default filename is too wordy) or type a short and useful name of your own, and then click the Add button.

 *If you have several Web pages that pertain to the same topic, start each Favorites name with the same word so that they're all grouped together in the Favorites list.*

When you want to visit that Web page again, either in Outlook or in your browser, or from the Windows Start button, click Favorites and then click the Web page name.

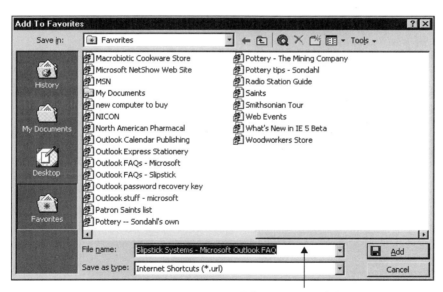

Edit or type a useful name

FIGURE 14-3 Add a Web page to your Favorites list

Double-click a folder to open it   Delete a selected Web page or folder

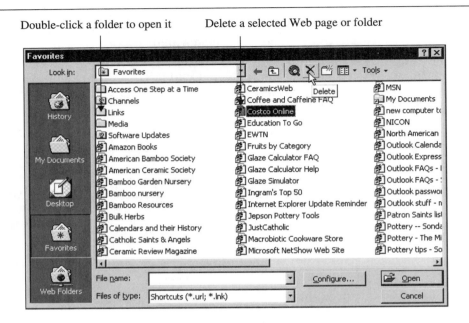

Delete Web pages that aren't your favorites

Delete a Web Page from Your Favorites List

When you want to clean out your Favorites list (because some of the Web pages aren't really your favorites), you can delete Web pages, like this:

1. In the Outlook window, click Favorites | Open Favorites.

2. In the Favorites dialog box, shown in Figure 14-4, click the name of a Web page you want to delete, and click the Delete button on the dialog box toolbar.

3. When asked if you're sure you want to send the shortcut to the Recycle Bin, click Yes. Then, click the Cancel button to close the Favorites dialog box.

Using Outlook's Newsreader

A *newsreader* is a program that can post, download, and read articles in *newsgroups,* which are like Internet bulletin boards. Each newsgroup has a particular topic that all the subscribers to that newsgroup want to share information about, and there are literally thousands of newsgroups. They aren't commercial sites—they're maintained by the users who want to share information about that particular topic.

To read and post messages to a newsgroup, you *subscribe* to the newsgroup, which is a fancy word for telling Outlook you want to participate in that particular newsgroup.

Set Up Your Newsreader

Outlook uses Outlook Express as its newsreader, and the first time you use the newsreader, you have to configure it with the Internet Connection Wizard. To configure your newsreader, you need your e-mail account name and address, and the name of the Network News Transport Protocol (NNTP) server that you'll use to access the newsgroups.

NOTE *The NNTP server is provided by your Internet service provider (ISP), if it has one (some don't), and your ISP can give you the name of the NNTP server to use to set up your newsreader. If you're using Outlook in a corporate network environment, ask your network administrator about access to Internet or local network newsgroups.*

When you know the name of your NNTP server, follow these steps to set up your newsreader:

1. Click View | Go To | News. Outlook Express and the Internet Connection Wizard open.

TIP *If you don't see the Internet Connection Wizard when you click View | Go To | News, click the Set Up A Newsgroups Account link under Newsgroups in the Outlook Express window, and the Internet Connection Wizard will start.*

2. Follow the wizard steps and fill in all the information it asks for (your name, your e-mail address, and the name of your ISP news server).

3. When you finish the wizard steps, a dialog box asks if you want to view a list of available newsgroups. Click Yes, and Outlook Express downloads a list of all the newsgroups available to you on your news server.

14

Once you have the list, you can subscribe to the newsgroups that you want to read and post to.

 *Whenever you send Outlook Express to get newsgroup information, it also picks up any waiting e-mail at that ISP—which means important messages may end up in your Outlook Express Inbox instead of your Outlook Inbox. See Chapter 16 to learn how to import mail from Outlook Express to Outlook, to keep all of your messages in one place.*

Find and Subscribe to a Newsgroup

After you download the initial list of newsgroups available on your news server, the Newsgroup Subscriptions dialog box, shown in Figure 14-5, appears.

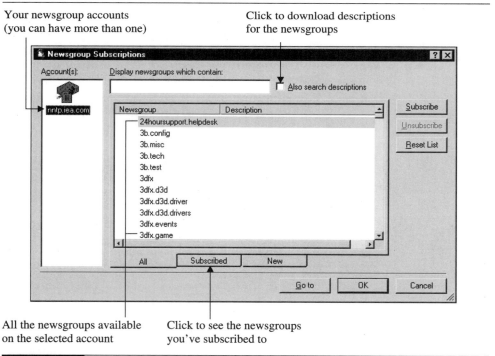

FIGURE 14-5   Search for and subscribe to newsgroups in the Newsgroup Subscriptions dialog box

The names of newsgroups are not always very intuitive, and descriptions will help you find those you might be interested in. Click the Also Search Descriptions check box, and a message appears.

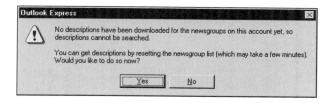

Click Yes, and Outlook Express goes back to your news server to download descriptions (so you can search descriptions as well as names). Don't be surprised if your new list doesn't appear to have descriptions, because not all newsgroups have descriptions attached—but if you scroll down the list a bit, you'll eventually come across some that do.

 *To download the list again in the future, click the Reset List button.*

Suppose you want to investigate newsgroups about computer network systems. Type **network** in the Display Newsgroups Which Contain box, and the list is instantly filtered for all newsgroups that have the word "network" in their name or description. You'll also get a lot of newsgroups that aren't about computer networks at all, but it's a place to begin your search.

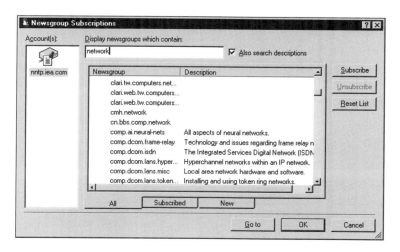

Click the newsgroups you want to subscribe to (use the CTRL and SHIFT keys to select multiple newsgroups), and click the Subscribe button. The subscribed newsgroups appear on your Subscribed tab.

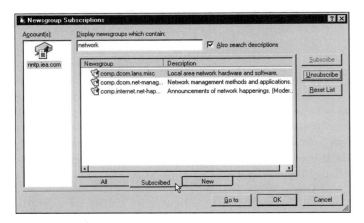

Read Newsgroup Postings

To download and read messages posted in a newsgroup, click the Subscribed tab, click a newsgroup name, and click the Go To button, shown in Figure 14-6.

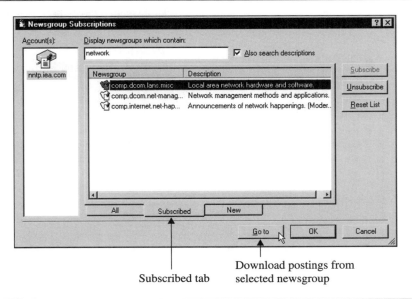

Subscribed tab

Download postings from selected newsgroup

FIGURE 14-6   Select newsgroups and click Go To to download

All the current postings in the newsgroup are downloaded into your news folder, shown in Figure 14-7.

To read the posted messages:

■ Click a message to read it in the Preview Pane.

■ Click the small plus symbol next to a message to read the *message thread,* all the replies posted back and forth in response to that message. The plus symbol becomes a minus symbol when the message thread is expanded.

■ Click the small minus symbol next to the original message to collapse the message thread.

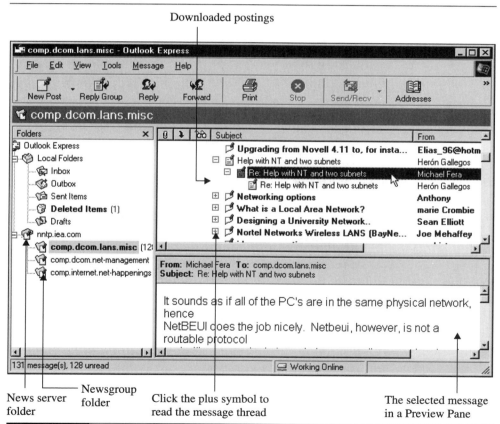

FIGURE 14-7   Newsgroup postings are downloaded into your news newsgroup

Get News After You Configure and Subscribe

After the first time you use your newsreader—when you configure it and download the list of newsgroups and subscribe to some of them—you'll see an Outlook Express window like the one shown in Figure 14-8 when you open your newsreader.

To open the newsreader, in Outlook, click View | Go To | News.

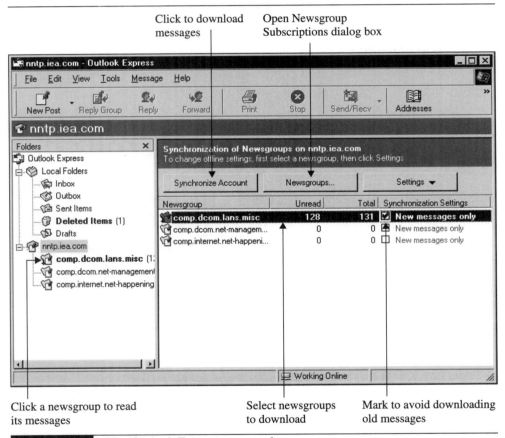

Click to download messages

Open Newsgroup Subscriptions dialog box

Click a newsgroup to read its messages

Select newsgroups to download

Mark to avoid downloading old messages

FIGURE 14-8 The Outlook Express newsreader

Reply to, Post, and Forward Newsgroup Messages

Lots of folks simply "lurk" on newsgroup sites, reading other folks' messages but not jumping into the fray. You might, however, want to participate at some point. You can reply to the message thread for all the other subscribers to read, reply privately to the individual who posted the message, post your own new message, or forward a scintillating message to some of your coworkers.

Reply to a Newsgroup Message

When you read a message that's crying out for a response, and you want to send a reply that will appear in the message thread for the newsgroup, click the Reply Group button on the Outlook Express toolbar.

If you want to send a personal reply to the person who posted the message, click the Reply button.

In both cases, an Outlook reply message opens. If you clicked Reply Group, the message is addressed to the newsgroup; if you clicked Reply, the message is addressed to the sender of the open message. Write your reply to the newsgroup message, and click the Send button in the message's upper-left corner.

Post a Newsgroup Message

Suppose you have a question yourself—perhaps you want to know what experiences others have had with a particular brand of network hub that you're having trouble with. You can post a brand new message posing the question, like this:

1. Click the New Post button on the Outlook Express toolbar. A new Outlook Express message opens, addressed to the newsgroup.

2. Fill in the Subject line with a brief but informative message topic—lots of folks download only message headers, and then download only the messages with interesting headers.

14

3. Write your message, and click the Send button on the message toolbar.

Forward a Newsgroup Message

Suppose you get a clear and helpful response to your posted question about network hubs, and you want to pass the message along to the rest of your company's network administration team. You can forward the open message to them by clicking the Forward button on the Outlook Express toolbar. In the new message that opens, click the To button, and then use the Select Names dialog box to add contact names to the message's To box. Click the Send button in the upper-left corner of the message to send the message out with your e-mail.

To learn about newsgroups in more detail, click Help | Contents And Index in the Outlook Express window, and read about Viewing And Posting To Newsgroups.

Use Your Browser with Outlook

Would you like to explore an open Web page in your browser rather than in Outlook? In your browser, you get a bigger view of the Web page, because you won't have an Outlook bar and extra toolbars taking up screen space. It's easy to switch to your browser, and it doesn't matter whether your browser is Internet Explorer or Netscape Navigator (or your cousin Jimmy-the-hacker's personal software creation), as long as Windows knows it's your designated default browser.

With a Web page open in Outlook, you can switch to viewing that same Web page in your browser by clicking File | Open In Default Browser.

Sometimes, Web pages ask for your responses (messages, orders, and such) via e-mail that you can send from a hyperlink in the Web page. The message is sent using your browser's default e-mail program, and if you use Internet Explorer, the default is probably Outlook Express.

If you want to switch Internet Explorer's e-mail program to Outlook, right-click the Internet Explorer icon on your Windows desktop, and click Properties. In the Internet Properties dialog box, on the Programs tab, select Outlook in the E-Mail list box, and click OK.

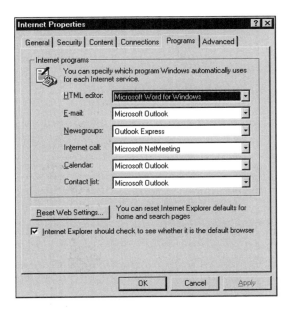

TIP *You can also switch your mail program from within your Internet Explorer window, by clicking Tools | Internet Options. The Internet Options dialog box is the same as the Internet Properties dialog box.*

In this chapter, you learned how to use Outlook as an on-ramp to the Internet. In the next chapter, you'll learn how to customize your Outlook window, Outlook bar, toolbars, views, and fields.

14

Part IV

Advanced Outlook Management

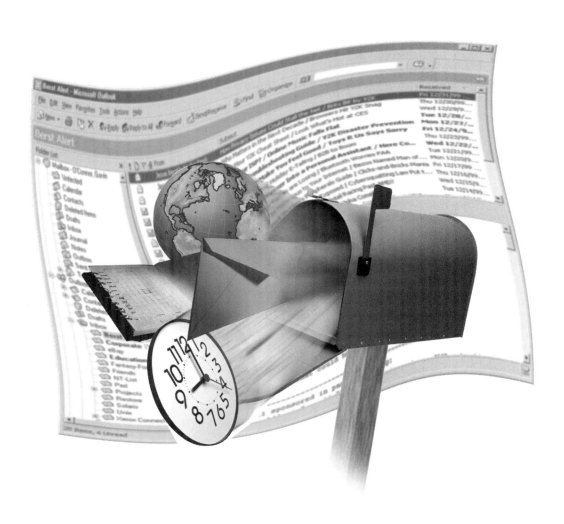

Chapter 15

Customizing Outlook

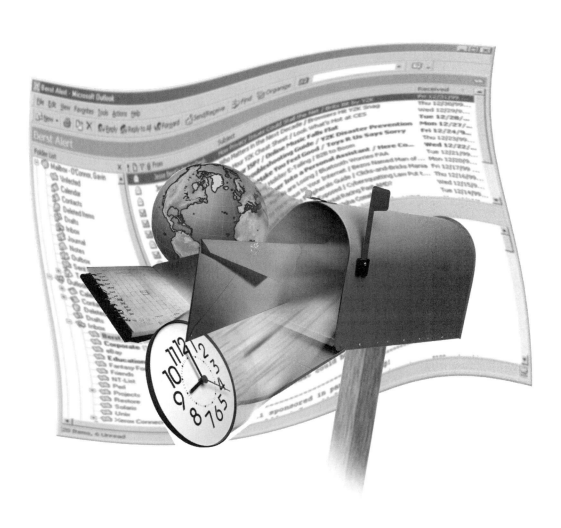

How to . . .

- Customize your Outlook bar
- Customize your toolbars
- Add hyperlinks to toolbars
- Customize views of your Outlook folders
- Create custom fields

Throughout the earlier chapters in this book, you've learned that Outlook is designed to help you work efficiently. You can make Outlook even more personally accommodating by customizing it: change your Outlook bar groups and shortcut icons, your toolbars, and your views for different Outlook folders, and create custom fields to store information that Outlook hasn't provided for (such as an employee number or year hired). You'll learn how to do all of these things in this chapter.

Customizing Your Outlook Bars

After you install Outlook, you'll have the following three groups in your Outlook bar:

- **Outlook Shortcuts**   Includes shortcut icons for most of the Outlook folders.
- **My Shortcuts**   Includes shortcut icons for Outlook's Drafts folder and the Outbox.
- **Other Shortcuts**   Includes shortcut icons for folders on your hard drive, including My Documents, Favorites, and My Computer.

You can add your own custom groups to the Outlook bar, rename any Outlook bar group (including the default groups), add shortcuts to folders and files, rearrange shortcut icons in a group, and delete icons or groups. Figure 15-1 shows some of these customized changes.

Create a Custom Group

When work is hectic, it's important to have information organized in a manner that makes everything easy to find when you need it. One way to organize Outlook information is to add custom groups to the Outlook bar. For example, suppose you're

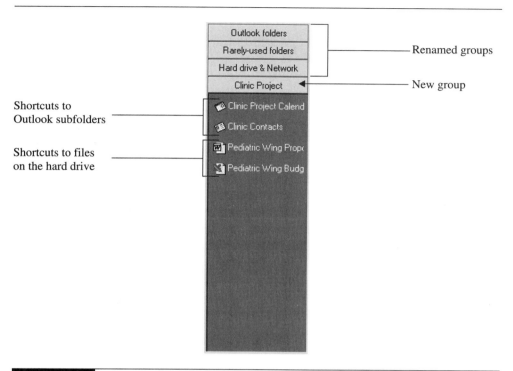

Renamed groups

New group

Shortcuts to
Outlook subfolders

Shortcuts to files
on the hard drive

FIGURE 15-1 A customized Outlook bar

working on a project that involves several contacts, lots of e-mail, tasks, and a separate
calendar to keep everything on schedule. You can create subfolders for the project's
contacts, messages, tasks, and calendar, and create a special Outlook bar group that
keeps the shortcut icons to all of the subfolders in one place.

*If you've lost one of your default Outlook bar groups (for example, the Other
Shortcuts group), you can use the following procedure to re-create it.*

1. Right-click in an empty area of the Outlook bar (in any
group), and click Add New Group. A new group button
appears at the bottom of the Outlook bar.

2. Type a name for the new group, and then press ENTER.
The white box changes into a group button.

15

 *If you inadvertently clicked away from the new button before you typed a new name, see the upcoming section "Rename an Outlook Bar Group" to rename the button.*

Add Shortcuts to a Group

After you create a new group, you'll want to add shortcut icons to it, as described next. You can also use this procedure to add shortcut icons to the default Outlook bar groups.

NOTE *Each Outlook bar group can contain a maximum of 11 shortcut icons.*

1. Open the group to which you want to add a shortcut icon (click the group button to open it).

2. Right-click an empty space in the Outlook bar and click Outlook Bar Shortcut. The Add To Outlook Bar dialog box appears. You can add shortcuts to folders on your hard drive or to folders and subfolders in Outlook.

3. In the Look In list box, select File System if you want to add a shortcut to a folder on your hard drive; select Outlook if you want to add a shortcut to an Outlook folder or subfolder.

4. Navigate to the folder you want to add to the Outlook bar. If you're creating a shortcut to an Outlook subfolder, click the plus symbols in the dialog box's Folder list to show the subfolder you want.

5. Click the folder name, and then click OK.

The new shortcut icon appears in your Outlook bar group.

TIP *To make the Outlook bar wider or narrower, point to the right border of the Outlook bar. When the mouse pointer becomes a two-headed arrow, drag the border to a new width.*

Here's another way to add shortcut icons to your Outlook bar: drag and drop them. This is the only way to add shortcuts to a specific file on your hard drive.

■ If you want to add an Outlook folder or subfolder to your Outlook bar, open the Folder list and drag the folder or subfolder to your Outlook bar.

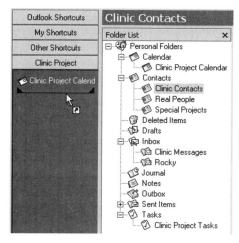

15

■ If you want to add a shortcut to a folder or file on your hard drive, display the name of the folder or file in the Outlook window and then drag it to the Outlook bar.

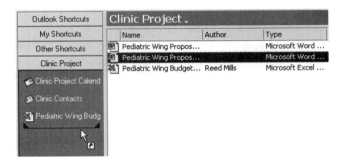

Rename an Outlook Bar Group

If you don't like the name of an Outlook bar group (even one of the default groups), you can change it like this:

1. Right-click the group button and click Rename Group.

2. Type a new name for the group, and then press ENTER.

Rearrange Shortcuts in a Group

If you've got several shortcut icons in a single group, you might find yourself repeatedly scrolling up and down in that group's list of icons. A more efficient way to get to your shortcut icons is to rearrange them, to place the shortcuts you use most often near the top of the group list. You can also rearrange shortcuts by moving them into different groups.

Rearrange Icons in a Group

To rearrange icons within a group, drag an icon up or down to a different position. As you drag an icon, a horizontal bar shows you where the icon will be inserted when you drop it.

Move or Copy an Icon into a Different Group

To move an icon to a different group, drag the icon onto the group button for the group into which you want to move the icon (don't release the mouse button yet). Hold the icon over the group button for a moment, and the group opens; then drag the icon into position and release the mouse button to drop it.

If you want to create a copy of an icon in a different group, follow the preceding procedure to drag the icon into a new group, but hold down the CTRL key while you release the mouse button. (When you press the CTRL key, a small plus symbol appears next to the mouse pointer to tell you that you're creating a copy.)

Delete Shortcut Icons and Groups

You can delete Outlook bar groups and shortcut icons within Outlook bar groups. When you delete a group, all the icons in it are deleted, too, so before you delete the group, move any icons you want to save. When you delete icons, you're only deleting shortcuts; all the folders and subfolders to which those shortcuts point are safe, and you can still find them in Outlook's Folder list (or on your hard drive if you're deleting shortcuts to files and folders on your hard drive).

To delete a shortcut icon from an Outlook bar group, right-click the icon and click Remove From Outlook Bar. When asked if you're sure, click Yes.

To delete an Outlook bar group, open the group and right-click in an empty area within the group. Click Remove Group. When asked if you're sure, click Yes.

Hide and Show the Outlook Bar

If you prefer to use the Folder list, the Outlook bar is extra clutter in your Outlook window. To hide the Outlook bar, right-click in an empty space in the Outlook bar and then click Hide Outlook Bar. Figure 15-2 (on the next page) shows the Outlook window with the Outlook bar hidden and the Folder list displayed.

If you change your mind after you hide the Outlook bar (or if someone else hid it), and you want to display it again, click View | Outlook Bar.

15

Customizing Your Toolbars

All Microsoft programs have versatile, customizable toolbars that you can change to fit your personal working style, and Outlook 2000 is no exception. You can add buttons and commands for procedures you use often, delete buttons and commands that you rarely use (to make more space on a toolbar), and create your own custom toolbars and menus that contain only the commands you want.

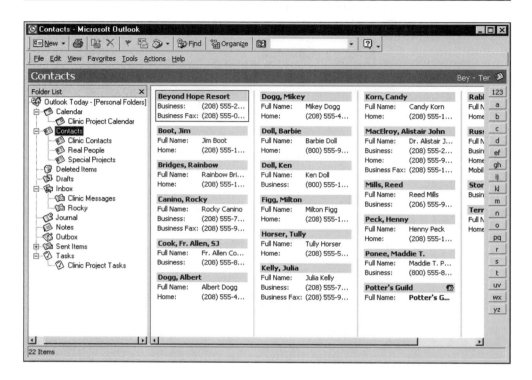

FIGURE 15-2 You can hide the Outlook bar and use the Folder list instead

Create a Custom Toolbar

A custom toolbar is essential if you share a computer with someone, because you can use your own efficient toolbar without affecting the toolbars that others need. A custom toolbar is also a good way to get all the buttons you want onto a single toolbar, instead of displaying multiple toolbars. Custom toolbars can be "floated" or "docked" just like the built-in toolbars, and can be displayed instead of the built-in toolbars.

To create a custom toolbar, follow these steps:

1. Right-click any toolbar or the menu bar, and click Customize. The Customize dialog box appears.

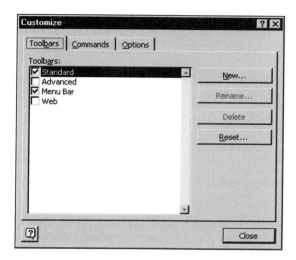

2. Click the Toolbars tab and then click the New button. The New Toolbar dialog box appears.

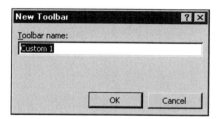

3. Type a name for your custom toolbar, and click OK. A small, empty toolbar appears next to the Customize dialog box.

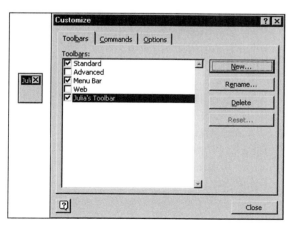

15

In the next section, you'll learn how to add buttons, menus, and commands to the new toolbar. Here are a few more tips for toolbars:

■ To "dock" a toolbar, drag it by its title bar up to a toolbar row. It loses its title bar and fits into the toolbar/menu bar area when it's docked.

■ To "float" any toolbar, drag the vertical bar at the left end of the toolbar into the Outlook window. It shows a title bar and floats on top of the Outlook window.

■ You can use the same techniques to dock toolbars at the sides and bottom of the Outlook window.

■ When a toolbar is floating, you can reshape it to a more efficient shape (tall or square) by dragging any side or corner of the toolbar.

■ To rename a toolbar, open the Customize dialog box. On the Toolbars tab, click the name of the toolbar you want to rename, and then click the Rename button. In the Rename Toolbar dialog box, type a new name and click OK. You cannot rename built-in toolbars, only custom toolbars.

■ To delete a toolbar, open the Customize dialog box. On the Toolbars tab, click the name of the toolbar you want to delete, and then click the Delete button. When asked if you're sure, click OK, and then click the Close button to close the Customize dialog box. You cannot delete built-in toolbars, only custom toolbars.

Add a Button or Command

You can add buttons and commands to any toolbar, custom or built-in, and to any menu. For example, it would be convenient to have an Empty Deleted Items Folder button on a toolbar, and if you send and receive faxes often, it would be convenient to have toolbar buttons to send and receive them with fewer mouse clicks and less searching of menus for the commands. You can customize your toolbars and menu bar to display any commands that you find convenient.

Commands you place on toolbars and the menu bar are active only when the appropriate Outlook folder is open. Also, when you customize a toolbar or the menu bar, you must first open the folder in which the commands will be active, because commands in the Customize dialog box are only available when the appropriate Outlook folder is open—for example, if the Journal is open, you won't find a Send or Send/Receive command in the Tools category under the Commands tab of the Customize dialog box, but you'll find both commands there if the Inbox is open.

Create a Menu Command

When the Inbox is open, the Actions menu shows a Junk E-Mail command. To add a sender to the Junk Senders list, you must open the Actions menu, point to Junk E-Mail, and click the Add To Junk Senders List command. It would be faster if you could simply select Actions | Add To Junk Senders List; you can do this by altering your Actions menu, as follows:

1. Open the Inbox. This command won't be available in the Customize dialog box unless the Inbox (or another mail folder) is open.

2. Right-click any toolbar or the menu bar, and click Customize. The Customize dialog box opens.

3. Click the Commands tab.

4. Under Categories, click Actions. All the Actions commands are listed under Commands.

5. In the Commands list, scroll down and select the Add To Junk Senders List command.

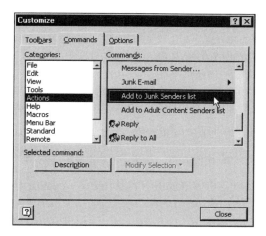

6. Drag the Add To Junk Senders List command from the Customize dialog box to the Actions menu on the menu bar, and hold it there (don't release the mouse button yet). The Actions menu opens.

15

7. Drag the command down the menu and drop it in place. While you drag the command up and down the menu, a horizontal bar shows you where the command will be inserted.

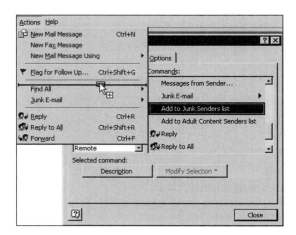

8. Click the Close button to close the Customize dialog box.

Now you can add senders to your Junk Senders list using fewer actions.

Create a Toolbar Button

You can also add the Add To Junk Senders List command to a toolbar, which makes using the command even faster than when it's on a menu. Follow these steps to add a command button to a toolbar:

1. Start with the appropriate folder open (in this example, the Inbox is open).

2. Right-click any toolbar or the menu bar, and click Customize.

3. In the Customize dialog box, click the Commands tab.

4. Under Categories, click Actions, and in the Commands list, select the Add To Junk Senders List command.

5. Drag the Add To Junk Senders List command to a toolbar. A vertical bar shows you where the button will be inserted.

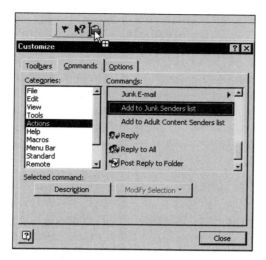

6. Release the mouse button when the vertical bar is in the position you want. The button is added to the toolbar. In this case, the button shows the lengthy name of the command, but you can change that.

7. Right-click the new button. The button shortcut menu appears.

8. Select the name in the Name box, and type a shorter name for your button.

15

9. Click away from the shortcut menu to close it. When you finish creating the button, click the Close button to close the Customize dialog box.

Here are some tips for changing button images (remember that the Customize dialog box must be open to make these changes):

- If you want to use an image instead of text, right-click the new button, click the Change Button Image command on the shortcut menu, and click a button picture.

- If you want the button to display only the picture, right-click the new button, and click the Text Only (In Menus) command on the shortcut menu. The text in the Name box will appear in a ToolTip when you point at the button.

- To change the button image (change colors, or draw your own), right-click the new button, and click the Edit Button Image command on the shortcut menu. The Button Editor dialog box opens. Click a color, click squares in the Picture to color the pixels, and then click OK when you finish.

- If you have a box-type button, such as the Find A Contact button on the Standard toolbar, that's too long or too short, you can change the length. With the Customize dialog box open, click the button to select it (a dark border appears around the box). Point to either end of the button, and when the pointer becomes a two-headed arrow, drag to change the length of the box. Close the Customize dialog box when you finish.

Create a Hyperlink Toolbar Button

Suppose you have a Web page, a folder, or a file on a network drive that you need to open often. It would be a time-saver to click a toolbar button that opens the Web page, folder, or file. You can create a toolbar hyperlink like this:

1. Create a custom button on a toolbar. You can use any command in the Customize dialog box to create the button, because you'll replace the button's command and name when you assign the hyperlink to it, and you can change the button image using the procedure for editing a button image in the preceding list of tips.

2. With the Customize dialog box still open, right-click the new button, point to Assign Hyperlink, and click Open. The Assign Hyperlink dialog box appears.

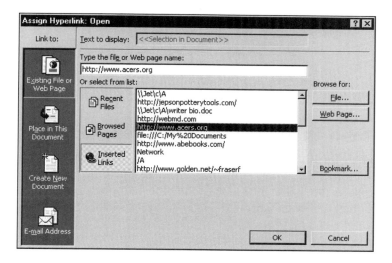

3. You can either select a link from lists of Recent Files, Browsed Pages, or Inserted Links, or type the path or URL in the Type The File Or Web Page Name box. You can also click the File button or the Web Page button and browse for files or Web pages that aren't listed in the Assign Hyperlink dialog box.

4. After you enter a file path or URL, click OK to close the Assign Hyperlink dialog box, and then click the Close button to close the Customize dialog box.

If you create a hyperlink to a folder, clicking the button opens a window into that folder. If you create a hyperlink to a file, clicking the button opens that file in its program. If you create a hyperlink to a Web page, clicking the button launches your browser and opens the Web page.

Delete a Button or Command

Deleting a button or menu command is quick (and important when you've got toolbars cluttered with buttons you never use).

To delete a button, hold down the ALT key while you drag the button away from the toolbar and drop it in the Outlook window. Release the mouse button when the mouse pointer displays an X, and the button is removed.

To delete a menu command, the Customize dialog box must be open (although you won't use it). Click a menu and drag the command away into the Outlook window. Release the mouse button when the mouse pointer displays an X, and the command is removed from the menu. Close the Customize dialog box when you're finished.

You can also rearrange toolbar buttons easily by holding down the ALT *key while you drag a button to a new position or to a different toolbar.*

Reset a Built-In Toolbar or the Menu Bar

If you've made lots of changes to your built-in toolbars and menu bar, you can reset them to their original configuration. Open the Customize dialog box and click the Toolbars tab. Click the name of the built-in toolbar or menu bar you want to reset, and click the Reset button. You cannot reset custom toolbars, only built-in toolbars and the menu bar.

Customizing Your Outlook Folder Views

There are several ways to customize and personalize the display of information in your Outlook window, such as changing field labels and display fonts, and creating and saving custom views so that you can display only the fields you want to see simply by switching the view.

Change a Field Label

Do you like all the field labels (the column headings) that came with your views, or do you sometimes wish that a field had a more intuitive label? Perhaps in the task list, the Subject field would be better labeled To Do.

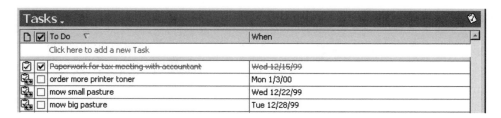

You can change the labels on your fields. Changing field labels is, admittedly, a trivial concern, but it's the little things that make a workday more enjoyable.

When you change the label on a field, the name of the field doesn't change (Outlook still thinks of Subject as Subject), but you get a personalized display of your information. Also, the label is specific to the view in which you made the change; for example, if you change the Subject field label in the Detailed List view in Tasks, the Subject field label remains "Subject" in all the other Tasks views.

To change a field label, follow these steps:

1. Right-click the field heading you want to change, and then click Format Columns.

2. In the Label box, type a new label, and then click OK.

Change Fonts and Formats for a View

You can alter the look of any view by changing the fonts and formatting, and then saving your changes. You can make formatting changes to a built-in view, or create a new custom view that is entirely your own. To change the look of a view, follow these steps:

1. Display the view you want to change.

2. Click View | Current View | Customize Current View. The View Summary dialog box appears.

3. In the View Summary dialog box, click the Other Settings button. The options you see in the Other Settings dialog box depend on what view is displayed (the Other Settings dialog box for a table-type view is shown next). You can change fonts for column headings and rows by clicking the appropriate buttons. The AutoPreview Font button allows you to change the color of the font as well as the typeface and size. In a table view, you also have the option of changing the gridline style and color (under Grid Lines in the Other Settings dialog box).

15

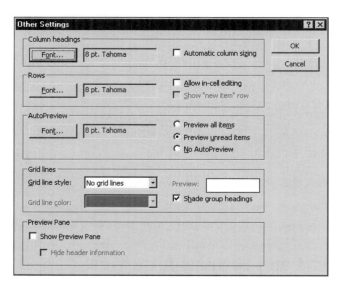

4. Make the changes you want, and then click OK twice to close both dialog boxes. The changes to the view are automatically saved.

Suppose you want to use two slightly different views of the same information, for two different tasks. You can create and save custom views in any Outlook folder. Refer to Chapter 3 to learn how to create and save custom views of your Contacts folder, and use the same procedure in other Outlook folders.

Creating Custom Fields

Suppose you work in the Personnel department of a large company, and you need to keep track of employee ID numbers. Outlook's Contact dialog box has no Employee ID field, so where can you keep a useful record of employee ID numbers? Likewise, how can you make data entry in that field as efficient as possible? You can create a new field.

The Contact dialog box (often called a Contact *form* when you're modifying it) has an All Fields tab. If you select All Contact Fields in the Select From list box, the All Fields tab displays a table of all the Contact fields available in Outlook.

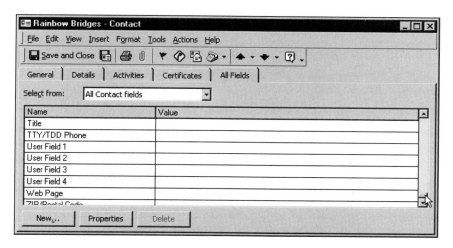

At the bottom of the list are four User Fields, which you can use for anything you like—the only problem is that User Field 1 isn't an intuitive field heading, which means it will take longer, for example, to train your vacation replacement to fill in at your desk while you're out of town.

NOTE   *You can use the following procedure to create custom fields in any of Outlook's folders.*

To create your own custom field for employee ID numbers:

1. Open the folder for which you want to create a custom field (in this example, the Contacts folder).

2. Right-click in an empty space in the window and click Show Fields. The Show Fields dialog box appears.

15

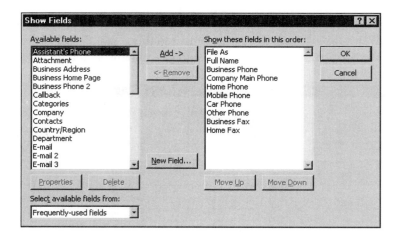

3. In the Show Fields dialog box, click the New Field button. The New Field dialog box appears.

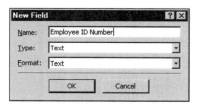

4. Type the field name in the Name box.

5. In the Type list box, select the type of data that the field will contain (for example, employee ID numbers won't be calculated, so the best option is Text).

6. In the Format list box, select a display format for the entries (if you select a data type of Text in the preceding step, the only available format is Text).

7. Click OK. The new field appears in the Show These Fields In This Order list in the Show Fields dialog box. Click OK to close the Show Fields dialog box.

To enter data in the new field (in this example, employee ID numbers), open an employee's Contact form and click the All Fields tab. In the Select From list box, select User-Defined Fields In Folder. The new field is listed. To enter data, click in the Value column, type the entry, and press ENTER.

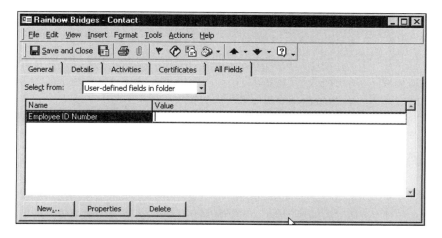

You can also enter and display the new field data easily by switching to a table-type view, such as Phone List. Use the Field Chooser to add the new field to the view (be sure you select User-Defined Fields In Folder in the list box at the top of the Field Chooser). The following is a Phone List view of Contacts, with the Employee ID field added, ready for efficient entry of employee ID numbers. You can use the new field to sort, group, filter, and search for information just as you can with any built-in field.

			Full Name	Employee ID Number	Company	File As /	Busines
			Click here to add a new C...				
					Beyond Hope Re...	Beyond Hope Resort	(208) 5
			Jim Boot	225	Mouses 'R Else	Boot, Jim	
			Rainbow Bridges	224	Beyond Hope Re...	Bridges, Rainbow	
	0		Rocky Canino	123	Two Dog Night (r...	Canino, Rocky	(208) 5
	0		Fr. Allen Cook, SJ	124	Beyond Hope Re...	Cook, Fr. Allen, SJ	(208) 5
	0		Albert Dogg	243	Two Dog Night (r...	Dogg, Albert	
	0		Mikey Dogg	116	Two Dog Night (r...	Dogg, Mikey	
			Barbie Doll	118		Doll, Barbie	
			Ken Doll	119		Doll, Ken	(800) 5
	0		Milton Figg		Mouses 'R Else	Figg, Milton	
	0		Tully Horser		JAK InfoWorks	Horser, Tully	

15

TIP *If you've forgotten how to locate the Field Chooser, right-click any column heading and click Field Chooser.*

In this chapter, you've learned several techniques for customizing Outlook to work best for you. In the next chapter, you'll learn how to archive your Outlook items for safe storage, and how to import and export information between Outlook and other programs.

Chapter 16

Archiving, Importing, and Exporting Data

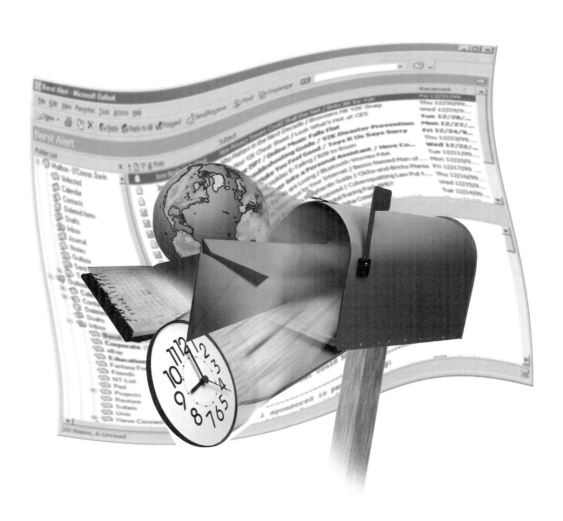

How to . . .

- Archive Outlook items for old-item storage

- Retrieve archived items

- Import information into Outlook from other programs

- Export Outlook information to other programs

- Move e-mail and addresses from Outlook Express into Outlook

Whether your office is based on paper or bytes, stuff accumulates. Outlook has a feature that preserves old items while getting them out of your way, called *archiving.* Archiving is similar to filing important but seldom used files (like the paperwork for the house you sold ten years ago) in a cardboard box and storing it in the back of a closet.

Archiving is not the same thing as exporting to another file. When you export items (for example, your Contacts list), the items are copied to a non-Outlook file, perhaps a text file or an Access table, where you can use them easily within another program. You'll learn how to export Outlook items in this chapter.

Archiving, on the other hand, does not copy items—it moves them out of Outlook and into a file called archive.pst. You can archive Outlook items manually, or you can have Outlook archive items automatically when they reach a specific age (called *AutoArchiving*), meaning you don't have to remember to archive them yourself. You can choose the age at which items are AutoArchived, and you can choose to have aged items either stored in an archive file or deleted. You'll learn how to archive Outlook items, both manually and automatically, in this chapter.

Archived items can be retrieved by importing them back into Outlook. In this chapter, you'll learn how to import archived Outlook items and information from other programs (such as Excel and Outlook Express) into Outlook.

Archiving Automatically

AutoArchive archives old files automatically every other week when Outlook starts up. The every-other-week schedule is Microsoft's choice; you can change it to a schedule you prefer, or turn it off entirely if you want to.

When AutoArchive fires up, it checks each Outlook folder to see whether it has AutoArchiving turned on, and, if so, what the folder's AutoArchiving schedule is. This is the default AutoArchive schedule for Outlook folders:

- The Inbox, Drafts, and Notes folders are not AutoArchived automatically.

- Items in the Sent Items folder that are more than two months old are AutoArchived.

- Items in the Calendar, Journal, and Tasks folders that are more than six months old are AutoArchived.

- Items in the Deleted Items folder that are more than two months old are deleted.

- Contacts cannot be AutoArchived, but they can be archived manually.

To determine whether an item is old enough to AutoArchive, Outlook uses the latest date/time associated with the item (sent, received, created, modified, and so forth). Tasks are not AutoArchived unless they're marked complete.

As an example of how AutoArchiving works, suppose you have messages that have been in your Sent Items folder for at least two months. Your Sent Items messages that are more than two months old will begin to disappear into an archive file named archive.pst. Later in this chapter, you'll learn how to retrieve those archived items if you need to look up a message you sent.

You can check and change a folder's AutoArchiving schedule by following the steps in the section "Set AutoArchive Properties for an Individual Folder," later in this chapter.

Turning AutoArchive On and Off

Turning on Outlook's AutoArchive feature is similar to turning on the water at a main water valve; you get no water at individual faucets unless the main valve is opened. Similarly, you get no AutoArchiving in individual folders unless the main AutoArchive valve is opened.

To turn AutoArchive on or off for all of Outlook, follow these steps:

1. Select Tools | Options, and click the Other tab.

16

2. On the Other tab, click the AutoArchive button. In the AutoArchive dialog box, mark the AutoArchive Every check box to turn on AutoArchive, and set a schedule for AutoArchiving (a schedule of 14 days tells Outlook to look for old items every 14 days).

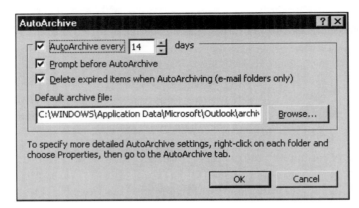

3. If you want to be asked before the old items are archived, be sure the Prompt Before AutoArchive check box is marked, and if you want expired messages to be deleted rather than stored, mark the Delete Expired Items When AutoArchiving check box. The path in the Default Archive File box tells you where you'll find the archived items if and when you want to retrieve them later.

NOTE *Expired messages are those that you set an expiration date for—refer to Chapter 4 to learn how.*

4. Click OK twice to close both dialog boxes.

Set AutoArchive Properties for an Individual Folder

You might not want all of Outlook to be on an AutoArchive schedule—the stuff you archive doesn't get compressed, it just gets stored elsewhere on your hard drive—so my advice is to be selective about what you archive, and delete what you know you don't need to save (like the list of Internet jokes a colleague sent you last week).

After you turn on the AutoArchive feature and set an AutoArchive schedule, you can turn AutoArchive on or off for individual Outlook folders:

1. Right-click the icon for the individual folder, and click Properties. You can right-click folders in either the Outlook bar or the Folder list, and you can set custom subfolders to be AutoArchived.

2. Click the AutoArchive tab. (If you run Outlook in Internet Mail Only configuration, the Administration and Forms tabs won't be available.)

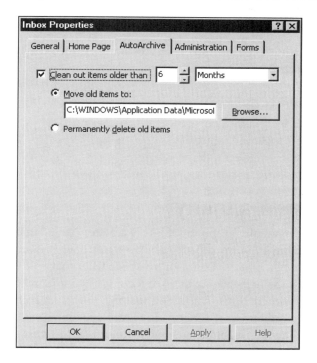

You won't find an AutoArchive tab for your Contacts folder, but you can archive them manually or export a copy of Contacts to a different file for safekeeping.

16

3. Mark the Clean Out Items Older Than check box to turn on AutoArchiving for the folder; clear the check box to turn it off. Here are a few other ways you can alter a folder's AutoArchive schedule:

■ If you want a folder's items AutoArchived but at a different age, type a number and then select Months, Weeks, or Days in the Clean Out Items Older Than list box.

■ Check the filename in the Move Old Items To box, so you know where to find them again. To archive a specific folder's items in a custom archive file, click the Browse button and type a new File Name in the Find Personal Folders dialog box (or click an existing custom filename) and then click OK.

■ If you want to delete old items instead of AutoArchiving them, click the Permanently Delete Old Items option button.

4. Click OK to close the folder's Properties dialog box.

When AutoArchive is turned on at the "main valve" (in the Tools | Options dialog box), Outlook automatically archives the items in those folders that have AutoArchive turned on (in the folder's Properties dialog box).

Archiving Items Manually

You may find that manually archiving items is a better choice than using AutoArchive. You have to remember to do it yourself, but you are less likely to automatically archive a bunch of hard-drive-space filler that you will never, ever need again, and it's the only way to archive a copy of your Contacts folder. You cannot archive individual items in a folder; instead, you must archive the whole set of aged items in the folder (so it's a good idea to delete unnecessary items first).

To archive the items in a folder manually, follow these steps:

1. Open the folder you want to archive.

2. Select File | Archive. The Archive dialog box appears.

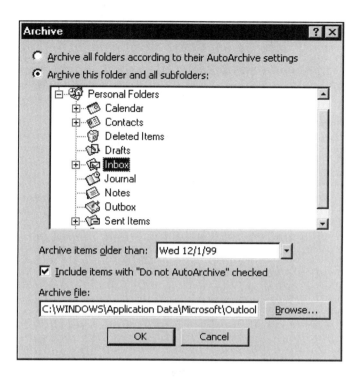

3. Click the Archive This Folder And All Subfolders option button.

4. Be sure the folder you want to archive is selected. The folder you opened in step 1 will be selected in the dialog box's list of folders.

5. In the Archive Items Older Than list box, choose an aging date. Everything older than the date you select will be archived. For example, if you want to archive today's stuff, select tomorrow's date (or type **tomorrow** in the list box and let AutoDate figure it out).

6. Take a look at the Archive File box—the default file for your archives is archive.pst. If you are on a corporate network, your archive file might be on the server—it's a good idea to remember the name and location of the file so that you can retrieve your archived items in the future.

16

To keep track of bits of information, such as the path to your archived items, copy the path into an Outlook note.

7. Click OK to start the archive process. This will take a few moments, depending on the length of your list of items and the speed of your computer. While the folder is being archived, Outlook's Status bar shows a message similar to the one shown next. If you need to cancel the archiving process for any reason, click the small arrow at the right side of the Archive icon, and click Cancel Archive.

138 Items   Archiving Inbox to C:\WINDOWS\Application Data\Microsoft\Outlook\archive.pst.

Any items that are older than the aging date you set in the Archive dialog box are moved from the Outlook folder to the archive file. If you archive a Contacts folder or subfolder, all the contacts are copied (not moved) into the archive file, regardless of the dates associated with the contact items.

If you notice items in your Inbox that have a Received date that's older than your archive date, but which haven't been archived, it's because they have Modified dates that are more recent than your archive date.

Retrieving Archived Items

You archive items because of the slight chance that one day you will need to see them again. To see an archived item, you can either retrieve the whole set from the archive file in which you stored it, or limit what's retrieved by filtering the items for a specific date range, sender, or other criteria.

To retrieve archived items, import them back into Outlook, at which point you can copy the information you need and delete everything else that was retrieved (the archive file retains everything you archived, and when you retrieve items, you retrieve copies of the items).

To retrieve archived items, follow these steps:

1. Open the folder for which you want to retrieve items.

2. Select File | Import And Export. The first step of the Import And Export Wizard appears.

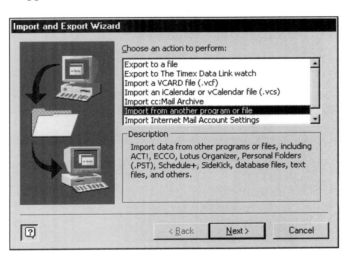

3. Click Import From Another Program Or File, and then click Next. The second step of the Import And Export Wizard appears.

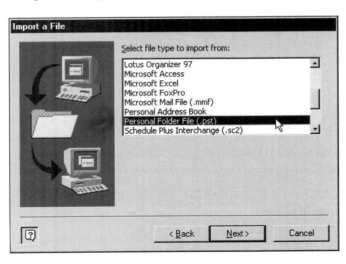

4. Scroll down and select Personal Folder File (.pst), and then click Next. The third step of the Import And Export Wizard appears.

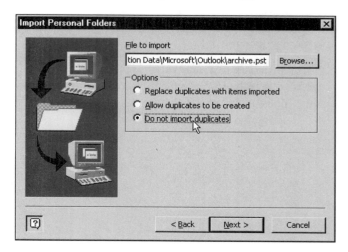

5. Look at the File To Import box—it should display a path to the PST file where you archived the files. If not, click the Browse button and navigate to the correct PST file in the Open Personal Folders dialog box, and double-click the filename to enter it in the File To Import box.

 When Outlook is in Internet Mail Only configuration, the path to the default archive file is C:\Windows\Local Settings\Application Data\Microsoft\ Outlook; in the Corporate/Workgroup configuration, the path to the default archive file is C:\Windows\Application Data\Microsoft\Outlook.

6. Be sure the duplicates option you want is selected, and then click Next.

7. Select the folder you want to import archived items for, and then click Finish. Here are a few hints for importing from an archive folder:

- The archive folder maintains a file list identical to your Outlook file list, so it's easy to find and import the archived items you want.

- You can import everything in the archive file, or you can import archives from an individual folder by selecting the folder name.

- You can limit the number of items imported by using filter criteria. Click the Filter button and set criteria to filter the imported items, and then finish the import procedure.

■ You can import archived items from a single selected folder by clearing the Include Subfolders check box (to select a single subfolder, click the plus symbol next to a main folder and then click the subfolder name). To import an archived folder and all of its subfolders, mark the Include Subfolders check box.

■ If you've modified an item and you want to retrieve a copy of the original item, choose either the Replace Duplicates With Items Imported option (to replace the modified item with the original), or the Allow Duplicates To Be Created option (to see the modified and original side by side). If you want only to retrieve an old item, the Do Not Import Duplicates option is faster.

■ If you want to get rid of archives that are years old (so you don't keep retrieving the whole set), you can delete the archive.pst file. Outlook will create a fresh new archive.pst file the next time you archive any folder. You can also save periodic archive files by renaming an archive file, perhaps with a date, and Outlook will start a fresh archive.pst file the next time you archive. To retrieve items from a renamed archive file, use the Browse button in step 5 to locate the file. To delete or rename the archive.pst file, Outlook must be closed.

Importing Data from Other Programs

Lots of us have lists of items (usually contacts) in programs other than Outlook. If you do much work in Access, for example, you probably have a table of contacts in at least one database; or perhaps you've always kept your Contacts list in Excel, or someone has sent you a list of items in a text file such as Comma Separated Values or Tab Separated Values. You can bring those lists into the appropriate Outlook folders by importing them.

NOTE   *To import and export items between Outlook and other programs, you need the Import/Export feature installed. If the Import/Export feature is not already installed in your computer, Outlook will ask if you want to install it, when you begin the import or export process. Click Yes, and the feature will be installed automatically (you may need to insert your Office 2000 CD-ROM).*

Suppose you keep a list of contacts in an Excel workbook. To import the list of contacts into your Outlook Contacts folder, follow the procedure in the next paragraph to set up the Excel workbook for importing, and then follow the steps below to import the list. (Importing lists from other programs is similar, and the Import And Export wizard will lead you through it.)

First, get your Excel worksheet set up for easy importing. Put all of your items in a table on a single worksheet (which shouldn't be a problem, because there are 65,536 rows in a worksheet). Make sure there are no blank rows or columns in the table; individual empty cells are fine. Give each column a logical heading (such as LastName or Phone) so Outlook can identify the field name. Make sure there's nothing else on the worksheet except your list. Finally, for easiest importing, name the Excel range you want to import.

If you don't know how to name an Excel range, here's an easy technique. Select the entire table, click in the Name box in the upper-left corner, type a one-word name, and press ENTER. *Then, save and close the Excel file and Excel.*

When your file is ready to be imported, follow these steps to import it:

1. Click File | Import And Export. The Import And Export Wizard appears.

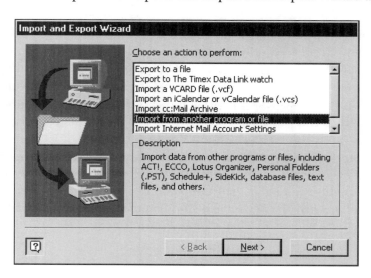

2. Click Import From Another Program Or File, and then click Next. The second step in the wizard appears, with the list of file types that Outlook can import.

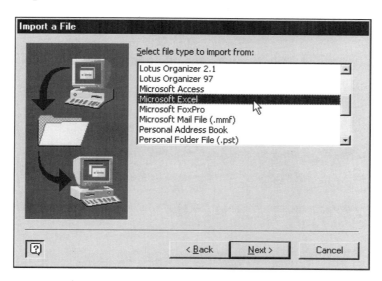

3. Select the program from which you are importing the list. In this case, I'm importing from Excel. Click Next, and the third wizard step appears.

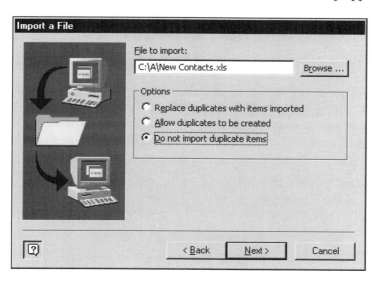

4. Click the Browse button and navigate to the file you want to import. Make a choice regarding duplicates—if you often update Outlook by importing data from the same file, you might want to choose Do Not Import Duplicate Items so that only fresh data is imported.

5. Click Next. The next wizard step appears.

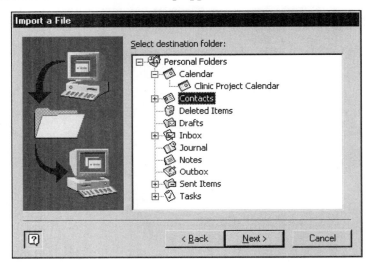

6. Click the folder you want to import your list into—in this case, I'm importing an Excel Contacts list into the Contacts folder. Then, click Next. The final wizard step appears.

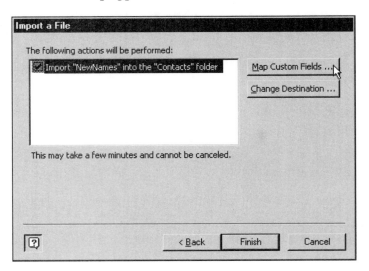

7. In the final step, the wizard detects the named range (in this example, "NewNames") and will import that range into the folder you selected in step 6. If this is the first time you have imported this list into Outlook, and your list uses field names that are different from the standard field names in Outlook (for example, if the field name in Contacts is "First" and your matching Excel field name is "FirstName"), then you'll need to *map,* or match up, your field names to Outlook's field names—don't worry, this is a lot easier than it sounds.

8. Click the Map Custom Fields button. The Map Custom Fields dialog box appears, shown in Figure 16-1, so you can match up your field names with those in the Outlook folder.

Take a look at the To area, on the right side of the dialog box. Some of the field names have plus symbols next to them, because Outlook's field names are organized by category (for example, the Name field is composed of First Name, Middle Name, Last Name, and so forth).

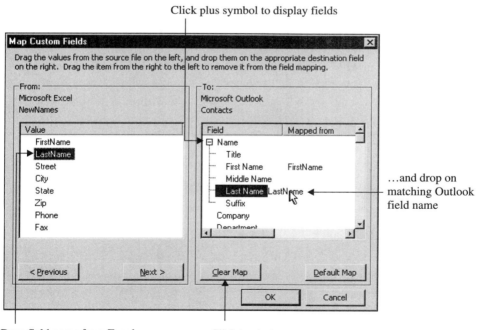

16

FIGURE 16-1   Mapping Excel field names to Outlook field names

9. Click the plus symbol next to a field category (for example, Name) so that you can see the Outlook fields that match your Excel fields.

10. Drag each of your Excel fields from the left side of the dialog box and drop it on a matching Outlook field on the right side of the dialog box (called *mapping*).

11. Click OK, and then click Finish.

The list is imported, and when the wizard is finished, it closes itself. Open the folder or subfolder you imported items into, and you'll find all the new items. Running the Import And Export Wizard is similar regardless of where you import from, and even with minor differences between programs, you'll figure the procedure out quickly.

Exporting Outlook Items and Lists to Other Programs

What if you want to go the other direction, and send information to another program? You might want to send your Contacts list to someone who doesn't have Outlook, or to your own Access database because Access mail-merge is easier to run when the data is wholly contained within Access.

In this section, I'll demonstrate exporting a Contacts list to an Access database, and I'll create a new database with the exported information. Exporting to any database-type file will be a similar procedure.

Because I'm creating a new database with the Contacts list, the process is faster and I don't need to map my field names (my Contacts field names will become my new Access field names), but if you export to an existing database, you'll need to map field names. To export Outlook data, follow these steps:

1. In Outlook, click File | Import And Export. In the first wizard step, click Export To A File, and then click Next.

2. In the second wizard step, click the type of file you want to create for your exported items. If you don't find the specific program type listed in the wizard step, choose either Comma Separated Values (in which column entries are separated by commas) or Tab Separated Values (in which column entries are separated by tab characters). Both are text files that can be opened in most programs.

To export to a new Access database, click Microsoft Access and then click Next.

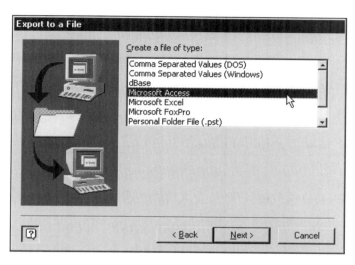

3. In the third wizard step, click the name of the Outlook folder you want to export, and then click Next.

4. In the fourth wizard step, click the Browse button and browse to the folder where you want to save the new database file. When you've located the folder you want in the Browse dialog box, type a name for the new file and click OK. The new filename and the path to it are displayed in the fourth wizard step; then, click Next.

5. The fifth (last) wizard step appears, where you can map field names if you want to. If you're exporting to an existing database or spreadsheet, you'll want to map the field names so that your Outlook items go into the correct fields; but if you're creating a new database, the field names in the new database table will be whatever they are in Outlook, and there's no need to map them.

6. Click Finish to export the data. The wizard closes itself when it's finished.

Now you can open the program and the new file to see what the exported data looks like. In the Contacts table that I exported to a new database, there's a matching field for every field in Outlook's Contacts folder, which is many more fields than I need in the database, but I can clean up my Access database by deleting the fields I don't want in the database table.

16

	Title	FirstName	MiddleName	LastName	Suffix	Company	Department	JobTitle	BusinessStreet	Busine
▶						Beyond Hope R			248 Beyond Hol	
		Chloe		Terriene		JAK InfoWorks		Guard	123 Ramblin Ra	
		Tully		Horser		JAK InfoWorks		Gadabout	123 Ramblin Ra	
		Mikey		Dogg		Two Dog Night (		Lead Howler	345 Hydrant Ave	
		Bunny		Rabbit		JAK InfoWorks		Housemother	123 Ramblin Ra	
		Albert		Dogg		Two Dog Night (		Percussionist	345 Hydrant Ave	
		Maddie	T.	Ponee		Pasture Ponies		Fancy Fixture		
		Milton		Figg		Mouses 'R Else		Dilletante	123 Ramblin Ra	
		Jack		Russel		Haven Farm		Ratcatcher	123 East Open	
		Barbie		Doll					3333 Deb Avenu	
		Ken		Doll					2222 Manley Rc	
		Reed		Mills		Julia's Mystery		Fictional Chara	123 Any Street	
		Jim		Boot		Mouses 'R Else			123 Ramblin Ra	

Record: ⏮ ◀ 1 ▶ ⏭ ▶* of 22

Switching from Outlook Express to Outlook

If you've been using Outlook Express before you installed Outlook, you'll want
to move your existing mail messages, contacts' e-mail addresses, and Internet
account information from Outlook Express to Outlook. This is a simple procedure
that's performed by the Import And Export Wizard.

Import Internet Account Information from Outlook Express to Outlook

If you've been using Outlook Express before you installed Outlook, there's no
point in re-entering all of your Internet service provider connection information,
because it's already set up in Outlook Express. Follow these steps to import your
Outlook Express mail service information into Outlook:

1. In Outlook, click File | Import And Export.

2. In the first step of the Import And Export Wizard, click Import Internet
   Mail Account Settings, and click Next.

3. Follow the remaining instructions in the wizard to finish setting up.

Outlook should be able to import all the information it needs from Outlook Express.

 *Don't uninstall Outlook Express—Outlook needs it
to function properly.*

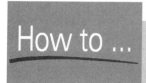 **Send Your Outlook Items into a New Computer**

If (or rather, when), you get a new computer you can move all of your Outlook items—Tasks, Messages, Journal, Contacts, everything—into the Outlook program on the new computer by following these steps:

1. Archive everything to an archive.pst file.

2. Bring the archive.pst file to the new computer (over the network, by floppy disk, or even by e-mail). If you're not on a company network, you'll probably find the archive.pst file in either C:\Windows\ Local Settings\Application Data\Microsoft\Outlook folder (in Internet Mail Only configuration) or C:\Windows\Application Data\Microsoft\Outlook (in Corporate/Workgroup configuration).

3. Regardless of the means you use to bring the archive.pst file into the new computer, copy the file into an easy-to-find folder on the new computer's hard drive.

4. Import the archived data into the new Outlook program in the same way you would import normal archives. The only difference will be the location of the archive file you're importing (it will be in that easy-to-find folder where you copied it).

As an alternative to using an archive file, you can also export all of your data to files in a program such as Excel in the old computer, and then transport those Excel files to the new computer's hard drive and import them to the new copy of Outlook.

16

Import Messages and Contacts from Outlook Express to Outlook

If you've been using Outlook Express and have accumulated e-mail messages and contact information there, you'll want to import them into Outlook so that all of your e-mail information will be in one place. To bring your messages and addresses into Outlook from Outlook Express:

1. In Outlook, click File | Import And Export.

2. In the first step of the Import And Export Wizard, click Import Internet Mail And Addresses, and click Next.

3. Follow the rest of the instructions in the wizard.

Every time you use Outlook Express instead of Outlook, any e-mail you send or receive will have to be imported into Outlook if you want to keep all of your messages in one place.

In this chapter, you learned how to store old Outlook items by archiving them, and how to retrieve archived items. You also learned how to import data into Outlook from other programs, and how to export Outlook data to other programs. In the next chapter, you'll learn how to set up Outlook for a small business network, and about the special things Outlook can do for you if you're using it in a network environment running on the Microsoft Exchange Server.

Chapter 17

Configuring Outlook for Your Business

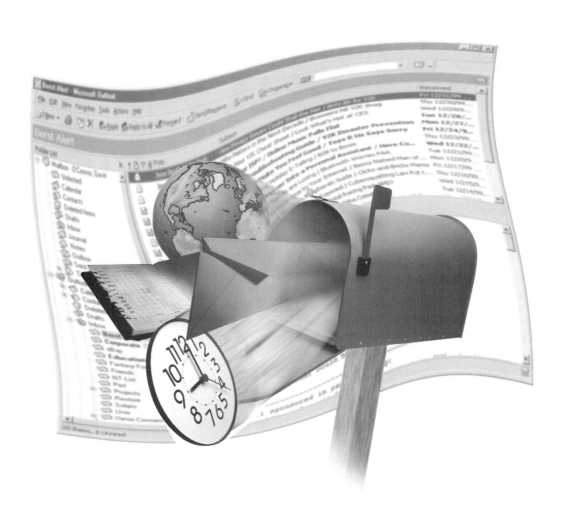

How to . . .

- Use Outlook to help you work as a team when you and your contacts are all on separate, Internet Mail Only computers
- Use Net Folders to share Outlook folders over the Internet
- Use Outlook to help you work as a team when you're using a local area network and Corporate/Workgroup configuration in Outlook
- Use Outlook workgroup features that are available when your network uses the Microsoft Exchange Server
- Use public folders (Exchange Server network)
- Take an e-mail tally of votes (Exchange Server network)
- Use the company's Global Address Book (Exchange Server network)
- Give others permission to work in your Outlook folders (Exchange Server network)

The tasks you can perform in Outlook depend on your configuration: Internet Mail Only, Corporate/Workgroup, or Corporate/Workgroup using the Microsoft Exchange Server. Regardless of your configuration, however, Outlook can be a useful tool in your business.

Throughout this book, you've learned how to use Outlook's available features in both Internet Mail Only configuration and Corporate/Workgroup configuration, and you can switch between them whenever you need to. In a small business, either configuration is suitable—Corporate/Workgroup if your small business is a group of computers using even a minimal peer-to-peer network in the same building, or Internet Mail Only if your small business is composed of partners or employees who work in separate offices or out of their homes.

When your business grows and your network requirements become more complex (and when you can afford the investment in time, equipment, and training), you'll want to upgrade your network to a corporate-sized system, possibly one that uses the Windows NT operating system and the Microsoft Exchange Server. Outlook makes this transition very well, and if your network uses the Exchange Server, there are a few more team-oriented features available in Outlook.

Using Outlook in a Home Office or Small Business

Suppose you and three colleagues have started a business that creates commercial Web pages for clients. You can work together as a team, yet work alone in your own home offices, by using Outlook in the Internet Mail Only configuration. You'll each have e-mail and Internet accounts with a local Internet service provider that uses POP3 mail servers—see the Section "Internet Mail Only Configuration" in the Appendix if you need to learn about setting up an Internet Mail Only mail account.

Using Outlook in a Small Business Without a Network

If all of your colleagues use Outlook 2000, you can confidently send each other e-mail in HTML or Rich Text format, even if you send e-mail to the rest of the world in Plain Text format.

TIP *To automate your e-mail formats, set the default format for your colleagues (HTML or Rich Text) in the Mail Format tab of the Tools | Options dialog box. Then, for every contact who needs e-mail in Plain Text, open their Contact dialog box, and on the General tab, mark the Send Using Plain Text check box.*

Another way to coordinate information within your non-networked small business is to use Net Folders, an Outlook 2000 feature that uses e-mail to automatically synchronize shared Outlook folders (such as a work Calendar or a Tasks folder) among computers that aren't linked by a network. You'll learn how to use Net Folders in the following section.

You can also publish a company calendar as a Web page on the Internet (see Chapter 9) and require a password to open the page to keep the information secure within your company. A colleague only needs a Web browser to see the Web calendar.

Using Net Folders

Net Folders give you a means of sharing an Outlook folder with another computer over the Internet. For example, you can use a Net Folder to post messages to a group of people, share a Contacts folder, or share a Calendar folder. When you

17

create a Net Folder, a copy of the folder is sent to everyone who subscribes to the folder, and the shared Net Folder becomes a folder in their Outlook Folder lists. The information in the folder is updated regularly, in the background, via e-mail. You can set different levels of access to a shared folder for each subscriber, or *member,* so that some members can only read what's in the folder and others can create new folder items or edit and delete existing items.

Net Folders can only be fully shared with others who use Outlook 2000. If a subscriber doesn't have Outlook 2000, they'll receive e-mail messages in their Inbox, but no shared folder, and you can only share e-mail messages with them (no Calendar, Contacts, or other Outlook items).

Suppose your small Web-page business is composed of four people who live in different parts of the country (which means many more potential clients, but more difficulty sharing information between partners). You can use Net Folders to share a company projects calendar and keep everyone aware of what everyone else is doing.

Creating and Sharing a Net Folder

When you create and share a Net Folder, you are the *owner* of the Net Folder, which puts you in control of who has access to the folder. To create and share a Net Folder, be sure everyone is using Outlook 2000, and follow these steps:

1. Create the folder you want to share. You cannot share your Inbox or Outbox, and you might find it best to share a subfolder that you create specifically to hold shared information. For this example, I'll create a Calendar subfolder named Webmaster Projects.

2. Open the folder you want to share (in this example, my Webmaster Projects calendar folder).

3. In the Outlook window, click File | Share | This Folder. The Net Folder Wizard starts.

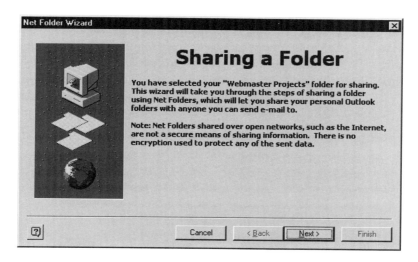

4. Read the wizard information, and click Next. The next wizard step appears.

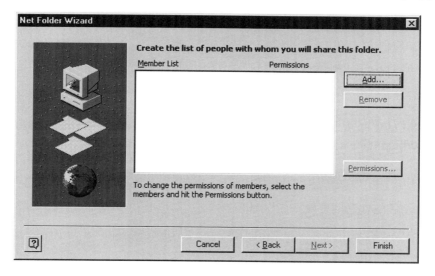

5. In this wizard step, you add members from your Contacts folders and subfolders, and assign permissions to each. Click the Add button. The Add Entries To Subscriber Database dialog box appears (it's just like your e-mail Select Names dialog box).

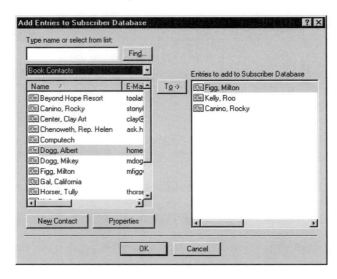

6. Double-click each name you want to add as a member of the shared Net Folder, and then click OK. All the names are listed in the Net Folder Wizard step, and each is assigned a minimal Reviewer permission level, which means they can only read items in the shared folder.

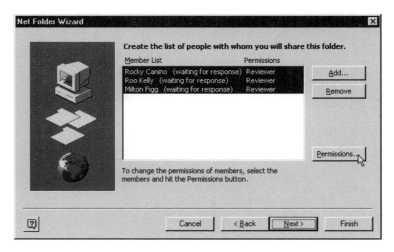

You want your partners to be able to add and edit information to this folder and delete their own entries, so you'll change the permission level for each of them to Author. Your default permission level will be Editor, because you own the folder, and you'll be able to create, change, and delete any item in the folder.

7. Click a name in the Member List, and then click the Permissions button. (To assign the same Permission level to several members in one step, use the CTRL or SHIFT key to select all their names.) The Net Folder Sharing Permissions dialog box appears.

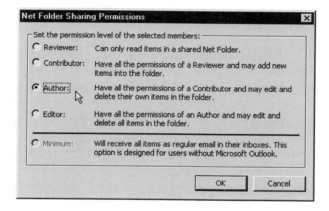

8. Click the Author option, and then click OK. You'll see the Net Folder Wizard again; and each name reads "(waiting for response)" because you haven't sent their invitations to the shared folder yet.

9. Click Next, and in the next wizard step, type a short description of the contents of the shared folder. Your description will be attached to the folder when it's sent to your partners.

10. Click Next, read the last wizard step, and then click Finish.

Invitations are sent out to all the names on your Member List (you might want to warn them that it's coming so they won't be surprised when it arrives), and a message tells you that invitations for your Net Folder have been sent successfully (click OK to close the message). If Outlook isn't online, the invitations go to your Outbox to await mailing.

Each e-mail invitation (see Figure 17-1) will have an Accept button and a long explanation of Net Folders, and each member will need to click the Accept button

17

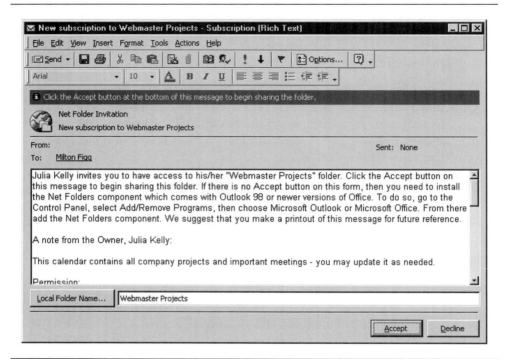

E-mail invitation to a shared-access Net Folder

to subscribe to the new Net Folder. The accepted e-mail invitation is returned to you automatically, and then the new Net Folder and all updates are sent to the subscribers automatically.

After a member accepts the Net Folder subscription, a copy of the Net Folder appears via e-mail in their Outlook Folder list. The shared Net Folder is automatically updated via e-mail on a regular schedule.

Maintaining a Net Folder

Here are a few more things to know about using Net Folders:

- To share your Net Folder as an e-mail list server (in which each member can post messages to other members), give each member Editor permission. To post a message, a member opens the shared folder and then clicks File | New | Post In This Folder.

■ To change your Net Folder's update schedule, right-click the shared folder (in the Folder list) and click Properties on the shortcut menu. On the Sharing tab, change the time interval in the Updates Will Be Sent Out Every drop-down list box.

■ To send out an update to your Net Folder immediately, right-click the shared folder (in the Folder list) and click Properties on the shortcut menu. On the Sharing tab, click the Send Updates Now button.

■ To change a member's permission level in your Net Folder, open the shared folder. Then click File | Share | This Folder, click Next, click the member name, click Permissions, and click the new permission level option.

■ To remove a subscriber from your Net Folder, open the shared folder. Then click File | Share | This Folder, click Next, click the member name, and click Remove.

■ To stop sharing your Net Folder, right-click the shared folder (in the Folder list) and click Properties on the shortcut menu. On the Sharing tab, click the Stop Sharing This Folder button.

■ To stop subscribing to a Net Folder someone else owns, right-click your copy of the shared folder, click Properties, click the Sharing tab, and then click the Cancel Membership button.

 If you or your subscribers use Outlook in a Microsoft Exchange Server environment and use Offline Folders, Net Folders are unavailable.

Using Outlook in a Small Business on a Network

If your small business is using a network and all your colleagues have Outlook set up in the Corporate/Workgroup configuration, you can send e-mail to each other through the network server and avoid ever sending your messages over the Internet (which means the messages move from place to place much more quickly and remain secure within the company network). You can create shared folders (see the Appendix to learn how) and post e-mail messages to the whole company in a shared folder, similar to using a bulletin board. You can also use Outlook's Remote Mail (see Chapter 18) without having to reconfigure Outlook before you leave the office. Of course, you can also send e-mail over the Internet in the Corporate/Workgroup configuration (see the Appendix to learn more).

17

The rest of this chapter focuses on the additional capabilities available to you when you use Outlook on a network that uses the Microsoft Exchange Server.

Outlook and the Microsoft Exchange Server

The Microsoft Exchange Server provides Outlook with its fullest potential for teamwork and workgroup communication. In addition to all the capabilities you have in the Corporate/Workgroup configuration, you can create and use public folders to share Outlook information on the server, send messages asking recipients to vote on a topic (they click a button, and send the message back to you, where Outlook automatically tallies the responses), and download the company's Global Address Book to maintain a current copy of all the mailbox addresses on the server.

If you're going to be out of town and need to temporarily delegate your responsibilities to someone else, you can let a colleague see your Outlook Calendar and accept meeting requests for you, and let her send e-mail in your name. If you're scheduling a meeting, the Exchange Server gives you access to everyone's Free/Busy information in the Plan A Meeting dialog box so that you can plan a meeting that everyone is available for; also, your network administrator can make schedules for company resources (such as meeting rooms and audiovisual equipment) available to your Plan A Meeting dialog box.

Using Public Folders

A *public folder* is an Outlook folder that others on your network have access to (if they've been given permission by the folder's owner). When your network administrator sets up public folders for your server, they appear in your Folder list under the main folder name Public Folders. Under Public Folders, you can create subfolders that serve as shared calendars and bulletin boards for posted messages, create a Favorites folder that's available when you work offline, and add anything else you need to share with team members on your network.

Creating a Public Folder

To create a new public folder, follow these steps:

1. Open your Folder list and right-click Public Folders.

2. Click New Folder, type a name for the folder, and select the type of items the folder will contain (such as Mail Items for a discussion group, or Appointment Items to share a calendar).

3. Click OK to create the new public folder.

> TIP *To give yourself or others access to the public folder when away from the office, drag a copy of the new folder into the Favorites folder (in the Create New Folder dialog box). This will give you offline access to the Favorites folder, and any changes you make in the Favorites copy will automatically appear in the original public folder.*

After you create a public folder, you'll want to set access permissions for people who are allowed to access the folder. By default, anyone with access to a public folder can read existing items and files in the folder, create new items, and change or delete any items they create. You can put limitations on these activities by setting specific permissions.

Setting Permissions for a Public Folder

To set or change permissions in a public folder that you own, follow these steps:

1. Right-click the folder and click Properties.

2. Click the Administration tab, and click an option—This Folder Is Available To All Users With Access Permission gives everyone with access full permission to alter the contents of the folder; Owners Only gives access only to those who are granted the highest level of permission.

3. To adjust permissions to users by name, click the Permissions tab.

> TIP *To understand the various levels of permissions, click the Help button at the bottom of the Properties dialog box.*

4. Click the Add button and add the names of individuals and the specific permission levels that you wish to assign them.

5. Click a name in the Name list, and then select a Role for the user in the Roles drop-down list box. Each Role has default settings in the check

17

boxes and options below the Roles list box; you can customize each user's permissions by changing the check box and option settings after you select a Role for the user.

6. Click OK to finish.

Taking a Tally of Votes

Suppose you are responsible for organizing a company-wide training session, and you have a choice of dates between June and July. Because you don't want to impact more summer vacations than necessary, you want to take a vote from all company employees on which month they'd prefer to have the training session scheduled.

In a Microsoft Exchange Server environment, Outlook can send out ballots and tabulate the returns automatically, which makes your job a lot less time-consuming.

Ask Others to Vote in Their Replies

To turn an e-mail message into a ballot, follow these steps:

1. Start a new message.

2. In the message's toolbar, click the Options button.

3. In the Message Options dialog box, mark the Use Voting Buttons check box.

4. Select a set of default voting choices in the drop-down list box to the right of Use Voting Buttons; if none of the generic choices meets your requirements (which is the case in this example), type your choices into the list box, separated by semicolons. In this example, type **June;July**.

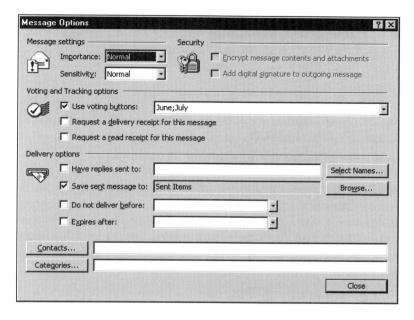

5. Click the Close button to close the Message Options dialog box. Your message has two buttons in the upper-left corner that read June and July.

6. Finish writing your message and send it to everyone in the company.

NOTE   *If you send this message outside the Exchange Server, the recipients will get a normal e-mail message without Voting buttons.*

Voting

If you receive a voting message, send in your vote by clicking the button for your choice. The message and your choice will be automatically returned to the sender.

17

View the Voting Responses

When the responses come rolling in, they're tallied on the Tracking tab of your original message.

By default, your original message is saved in the Sent Items folder. Open the message and click the Tracking tab. All of your message recipients' names are listed in the Recipient column, and their responses (or lack of response) are listed in the Message Status column. You can print the list of responses by printing the message, and then tally the votes by counting them manually.

If you want to keep only the list of responses that accumulate in the Tracking tab of the original message, and don't want to keep (or even see) all the response messages as they arrive, click Tools | Options, and on the Preferences tab, click the E-Mail Options button. In the E-Mail Options dialog box, click the Tracking Options button. In the Tracking Options dialog box, mark the Delete Blank Voting And Meeting Responses After Processing check box, and click OK to close each of the dialog boxes.

Using the Company's Global Address Book

When you use the Exchange Server, your network administrator can set up a Global Address Book that contains the e-mail addresses for everyone who has a mailbox on the server. You can download the Global Address Book to your copy of Outlook, and you can create distribution lists for sending group mailings to addresses on the server.

To download the Global Address Book, click Tools | Synchronize | Download Address Book. When you create a new e-mail message, the Select Names dialog box will include the Global Address Book in the Show Names From The list box of address books.

 *To use the Global Address Book when you're away from the office, make sure that your copy of the Address Book has Internet e-mail addresses, not just internal server addresses (coordinate this with your network administrator).*

Delegating Permissions for Other People

The Microsoft Exchange Server is designed for maximum teamwork, and one of the results of that design is the ability to delegate permission to other people to see and change items in your Outlook folders, accept meeting requests for you, and send e-mail in your name. This way, if you're going skiing in Gstaad and there's a work project that can't wait for your return, you can let someone else handle your workload while you're gone.

To make someone a delegate, follow these steps:

1. Click Tools | Options, and on the Delegate tab, click the Add button.

2. Select the name of the person to whom you're delegating access to your copy of Outlook.

3. If you want meeting requests and responses to be diverted to your delegate, mark the Send Meeting Requests And Responses Only To My Delegates, Not To Me check box.

4. To set specific permissions for your delegate, click the Permissions button.

5. Set permission levels for each Outlook folder that you want your delegate to have access to.

6. Click OK to close each open dialog box.

When your delegate needs to access your Outlook folders, they open their own copy of Outlook and click File | Open | Other User's Folder. Then they enter your name, select the Outlook folder of yours that they want to open, and click OK. Your Outlook folder opens in a separate window in their computer.

> **TIP** *If you're delegating access to one of your Outlook folders and there are specific items in the folder that you want to keep private, open each item and mark the Private check box in the lower-right corner of the item, and then click the Save And Close button.*

In this chapter, you've learned how to use Outlook to help you run or participate in a business, whether the business is small or large. At each level of business, Outlook has plenty of features to help you be more efficient. In the next chapter, you'll learn about taking Outlook on the road and working away from your desk.

17

Chapter 18

Using Outlook Away from the Office

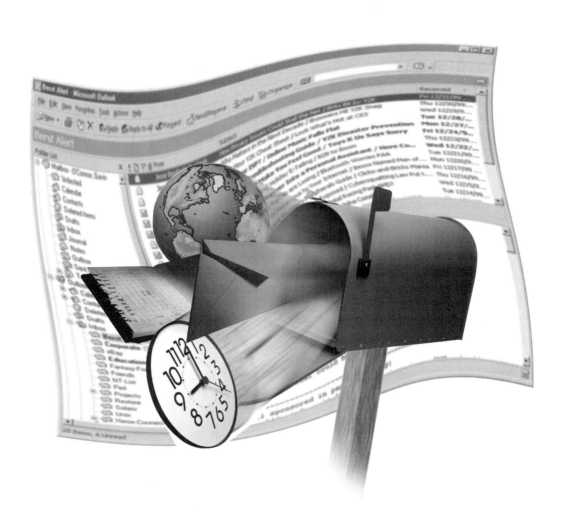

How to . . .

- ■ Get your e-mail when you're away from the office
- ■ Use the Exchange Server's Out Of Office Assistant to answer e-mail for you automatically
- ■ Use the Exchange Server's Offline Folders when you're away from the office
- ■ Integrate your Outlook data with a handheld personal digital assistant (PDA)

If you need to leave your office and computer to travel on business, (or even on vacation), you don't have to disconnect yourself from electronic communications. There are several ways to remain connected while you're on the road.

No matter what your Outlook configuration is, you can send and receive e-mail away from home (but if you're in Corporate/Workgroup configuration, you have a few more options than in Internet Mail Only configuration). If you work in a Microsoft Exchange Server environment, you can do more than pick up e-mail; you can also send automatic out-of-office replies to messages that come in, and connect to your company server to pick up current data and info.

Another popular way to work away from the office is to use a hand-held computer or a personal digital assistant. Examples of these devices are the Windows CE-based palm computers and the 3Com Palm PDAs. You can integrate and transfer data between your hand-held device and Outlook by using the device's software, and sometimes a third-party software program is also helpful.

Picking Up E-Mail Away from the Office

You can send and receive e-mail away from the office no matter what your Outlook configuration is, although the procedures differ somewhat.

 *You can switch your configuration between Internet Mail Only and Corporate/Workgroup at any time. See the section "Switching to a Different Configuration" in the Appendix to learn how.*

Internet Mail Only Configuration

If you have Outlook set up in the Internet Mail Only configuration, you can get e-mail away from the office in the same way that you receive it at the office (for example, lots of folks like to take their laptop computers home with them and get e-mail at home). The only difference between getting e-mail at the office and getting e-mail away from the office might be the telephone connection charges.

If your away-from-office location is in the vicinity of your office, there won't be any difference between dialing into your ISP from the office phone line and dialing in from a nearby phone line—it's still a local call and Outlook dials the same phone number. If you're dialing in from across the country, however, you'll need to change the phone number that Outlook dials (either to a long-distance number that includes the area code, or to a local number that your ISP has provided for that area). The easiest way is to create another connection that you can switch to whenever you need to.

TIP *If you're dialing in for mail and it's a toll call, you may want to limit the size of your downloaded messages to minimize the time you spend online. Click Tools | Options. On the Mail Delivery tab, mark the Don't Download Messages Larger Than check box, and type a maximum message/attachment size in the KB box. Remember to clear the check box when you return to the office.*

To create an away-from-office connection:

1. Click Tools | Accounts.

2. In the Internet Accounts dialog box, click the name of your e-mail account, and click the Properties button.

3. In the account's Properties dialog box, on the Connection tab, under the Use The Following Dial-Up Networking Connection list box, click the Add button.

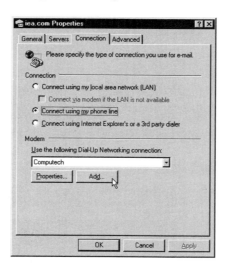

4. In the first dialog box of the Make New Connection wizard, type a name for the connection and click Next.

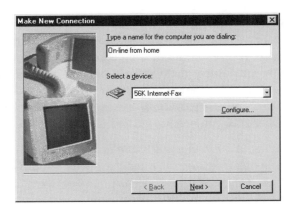

5. In the next step, type the telephone number, and the area code and country, if necessary. Then click Next.

6. In the last step, click Finish. The new connection is added to your list of connections, and you can select it when you dial in for e-mail from your away-from-office location.

7. Click OK and then Close to close all the dialog boxes.

After you've set up the away-from-home connection, you won't have to remember the phone number; instead, you can select the connection before you dial in for your e-mail. To select the connection, follow these steps:

1. Click Tools | Accounts.

2. In the Internet Accounts dialog box, click the name of your e-mail account, and click the Properties button.

3. In the account's Properties dialog box, on the Connection tab, in the Use The Following Dial-Up Networking Connection list box, select your away-from-office connection.

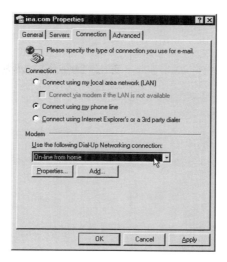

4. Click OK and then click Close to close the dialog boxes. Then click the Send/Receive button on the Outlook toolbar to dial in to your e-mail server.

   *Your new connection is also available to Internet Explorer for connecting to the Web. If you double-click the Internet Explorer icon to go online, you can select the away-from-office connection in the Dial Up Connection dialog box that appears when Internet Explorer dials out.*

Corporate/Workgroup Configuration

If you have Outlook in the Corporate/Workgroup configuration, you have the option of using Remote Mail. Remote Mail allows you to dial in and download only message headers, and then dial in again to pick up only the waiting messages that you want to download (which can save you quite a bit in connection-time charges if the call is costing you money). You can dial in to an ISP or to your company network server.

Dial Up a Remote Mail Connection

To use Remote Mail, you must be in the Inbox or another Outlook mail folder. Then follow these steps:

1. Click Tools and point to Remote Mail. You can use the Remote Mail commands on the submenu, or click the Remote Tools command and use

18

the Remote Mail toolbar to access those commands more quickly. For this example, I'll use the commands on the submenu.

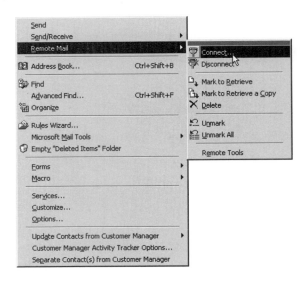

2. On the submenu, click Connect. The Remote Connection Wizard may ask you to confirm your connection. Click the mail service you want to connect to, and then click Next.

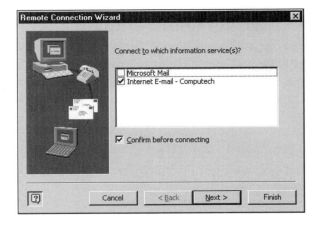

TIP   *If this is not the first time you've dialed from this location, you can skip all the interim checking and simply click Finish to dial up your mail server.*

3. In the next wizard step, choose a While Connected option. To reduce your connection time, leave the Do Only The Following option selected, and leave the Retrieve New Message Headers check box marked. Then click Next.

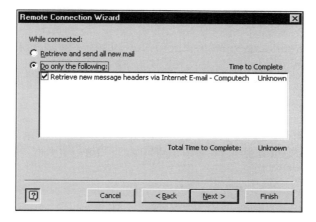

4. In the next step, select the location you're dialing from.

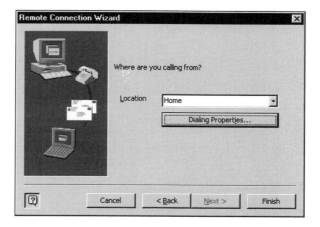

5. To see what the dial-out properties are for a location, click the Dialing Properties button. The dial-out properties tell Outlook whether or not to dial a number to access an outside line, use a calling card, disable call waiting, and so forth, each of which might be a factor, depending on where you're dialing from.

6. If you need to create a new dial-out location (for example, if you're dialing from an airport for the first time), click the Dialing Properties button, click the New button in the Dialing Properties dialog box, fill in the appropriate information, and click OK.

7. When the correct dial-out location is selected, click Finish.

Outlook dials up your connection and retrieves message headers for all of your waiting messages.

Download Remote Messages

After Outlook retrieves message headers, you'll need to decide which ones to download (if the call is costing money, you probably won't want to download any lists of Internet jokes or junk e-mail). To select and download the messages you want, follow these steps:

1. For each message you want to retrieve, click the message header to select it, and then click Tools | Remote Mail | Mark To Retrieve. A Retrieve icon, like those shown in Figure 18-1, appears next to each message header that Outlook will retrieve. These are your options for marking message headers for retrieval:

   ■ To retrieve the message from the server, click the Mark To Retrieve command.

   ■ To retrieve a copy of the message from the server (if you're retrieving messages from a company network server rather than an ISP), click the Mark To Retrieve A Copy command. The original message remains on the network server.

Downloaded header icon

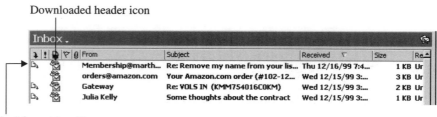

Marked-for-retrieval icon

FIGURE 18-1   Downloaded headers have different icons

■ To delete a message (if you're retrieving messages from a company network server rather than an ISP), click the Delete button on your Outlook toolbar.

■ To unmark a message you've marked for retrieval, click the Unmark command. To unmark all the messages you've marked, click the Unmark All command.

2. Click Tools | Remote Mail | Connect. Make sure the correct connection is selected in the first wizard step, and click Next.

3. In the second wizard step, select the appropriate options and click Next.

4. In the third wizard step, be sure the correct dial-out location is selected, and click Finish.

Outlook dials out and picks up all the complete messages for each header you selected for downloading.

Using the Out Of Office Assistant

This section is only for Outlook users who are connected to a Microsoft Exchange Server. If you're out of the office for a week (or even for a day), you can have Outlook reply to all incoming mail with a polite automatic response. The incoming mail will wait in your Inbox for your return, but your correspondents won't think you're ignoring them.

To set up automatic responses by the Out Of Office Assistant, follow these steps:

1. Open your Inbox, and then click Tools | Out Of Office Assistant.

2. Click the I Am Currently Out Of The Office option, and then type a polite message for your correspondents in the AutoReply box.

3. If you want special rules to apply to messages from specific senders or about specific subjects, click the Add Rule button at the bottom of the Out Of Office Assistant dialog box. In the Edit Rule dialog box, specify which messages the rule applies to in the upper part of the dialog box, and what actions should be performed on those messages in the lower part of the dialog box. Then click OK to return to the Out Of Office Assistant dialog box.

4. Click OK to close the Out Of Office Assistant dialog box.

18

When you return to the office, follow these steps to turn off the Out Of Office Assistant:

1. Open your Inbox, and then click Tools | Out Of Office Assistant.

2. Click the I Am Currently In The Office option, and then click OK.

Outlook retains the message and any rules you set up, so the next time you leave the office, all you need to do is click the I Am Currently Out Of The Office option in the Out Of Office Assistant dialog box.

In addition to sending an automated reply, you might want to divert incoming mail to an assistant by using the Rules Wizard. For example, you can create a rule that checks messages when they arrive, at the spot where your name is in the To box, and forward it to your assistant.

> NOTE *Be cautious using the Out Of Office Assistant if you subscribe to e-mail discussion lists. Your automatic responses get posted to any discussion list messages you receive, which respond automatically, and which trigger more automatic responses from you, and irritate everyone involved. You can always unsubscribe or put your list accounts on hold while you're away.*

Working Offline

This section is only for Outlook users who are connected to a Microsoft Exchange Server. Outlook's *offline folders* are Outlook folders on your computer that can be synchronized with matching folders on your company's Exchange Server. For example, if your network administrator has set up a Global Address Book for the company, you can download a copy of the Global Address Book from the network server to your computer, where it becomes an offline folder. Periodically, you can update your copy by synchronizing it with the Global Address Book on the network server, which makes both copies of the folder identical.

To use offline folders, you need to do three things: set up Outlook to work offline, establish a dial-up network connection, and synchronize your offline folders with those on the network.

Setting Up Outlook to Work Offline

First, you must create an offline folder file on your computer:

1. Open your Inbox, and then click Tools | Services.

2. Select Microsoft Exchange Server in the list of services (if it's not there, you'll need to add it—see "Microsoft Exchange Server" in the Appendix) and click the Properties button.

3. In the Microsoft Exchange Server dialog box, on the Advanced tab, click the Offline Folder File Settings button. The Offline Folder File Settings dialog box appears.

4. Take a look at the path to your offline folder file (outlook.ost) location, and either accept the default path or enter another path (if you don't have a specific reason to choose another path, it's best to accept the default).

5. Click an Encryption Setting option (you must choose one of these three options, and once you set it, it cannot be changed):

   ■ **No Encryption**   Means the offline folder file is neither encrypted nor compressed.

   ■ **Compressible Encryption**   Means you can compress your data to save space and still encrypt it for security.

   ■ **Best Encryption**   Means you get the best security, but can't compress the data as much as with Compressible Encryption.

> NOTE
>
> *The Compact Now button is for compacting (not compressing) offline files after you begin using them, enabling you to work faster. The Disable Offline Use button is for turning off offline folders when you're back in the office and reconnected to the network.*

6. Click OK.

7. Outlook tells you it can't find the OST file (because it doesn't exist yet). Click Yes, and Outlook creates the offline folder file.

8. On the Advanced tab of the Microsoft Exchange Server dialog box, click the Enable Offline Folders button to activate your new offline folders.

Don't close the Microsoft Exchange Server dialog box yet, because next you need to create the dial-up connection to the server.

Dialing Up the Network Connection

If you already have a dial-up connection to your company's Microsoft Exchange Server, there's not much to do here other than specify which connection Outlook should use. To specify the dial-up connection, click the Dial-Up Networking tab in the Microsoft Exchange Server dialog box, select the connection in the Dial Using The Following Connection list box, enter your User Name, Password, and Domain Name, and click OK

If you need to set up a dial-up connection to the server, follow these steps:

1. On the Dial-Up Networking tab, click the New button. The Make New Connection wizard starts.

2. In the first wizard step, enter a name for the server you're dialing up (a name you'll recognize—it doesn't have to be anything official). Then click Next.

3. Enter the telephone number for the server, and click Next.

4. Click Finish to create the connection and return to the Microsoft Exchange Server dialog box.

5. On the Dial-Up Networking tab, select the name of the new connection in the Dial Using The Following Connection list box. If you need to change any dialing properties for the new connection, such as entering a calling-card number or dialing a number to access an outside line before dialing your connection, click the Properties button and make those changes.

6. Close all the dialog boxes.

Synchronizing Offline Folders

This section is only for Outlook users who are connected to a Microsoft Exchange Server. When you set up offline folders, your Inbox, Outbox, Deleted Items, Sent Items, Calendar, Contacts, Tasks, Journal, Notes, and Drafts folders are automatically made available offline. To use any other folder (such as a subfolder) offline, you can make it available for offline use by following these steps:

1. Open your Inbox, and then click Tools | Options.

2. On the Mail Services tab, mark the Enable Offline Access check box, and then click the options you want.

3. Click Offline Folder Settings, and then select the additional folders you want to use offline. To speed up offline synchronization, try these additional settings:

   ■ To filter the downloads to a specific folder, click the folder and then click Filter Selected Folder. Set your filter criteria.

   ■ To limit the size of messages that are downloaded when you synchronize folders, click Download Options, and then click the options that you want.

   ■ Click the Quick Synchronization tab to select folders to synchronize as a group.

4. Click OK twice to close the dialog boxes, and then synchronize your offline folders manually the first time.

Manually Synchronizing Offline Folders

If you're on the road, you need to be able to synchronize your offline folders on your schedule rather than on the automatic schedule you may have set in Outlook. To synchronize offline folders manually, do one of the following:

■ To synchronize a single folder, open the folder in Outlook and then click Tools | Synchronize | This Folder.

■ To synchronize all of your offline folders, click Tools | Synchronize | All Folders.

■ If you created a Quick Synchronization group (earlier in this section), synchronize the group of folders by clicking Tools | Synchronize | *the group name*.

Automatically Synchronizing Offline Folders

If you want to keep your offline folders synchronized (and your data up-to-date) on a regular schedule without having to remember to do it yourself, you can set up an automatic synchronization schedule.

18

To set an automatic synchronization schedule, follow these steps:

1. Click Tools | Options.

2. On the Mail Services tab, mark the Enable Offline Access check box. Then do one of the following:

   ■ To synchronize all of your folders every time you exit Outlook, mark the When Online, Synchronize All Folders Upon Exiting check box.

   ■ To control how often your data is synchronized with the server while you're connected, mark the When Online, Automatically Synchronize All Offline Folders Every check box, and enter a number in the Minutes box.

   ■ If you're working offline and want Outlook to connect to the server and synchronize in the background regularly, mark the When Offline, Automatically Synchronize All Offline Folders check box, and enter a number in the Minutes box.

3. Close all open dialog boxes.

Adding the Global Address Book

This section is only for Outlook users who are connected to a Microsoft Exchange Server. If your network administrator has set up a Global Address Book on your company's Microsoft Exchange Server, you can add it to Outlook.

Click Tools | Synchronize | Download Address Book. Outlook connects to the server, downloads the Global Address Book, and then disconnects. The Global Address Book (now called a Global Address List) appears in the Show Names From The list box in the Select Names dialog box when you create a new e-mail message.

Integrating Outlook with Hand-held Devices

Lots of folks are taking hand-held computers or personal digital assistants (PDAs) with them when they leave the office, instead of much-larger laptop computers. A wide variety of hand-held computers and palm-sized PCs are on the market nowadays, and most of them can import and export data with Outlook.

Whatever system your hand-held PC uses to transmit data (it might be a dock-and-cable connection, or it might be a wireless infrared transmission system—and who knows what it will be by next year), either the hand-held PC will have its own software for trading data with Outlook or third-party software will be available that acts as a conduit for data between Outlook and the hand-held PC.

The first thing to do is check the *User's Guide* that came with your hand-held PC for instructions about transferring data between the device and your computer. Next, here are some Web sites that offer third-party software and help that might make the data transmission easier and more accurate, even if your device has its own data-transfer software:

- **Chapura**   www.chapura.com

- **DataViz**   www.dataviz.com

- **Puma Technology**   www.pumatech.com

- **TUCOWS PDA**   www.pda.tucows.com

Whatever help you need with your PDA or hand-held PC, these Web sites are a good place to begin your search.

In this chapter, you learned how to use Outlook away from the office, whatever configuration you have Outlook set up in. In the final chapter, you'll find lots of real-life questions (and answers) about Outlook that might come in handy.

Chapter 19

Questions and Problems in Outlook

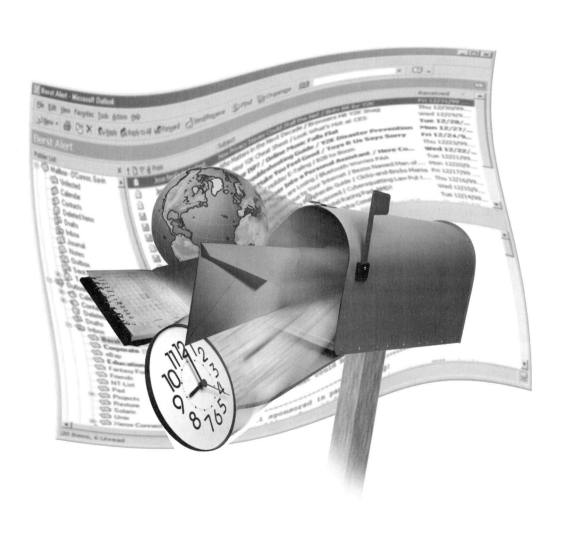

How to . . .

■ Troubleshoot Outlook Express

■ Troubleshoot E-Mail

■ Troubleshoot Contacts

■ Troubleshoot the Calendar

■ and more . . .

In this chapter, I've collected questions and problems from Outlook users (students, businesspeople, and others), and my answers. You may find an answer you've been looking for, or an answer to a question you hadn't though to ask yet.

Outlook Express

Q: I currently have Outlook Express as my default e-mail system. How do I switch to Outlook 2000? Or is it possible to keep and use both?

A: You can use both, no problem. Just click or double-click the desktop or taskbar icon for the program you want to use. Since Outlook Express is already set up, you can import your e-mail account settings, e-mail addresses, and any messages you receive from Outlook Express into Outlook (see Chapter 16 to learn how). Whatever you do, don't uninstall Outlook Express, because it needs to be installed for Outlook to work properly.

Q: The Send button does not appear on my new messages. When I click Help | About Outlook, the message reads "Outlook 2000, no e-mail." I've been using Outlook Express for e-mail, and I can't seem to transfer my address book from Outlook Express to Outlook. How can I send mail from Outlook?

A: It sounds like your copy of Outlook was installed in a No-Email configuration, which would explain why there's no Send button on your messages. See the section "Switching from Outlook Express to Outlook" at the end of Chapter 16, and follow all the procedures provided there to import your account information, e-mail, and addresses into Outlook.

E-Mail

Q: **When I type a contact name in the To field and press CTRL-K, Outlook doesn't recognize the name, and I have to select it from the Select Names dialog box. Why?**

A: In Corporate/Workgroup configuration, AutoName (described in Chapter 4) checks only the Contacts folder for names that have e-mail addresses, and none of the other folders. Names in other folders must be selected from the Select Names dialog box.

Q: **I have a friend who has two e-mail addresses, one at work and one at home. If I create a message and click the Address Book button to get the address, how can I get the second address?**

A: How you choose between two or three e-mail addresses depends on your Outlook configuration (Corporate/Workgroup or Internet Mail Only).

In Corporate/Workgroup configuration, the name is listed with each e-mail address (E-Mail, E-Mail 2, and E-Mail 3) in the Select Names dialog box. If you can't remember which is which, right-click a name/e-mail listing—for example, Joe Shmoe (E-Mail 2)—and then click Properties on the shortcut menu to see what the actual e-mail address is for that listing of the name. If that's the one you want, add it to the To box in your message.

In Internet Mail Only configuration, the name is listed only once in the Select Names dialog box, so add that name to the To box in your message. Then, in the message, right-click the name you added. If there are two (or three) e-mail addresses for that contact, you'll see them all listed in the shortcut menu. Click the one you want. If you choose the e-mail address that's not the default address for the name, you'll see the e-mail address in the To box instead of the contact's name, but that's okay.

Q: **How can I change the default e-mail address for a contact who has more than one e-mail address?**

A: This is an Internet Mail Only configuration question. To change the default e-mail address for a contact (so that the most-used e-mail address always has the display name, and is always the address Outlook uses unless you change it), follow these steps:

1. Open a new message and click the To button to open the Select Names dialog box.

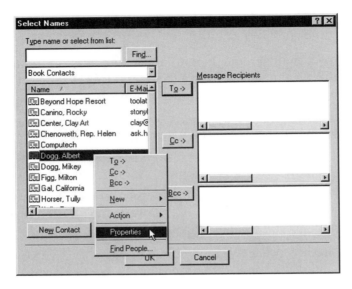

2. Right-click the name in the list of contacts, and click Properties.

3. In the Properties dialog box, on the Name tab, you'll see both (or all three) e-mail addresses listed, with the default address in bold type.

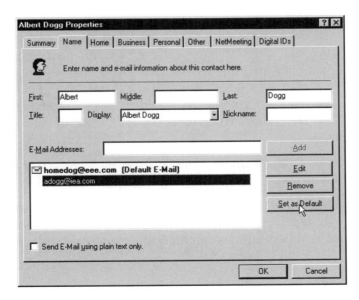

4. To switch the default to a different listed address, click the address, click the Set As Default button, and then click OK.

Q: My Contacts list contains hundreds of names, only a few of whom have e-mail addresses. Is it possible to filter the Contacts list so that only those contacts with e-mail addresses appear when I click the To button?

A: This is an Internet Mail Only configuration question. Filtering the names in the Select Names dialog box isn't possible. But try this: click the To button in a message to open the Select Names dialog box. Click the E-Mail Address column heading button to sort all the e-mail addresses to the top or bottom (click it a second time if they go to the bottom and you want to bring them to the top). If you've only got a few e-mail addresses, sorting will narrow your search by grouping together the contacts with e-mail addresses. Also, point to the border between the Name and E-Mail Address heading buttons (as shown in Figure 19-1), and when the mouse pointer becomes a two-headed arrow, slide the border to the left, to narrow the Name column and make it easier to see the e-mail addresses.

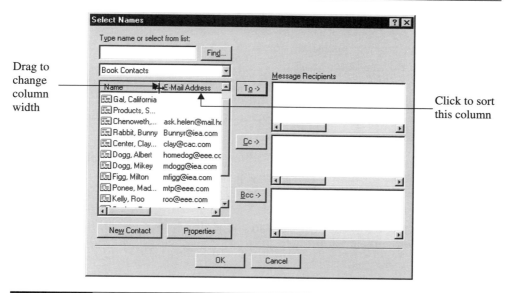

FIGURE 19-1   Sort the E-Mail Address column to locate e-mail addresses more easily

19

> TIP
>
> *If you create a Contacts subfolder and place copies of the contacts who have e-mail addresses in the subfolder, you can select that subfolder from the list box at the top of the Select Names dialog box, and only the names in that subfolder will appear.*

Q: When I select names for my e-mail messages, they're listed as first-name-first, even though I selected last-name-first in the File As field in my Contacts entries. How do I get them displayed last-name-first in the Select Names dialog box?

A: You probably have Outlook installed in Corporate/Workgroup configuration, which means you have an extra option in your address books. To change the address book listings:

1. Click Tools | Services. (Internet Mail Only configuration doesn't have a Tools | Services command).

2. In the Services dialog box, click Outlook Address Book, and then click the Properties button.

3. Click the File As (Smith, John) option, click the Close button, and then click OK.

4. Close Outlook and open it again. Your Select Names dialog box will list all names in File As order.

Q: I'm writing a new message and want to switch it to Rich Text or HTML format, but I can't find them on the Format menu. How can I change the format for this message?

A: If you're using Word as your e-mail editor, you won't have the option to change the format of open messages (which is one of the reasons why I don't use Word as my e-mail editor). To stop using Word as your e-mail editor, click Tools | Options, and on the Mail Format tab, clear the Use Microsoft Word To Edit E-Mail Messages check box. Then you can choose the format for individual messages when you create them.

Q: **When I try to send a file as text in an e-mail message, Insert As Text is not offered as an option. I only have Insert and Insert As Attachment. How can I make Insert As Text available?**

A: You're probably using Word as your e-mail editor, because when the Word e-mail editor is turned on, you lose the option to insert files as text. To regain the option to insert files as text, click Tools | Options, and on the Mail Format tab, clear the Use Microsoft Word To Edit E-Mail Messages check box.

Q: **Why is my Signature Picker disabled?**

A: If you use Word as your e-mail editor, you won't be able to insert signatures. To get your Signature Picker back, click Tools | Options, and on the Mail Format tab, clear the Use Microsoft Word To Edit E-Mail Messages check box.

Q: **Received messages often lose their "wrap-around" format, and one sentence is broken into two or three lines. Can I prevent this from happening when I'm preparing or receiving e-mail?**

A: If you use Plain Text or HTML, you can set the number of characters to wrap at. If you set the line length (the number of characters) shorter, it's less likely to break lines into tiny pieces when someone receives it; if you set the line length longer, messages you reply to are less likely to have their original text broken into short pieces. A line length of 90 characters works well for me. The procedure for setting the line length depends on your configuration.

If you're working in Internet Mail Only configuration, click Tools | Options, and click the Mail Format tab. Make sure your message format is Plain Text or HTML, and click the Settings button below the format. In the format's Settings dialog box, set a different number in the Automatically Wrap At box.

If you're working in Corporate/Workgroup configuration, click Tools | Options, and click the Internet E-Mail tab. Set a different number in the When Sending Messages, Wrap Text box.

Q: **My e-mail account is with AOL. Can I use Outlook to get my AOL e-mail?**

A: You cannot use other e-mail software (such as Outlook) to access your AOL e-mail account. AOL doesn't play well with others, and wants you to use its software exclusively. If you prefer the AOL e-mail software, you can still use most of the other features of Outlook, such as Calendar and Tasks, without using Outlook for your e-mail (and you won't be able to use your Contacts list as an e-mail address book). If you'd rather use Outlook fully, switch to a local Internet service provider (ISP).

Q: How do I set up a personal e-mail account if I'm in Corporate/ Workgroup configuration?

A: To set up a separate e-mail account that dials out from your modem (instead of using the network connection), follow this procedure:

1. Click Tools | Services.

2. In the Services dialog box, on the Services tab, click the Add button.

3. In the Add Service To Profile dialog box, click Internet E-Mail, and then click OK.

4. In the Mail Account Properties dialog box, fill in all the information about your Internet account. Don't mess with the Advanced tab; those default settings are probably fine.

5. On the General tab, type a recognizable name for your account (such as the ISP name) in the top box, and then fill in your name and e-mail address (use the Reply Address only if you want replies to your messages to be mailed to a different account, not your e-mail account—otherwise, leave it blank).

6. On the Servers tab, your incoming and outgoing mail (POP3 and SMTP) will both be the portion of your e-mail address that follows the @ symbol (unless your ISP gives you different server addresses). Your Account name is the portion of your e-mail address that comes before the @ symbol. And your password is the password you use to get your mail at your Internet service.

7. On the Connection tab, click the Connect Using My Phone Line option (I'm assuming your computer dials directly out on your phone line). If there's not already a Dial-Up Networking Connection listed under Modem, click the Add button and follow the steps in the Make A Connection wizard to fill in the phone number you dial to connect to your Internet service (and configure your modem, if you need to).

8. Click OK in all the dialog boxes that need closing, exit Outlook, and then restart Outlook.

Q: Why do attachments disappear when I reply to a message, but not when I forward a message?

A: People don't usually want to return the attachments in their replies (nor does the sender usually want to receive their unaltered attachments back), although people do often want to forward messages with the included attachments. To return a copy of an attachment in a reply, open both the original message and the reply, and drag the attachment icon from the original message to the reply message.

Q: Why are the formatting toolbar buttons (such as bullets, color, and font) unavailable when I forward a message, even though they're available when I reply to a message?

A: The formatting buttons aren't active unless you've clicked in the body of the message, where there's something to format. When you open a reply, your insertion point is blinking in the body of the message (and if you click in the To box to add another recipient, the Formatting buttons are grayed out). When you open a forwarded message, your insertion point is in the To box, waiting for an address; when you click in the body of the message, the buttons are available again.

Q: Why is my e-mail returned "Host unknown"?

A: You've sent a message to a nonexistent e-mail address—check the spelling of the address and send it again.

Q: My recipient got my message, but it was full of meaningless gibberish. What's the problem?

A: What they received was garbage ASCII files, because their e-mail program can't read the encoding format of the message you sent (this is not unusual in CompuServe and some older, bare-bones e-mail programs). If you sent the message encoded as MIME, you might try resending it after switching your message encoding to UUEncode. See Chapter 6 to learn how.

Q: Why did my recipient receive a winmail.dat attachment to a message I sent?

A: If you send a message with Rich Text formatting to someone whose e-mail program can't read Rich Text, they'll get this attachment. To prevent this, send e-mail to that recipient in Plain Text.

19

Q: Why can't I open a file I received in a message?

A: You can't open an attached file unless you have a program in your computer that can open that file, and the program must be the correct version. For example, if someone sends you a Word 2000 file and you are running Word 95, you won't be able to open the file; but you can ask your correspondent to save the file as a Word 95 or earlier version file type, and then you'll be able to open it.

Q: How can I turn off New Mail notification?

A: Click Tools | Options, and on the Preferences tab, clear the Display A Notification Message When New Mail Arrives check box.

Q: How do I limit the size of e-mail attachments that get downloaded?

A: In Internet Mail Only configuration, click Tools | Options. On the Mail Delivery tab, mark the Don't Download Messages Larger Than check box, and type a maximum-kilobytes number in the KB box. Be sure you make this number large enough to receive any important files you expect from colleagues.

In Corporate/Workgroup configuration, use Remote Mail and download only message headers first; then decide which actual messages to download, to avoid any with large attachments (see Chapter 18 to learn how to use Remote Mail).

Q: Why can't Outlook connect to my ISP and send my e-mail?

A: ISP mail servers occasionally get overloaded, especially when some pigheaded geek who needs a life decides to spam the world with thousands of automated messages. If you have a lot of trouble getting connected to your mail server, give it up and try again in a few hours, or the next day. If your message is really urgent, use the telephone.

Q: Why didn't the message in my Outbox go out?

A: If you're not online when you click the Send button in your message, the message goes into your Outbox and waits until you go online to send and receive mail. If you are online and the message doesn't go out, click Tools | Options, and on the Mail Delivery tab, mark the Send Messages Immediately When Connected check box.

Contacts

Q: When I search for a Contact using one word, I get the message, "There are no items to show in this view." Yet the word I've chosen is in five of the six Contacts entries I've saved. Why doesn't the search find items that I know are there?

A: In the Find pane, check whether you have the Search All The Text In The Contact check box marked (it's marked by default, but if it was inadvertently clicked and cleared, your search only looks at Name, Addresses, Company, and Category).

Q: All of my Ca (California) contacts are defaulting to Ga (Georgia) locations when I click the Display Map Of Address button in the contact dialog box toolbar. How can I display a map of my Ca contacts?

A: Be sure you're entering the state's two-letter abbreviation in uppercase letters (like CA and GA). Even if you use correct, uppercase state entries, the Microsoft Expedia Map search engine sometimes won't recognize them. Instead, an Expedia Map Address Finder Web page comes up, and reads Any State. Change the Any State entry to the correct state, and it should work. Microsoft software and Web pages are not without their bugs.

Q: I have asked Outlook to find several map addresses in Eugene, Oregon. It comes up with places in Pennsylvania and other states, but never Eugene, Oregon. What am I doing wrong?

A: The problem lies in the Microsoft Expedia map-search engine at its Internet site. It gets confused with state addresses. First, enter your contacts' state addresses as the two-letter state identifier, in capitals—for example, Oregon addresses should have OR for the state. Then, once you're at the Web map site, use the Web site's search engine to find the correct state (it's a problem at the Web site, not in your Contacts).

Q: Our corporate office has recently moved and I need to change the company address for all my contacts in that office. It's too tedious to do it individually—is there a way to do it "globally" within Outlook?

A: No direct method is available, but here are a couple of workarounds:

- To change contacts one at a time, but more quickly, click a contact that contains the new info (don't open it, just click it in the Contacts window), and then click Actions | New Contact From Same Company. Type the name of a contact who needs to be changed (type the name exactly the way it's entered in your existing contact), and then click Save And Close. In the Duplicate Contact Detected dialog box that appears, make sure the Update New Information option is marked, and then click the OK button. Do that for every contact whose company information needs to be updated.

- Export into an Excel file the whole group of contacts that needs to be changed. Then, use any of Excel's many methods to change the company data all at once. Finally, import the file back into Outlook, to replace existing contacts. You might want to do this using a custom Contacts subfolder in Outlook, so that you can work with only those contacts who need to be changed.

Q: Half of my contacts have the Holiday Cards category applied to them. How do I get the printer to print only those contacts falling within the Holiday Cards category?

A: If you apply a filter to the view, only those items displayed in the filtered view should be printed when you select All Items.

To filter by a category, click View | Current View | Customize Current View. In the View Summary dialog box, click the Filter button. In the Filter dialog box, click the More Choices tab, and click the Categories button. In the Categories dialog box, mark the check box for your Holiday Cards category, and then click OK three times to close all the dialog boxes. Your Contacts folder will show only those contacts in the Holiday Cards category, and the Outlook status bar will read Filter Applied on the left side.

Now you can print "all items" in the Print dialog box. To remove the filter, repeat the preceding steps until you get the Filter dialog box open; then click the Clear All button, and click OK to close each dialog box.

Q: When mapping my fields to import contacts from an Access database, my Access table has a field labeled Nickname. I don't see this field under the Outlook field names that are available (even though there's a Nickname field on the Details tab of the Contact dialog box). How do I add a field so that I can map it from one program to the other?

A: Unfortunately, you can't import data into any fields that aren't listed in the Map Custom Fields dialog box (and Nickname isn't listed, as you've seen). You can get around this limitation by mapping your Nickname field to one of the four User fields (for example, to the User 1 field) at the bottom of the list of Outlook fields.

You'll only see the nickname (the User 1 field) in the Contact dialog box if you click the All Fields tab and then select the Miscellaneous Fields list in the Select From list box—you'll have to enter the nicknames individually if you want them to appear in the Nickname field on the Details tab of the Contact dialog box. But even if you leave the nicknames in the User 1 field, you can still use the nicknames in a mail merge by inserting the User 1 field when you set up your mail merge.

Q: How can I make a public Contacts folder my default e-mail address book, so that if I have multiple users sharing the same Outlook Contacts list, we all use the same address book, too?

A: In Corporate/Workgroup configuration, set your default e-mail address book as follows:

1. Open your Inbox, click Tools | Services, and click the Addressing tab.

2. In the Show This Address List First list box, click the name of the Contacts folder you want to use as your default.

3. Click the Apply button, and then click the OK button.

Make sure each person sets the same default Contacts folder, and that each person has that Contacts folder available as an address book, like this:

1. In the Folder list, right-click the folder name and click Properties.

2. In the folder's Properties dialog box, on the Outlook Address Book tab, mark the Show This Folder As An E-Mail Address Book check box.

Q: **I know I can create subfolders within my Contacts folder, but contacts in those subfolders don't appear in the Select Names dialog box. The contacts in the Outlook Contacts folder are the only ones available. How can I display my Contacts subfolders in the Select Names dialog box?**

A: You need to make each Contacts subfolder available as an address book (refer to the two-step procedure in the preceding question, or to Chapter 3, to learn how).

Calendar

Q: **My calendar is not showing the TaskPad. How do I get it displayed?**

A: First, click View | Current View | Day, Week, Month and then click the Day, Week, or Work Week button on the toolbar to be sure you're looking at Calendar in a view that can display the TaskPad. If it's still hidden, it has probably been dragged out of view. You need to drag it back into view (and this will seem confusing until you do it the first time).

If you see thumbnail months all down the right side of Calendar, the TaskPad is off the screen at the bottom. Move your mouse pointer slowly between the lowest month borders and the bottom of the Outlook window; when your pointer becomes a two-headed arrow with the split lines in the middle (not the window-resize arrow), hold down your left mouse button and drag upwards at least two inches (if you drag higher, you get a taller TaskPad).

If you don't see thumbnail months on the right side of Calendar (just a full-screen Daily or Weekly calendar), the TaskPad and months are off the screen at the right. Move your mouse pointer slowly across the right border of the Outlook window; when the pointer becomes a two-headed arrow with the split lines in the middle (not the window-resize arrow), hold down your left mouse button and drag to the left at least two inches to bring a column of months and the TaskPad into view.

Q: **While dragging around in my Calendar window, I lost my TaskPad title bar and the actual tasks. The TaskPad space and the check box column are there, but no tasks. How do I get my tasks back?**

A: If you were dragging around in the window, you probably dragged the Subject field out of the TaskPad table by accident. Here's how you get it back: right-click the field header for the check-box field (the Completed field)—it's the gray box with the marked check box at the top of the check-box column. In the shortcut menu that appears, click Field Chooser.

In the Field Chooser dialog box, select All Task Fields from the list box at the top. Then, scroll down the list of gray field-header buttons until you find the Subject button.

Drag the Subject button over to the TaskPad area, and drop it on the right side of the Completed field-header button (the one with the check box). Before you drop it, you'll see two red arrows pointing to the spot where the new field header will be inserted, so you'll know you're in the right place. After you drop the Subject field header, it'll say "TaskPad" and all of your tasks will reappear.

Q: Is there any way to make the font displayed on the Daily calendar bigger so that I can read the appointments more easily?

A: Switch to Daily view, right-click in the Daily calendar, and click Other Settings on the shortcut menu. The Format Day/Week/Month View dialog box appears. To change the Daily Appointments font size, click the Font button under Day and select a new font size.

Q: I added lots of holidays to my calendar, just to practice. How can I remove them without going through the whole calendar and deleting the holidays one at a time?

A: You can't remove holidays from the calendar automatically, but you can remove them quickly, like this:

1. Click View | Current View | Events. Your calendar switches to a table-type view.

2. Click the Location header button to sort all the events (and holidays) by location. Each set of holidays is sorted together into a group according to the country of origin.

3. Drag down the left side to select all the holidays in the group you want to remove, and then click the Delete button on the toolbar. That set of holidays is removed, and you can switch your view back to the view you work most comfortably in. The deleted holidays are moved into the Deleted Items folder, and you can delete them permanently by emptying your Deleted Items folder.

19

Miscellaneous

Q: I want Outlook to start automatically when I start my computer, but I can't find the C:\Windows\StartMenu\Programs\StartUp folder. Where is it?

A: Individual computers are often set up differently; to search for the StartUp folder, click Start | Find | Files or Folders, and search on the Named tab for a folder named StartUp in the C drive (mark the Include Subfolders check box in the Find dialog box). You'll probably find a few folders named StartUp, and need to experiment a bit to locate the one that starts a program when Windows starts.

Q: If I want to use AutoDate, where do I type *week from tomorrow*?

A: In any box where you would normally type or select a date, you type the words instead. For example, open a new Appointment dialog box. In the Start Time date box, where you'd enter or select a date, drag the existing date entry to highlight it, and then type the words **wk from tomorrow**. Press ENTER, and the actual date of a week from tomorrow, whatever that is, is entered in the Start Time date box.

Q: On my Outlook bar, I have the Outlook Shortcuts and My Shortcuts groups, but Other Shortcuts is not there. How can I add that group and the icons that should be under it?

A: Sounds like someone may have inadvertently deleted the group. Here's how you add it (and the icons) back to your Outlook bar:

1. Right-click in the Outlook bar and click Add New Group. A new group button appears that says New Group. Type **Other Shortcuts**, and press ENTER. You now have an Other Shortcuts group, and you need to add the My Computer shortcut icon to it.

2. Click your new Other Shortcuts button to open the group. Right-click in the Outlook bar (below the Other Shortcuts button), and click Outlook Bar Shortcut. In the Add To Outlook Bar dialog box that appears, in the Look In list box, select File System. The top of your hard drive file tree, including the My Computer icon, appears in the list in the big box. Click the My Computer icon and then click OK. The shortcut is added to your Outlook bar.

3. The other default shortcut icons in the Other Shortcuts group are the My Documents and Favorites icons. Add them the same way as in step 2, but in the Add To Outlook Bar dialog box, you need to click the plus symbol next to the My Computer icon, and then next to the hard drive icon, and so forth until you locate the My Documents and Favorites folders (My Documents is usually at the root of your hard drive, and the Favorites folder is in the Windows folder).

Q: Why isn't my notification chime chiming?

A: There are two places where your reminder sound might be turned off. First, click Tools | Options, and on the Other tab, click the Advanced Options button; click the Reminder Options button, and mark the Play Reminder Sound check box to turn on all Outlook reminder sounds. Second, your speaker's Volume Control may be muted—double-click the speaker icon on the right end of the taskbar, and clear the Mute All check box.

Q: Why am I not getting task and appointment reminders?

A: Outlook must be open for you to be reminded about tasks and appointments. If Outlook is closed during the reminder time, the reminder appears the next time you start Outlook.

Q: How can I transfer contacts and other items to a new computer?

A: You can export contacts to an Excel file or to a text file, and then import the file into your Contacts folder in the new computer. Other items can be archived and then imported. See Chapter 16 to learn how.

Q: How can I tell Journal to stop AutoRecording everything?

A: Click Tools | Options, and on the Preferences tab, click the Journal Options button. In the Journal Options dialog box, clear the check boxes for everything you don't want recorded automatically.

Q: If I keep Outlook open and minimized, does that mean I'm online?

A: No, Outlook doesn't have to be online to be open—but you can tell Outlook to stay online or disconnect after you pick up your e-mail. See the answer to the following question.

19

Q: **How can I tell Outlook to stay online (or not) after mail delivery?**

A: In Corporate/Workgroup configuration, click Tools | Options, and click the Internet E-Mail tab. To tell Outlook to hang up when it's finished getting mail, mark the If Using A Dial-Up Connection Hang Up When Finished Sending And Receiving Mail check box (clear the check box if you want to keep the connection open).

In Internet Mail Only configuration, click Tools | Options, and click the Mail Delivery tab. To tell Outlook to hang up when it's finished getting mail, mark the Hang Up When Finished Sending, Receiving, Or Updating check box (clear the check box if you want to keep the connection open).

Q: **Why am I always asked if I want to empty my Deleted Items folder when I exit Outlook?**

A: Because someone has told your copy of Outlook to do that. To change the setting, click Tools | Options, and on the Other tab, clear the Empty The Deleted Items Folder Upon Exiting check box.

Q: **I don't use (or ever want to use) Microsoft Network, so how can I get rid of that MSN icon on my Windows 98 desktop?**

A: There's a helpful file (created by Microsoft itself) that will remove that icon and do lots more customizing for you. It's called TweakUI; you can find the TweakUI.inf file in the TweakUI folder on your Windows 98 CD-ROM, or you can download it quickly and for free from the Web site **http://www.annoyances.org/win98**.

Appendix

Installation

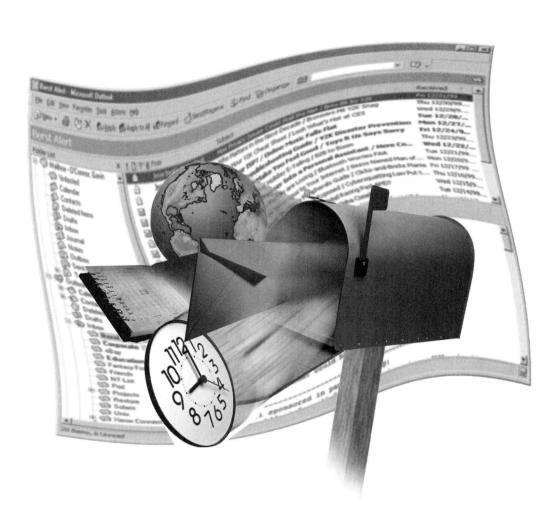

Installing Outlook

If you haven't installed Outlook yet, this material will help you make the right installation decisions for your work environment. If you've already installed Outlook, but want to change your configuration, the last section in this introduction, "Switching to a Different Configuration," will show you how.

According to Microsoft, Outlook 2000 has these computer system requirements:

- A PC with Pentium 75 MHz or higher processor

- Windows 95 or later, or Windows NT 4 or later

- 16MB RAM for the operating system plus 8MB RAM for Outlook in Windows 95/98; 32MB RAM for the operating system plus 8MB RAM for Outlook in Windows NT 4 or later

- CD-ROM drive

These are minimum requirements, however; you'll find that Outlook runs much better on a PC with a Pentium II processor and 64MB RAM (in Windows 95/98) or 96MB RAM (in Windows NT 4 or later).

Some Outlook features are only available in a network environment that uses the Microsoft Exchange Server. To use the Exchange Server as your network server, you must be running the Windows NT operating system.

You can get Outlook as a standalone product or as part of any Microsoft Office 2000 suite. I'll show you how to set up Outlook when you install Office 2000; and installing Outlook alone will be quite similar.

Microsoft Office 2000 installs itself, except for a few questions you'll need to answer and a few modifications you'll want to make. Follow these steps to begin the installation process:

1. Insert Disk 1 of Microsoft Office 2000 into your CD-ROM drive. The CD-ROM will load itself unless you've turned off the Auto Insert Notification in your CD-ROM Properties dialog box. If, after a few moments, the Office 2000 CD-ROM hasn't loaded itself, click Start | Run and click the Browse button; then browse to your CD files, and double-click Setup.exe to load the CD Installer.

2. Type your user and CD Key information on the first page, and click Next.

3. On the License Agreement page, check that your user information is entered correctly at the top of the page, click the I Accept option at the bottom of the page, and click Next.

4. In the Ready To Install page, you can click the Install Now button to install all of Office 2000, or click the Customize button to install only the parts of Office 2000 you want. Because this procedure is about installing Outlook, click the Customize button to focus on installing Outlook.

5. In the Installation Location page, it's best to accept the default hard drive location for Outlook (if you have a reason for locating Outlook elsewhere on your hard drive, click the Browse button and choose a different folder). Then click Next.

6. In the Select Features page (shown in Figure A-1), select the features you want to install and deselect the features you don't want to install at the moment.

> TIP   *If you're low on hard drive space, or expect you'll never use a certain feature, deselect it. You can always install it later.*

A

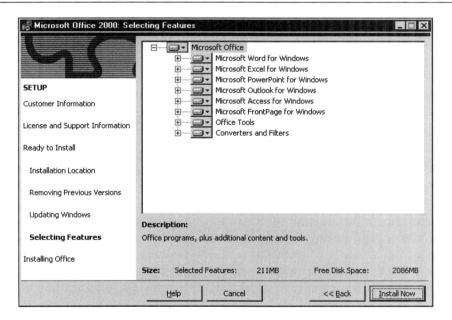

| FIGURE A-1 | Select the features you want to install, and deselect the features you don't want |

The Office 2000 programs on the CD-ROM are listed, and next to each is a small plus symbol that, when clicked, becomes a minus symbol, and expands to show a list of the features in each program that you can install.

7. If there are any programs you don't want to install at the moment, click the icon next to the program name (not the plus symbol) and click Not Available, as I've done for Microsoft PowerPoint here. The options for most programs and features are Run From Computer, Run From CD, Installed On First Use, and Not Available.

8. Click the plus symbol next to Microsoft Outlook For Windows to see what's installed by default. For now, you can leave all the default Outlook features set up as they are (you can make changes later, if you want to).

9. Click Install Now. The CD-ROM spins and installs all the selected programs and features.

10. When you're asked if you want to restart Windows now, click Yes. The Installer finishes and configures the installation.

If you're given the option to install Internet Explorer 5, click Yes, because Outlook needs it to be fully functional, even if you prefer to use a different Internet browser.

When you start Outlook the first time, you may be given the option to import e-mail messages, address books, and Internet connection settings from existing e-mail programs into Outlook. Click Yes, and Outlook will set itself up to use your existing mail accounts.

Next, you decide on your Outlook configuration: Internet Mail Only, Corporate/Workgroup, or No E-Mail. If you use another program to send and receive e-mail, such as AOL (which is incompatible with Outlook), you can choose the No E-Mail option. If you decide later to use Outlook to send and receive e-mail, you can set up your new e-mail account at that time.

Internet Mail Only Configuration

Choose the Internet Mail Only option in the E-mail Service Options dialog box if you send and receive e-mail and faxes from a modem in your computer rather than through a network server. Your modem dials up and connects directly to your Internet service provider's mail server. Outlook will be configured to use SMTP/POP3 (Simple Mail Transport Protocol/Post Office Protocol 3) mail servers and IMAP (Internet Message Access Protocol) servers to send and receive e-mail, and to send and receive faxes from your computer's fax/modem using Symantec Fax Starter Edition as a fax program.

A

About SMTP and POP3

SMTP and POP3 are *protocols,* or sets of rules, that your modem and your Internet mail server agree on so that mail can be sent back and forth and read. All you need to know about them is what to enter when a dialog box asks for your SMTP or POP3 server address.

Your POP3 server is the server for your incoming messages. Your SMTP server is the server for your outgoing messages. In most cases, they'll be the same server. If you use a local Internet service provider (ISP), your POP3 and SMTP server addresses will be the *domain name* portion of your e-mail address, which is the part of your e-mail address that comes after the @ symbol. For example, if my e-mail address is julia@eee.com, my POP3 and SMTP server addresses are both eee.com. In any case, your ISP will supply you with the information you need.

You can set up Outlook in the Internet Mail Only configuration even if your computer is on a network, as long as you have a modem or fax/modem in your computer. You won't have as many Outlook network interconnectivity options as in the Corporate/Workgroup configuration, but sending and receiving e-mail and faxes is simpler and faster. If you already have an e-mail account set up in your computer, Outlook will use that information to set up your e-mail service.

After you install Outlook and restart your computer, you'll have the option to set up Symantec WinFax Starter Edition. You can set it up at that point, or cancel the WinFax setup and set it up later. Either way, see Chapter 7 for details on how to set up WinFax.

After you set up your e-mail account in the Internet Mail Only configuration, you're finished with installation.

Set Up an E-Mail Account

If you don't already have an e-mail account set up in your computer, or if you want to set up a new account, you need to give Outlook the information it needs to use that account. Follow these steps to set up a new account:

1. Click Tools | Accounts. The Internet Accounts dialog box appears.

2. Click the Add button, and then click Mail on the submenu that appears.

3. The Internet Connection Wizard starts. Follow the steps in the wizard to set up your account. You'll need information provided by your ISP, such as the name and password for your account, and the POP3 and SMTP server addresses.

4. When you finish, the new account will appear in your Internet Accounts dialog box.

If you have more than one account, you can set or change the default account by clicking the account name and then clicking the Set As Default button. To remove an account, click the account name and then click the Remove button.

Import an Existing E-Mail Account

If you've been using Outlook Express, Netscape, or Eudora for e-mail, you can import those Internet account settings instead of reentering the data in the wizard. See Chapter 16 to learn how.

Corporate/Workgroup Configuration

If you're on a network and use a network server to send and receive e-mail and faxes, and/or need the interactive components provided in the Corporate/ Workgroup configuration, choose the Corporate Or Workgroup option in the E-mail Service Options dialog box that appears when you finish installing Outlook. This configuration is a bit more trouble to set up, but one of the advantages it provides is the ability to send and receive e-mail remotely and download only selected messages. You can continue to use your computer's own modem and phone line to send and receive Internet e-mail in this configuration, but it will take a bit longer.

To send and receive e-mail in Corporate/Workgroup configuration, whether you're sending mail over your network or over the Internet, you need to set up a post office for the network and a mailbox for each user on the network, and add Microsoft Mail to each user's Outlook profile.

 *These procedures assume that you are the network administrator for your network; if you are not, don't run these procedures without first checking with your network administrator.*

Create a Shared Network Folder to Hold the Post Office

The post office needs to be in a shared folder on the network so that other users can use it. Follow these steps to create a shared folder:

1. Click Start | Settings | Control Panel, and double-click the Network icon. The Network dialog box opens.

2. On the Configuration tab, click the File And Print Sharing button.

3. In the File And Print Sharing dialog box, click the I Want To Be Able To Give Others Access To My Files check box, and then click OK.

4. Click OK to close the Network dialog box.

5. Create a new folder in the network drive (use any technique you like to create the new folder) and give it an intuitive name, such as **Post Office**.

6. Right-click the new folder and click Sharing on the shortcut menu.

7. In the folder's Properties dialog box, on the Sharing tab, click the Shared As option, and under Access Type, click the Full option.

8. Click OK to close the Properties dialog box.

Next, you'll create a post office in the new shared folder.

Create the Post Office

The post office will be the network location for all the network users' mailboxes. Follow these steps to create the post office:

1. Click Start | Settings | Control Panel, and double-click the Microsoft Mail Postoffice. The Microsoft Workgroup Postoffice Admin wizard starts.

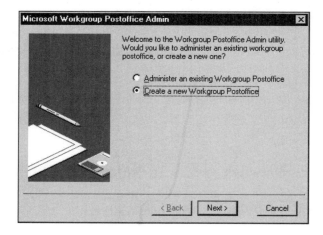

2. Click the Create A New Workgroup Postoffice option, and click Next. (If you need to change post office settings later, click the Administer An Existing Workgroup Postoffice option.)

3. In the second wizard step, click the Browse button, browse to the location of your new shared folder, and double-click it. When the wizard step reappears, the path to the shared folder is displayed. Click Next.

4. The next wizard step shows the path, along with a post office filename that you mustn't change. Click Next to continue.

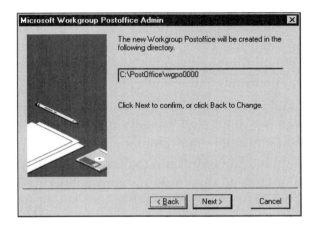

5. In the Enter Your Administrator Account Details dialog box that appears, you need to enter at least three items: your name (the administrator), a mailbox name for the post office, and a password. You'll use the mailbox name and password to get into the post office and set up mailboxes for other users on the network, and any time you need to make changes in the post office or mailboxes.

6. Click OK. A message tells you that the post office was created and that the folder must be shared, which you already did, so click OK to close it.

Next, create mailboxes for each user on the network so that they can get their e-mail.

If you're setting up Microsoft Mail on a single computer (for example, on your laptop, so that you can use Remote Mail away from your office), your administrative post office mailbox is all you need (you don't need to set up a separate mailbox just for yourself).

Create a Mailbox for Each User

To create more mailboxes on your network, follow these steps:

1. Double-click the Microsoft Mail Postoffice icon in the Windows Control Panel, click the Administer An Existing Workgroup Postoffice option in the wizard step, and click Next.

2. If there's only one post office on your network, the correct post office file will probably appear in the next wizard step. If not, click the Browse button, browse to find the post office file, and then click Next.

3. Enter your administrative mailbox name and password, and click Next.

4. In the Postoffice Manager dialog box, click the Add User button.

If you need to change a user's password, click the user's name and then click the Details button. Type a new password, and click OK.

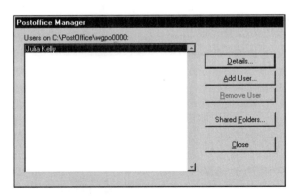

5. In the Add User dialog box, enter at least the user's name, mailbox name, and password, and click OK. Continue adding user mailboxes for each user

on the network, and be sure you keep a record of their mailbox names and passwords so you can let each person know how to get their mail.

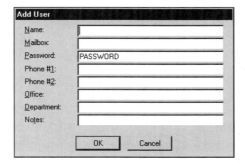

6. When you've added all the mailboxes you need, click the Close button in the Postoffice Manager dialog box, and then close the Control Panel.

Set Up Microsoft Mail for Each User

At this point, your physical mailbox structure is in place. Now you need to configure each user's computer/workstation to use the Microsoft Mail service. Follow these steps to set up Microsoft Mail in a computer:

1. Click Tools | Services, and click the Services tab.

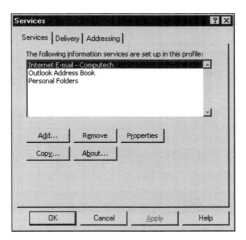

2. If Microsoft Mail is listed, you'll need to configure it. If not, you'll need to add it and then configure it.

3. To add Microsoft Mail, click the Add button. In the Add Service To Profile dialog box, click Microsoft Mail, and click OK.

4. To configure Microsoft Mail after it's been added, click Microsoft Mail in the Services dialog box, and click the Properties button. (If you've added Microsoft Mail in step 3, the Microsoft Mail dialog box may open automatically.)

5. In the Microsoft Mail dialog box, you have lots of decisions to make as the network administrator. To understand what each option does for you, click the Help button at the bottom of the Microsoft Mail dialog box. A list of explanations for each option on the displayed tab appears in a help file.

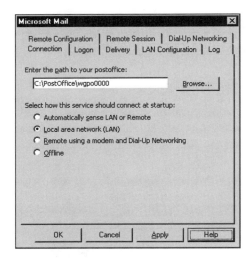

6. When you've finished configuring the Microsoft Mail service, click OK to close each dialog box. You'll need to exit (click File | Exit And Log Off) and then restart Outlook for all of your settings to take effect.

Now you can send e-mail to other mailboxes on your network without using the Internet, as well as send and receive e-mail outside your network.

Reinstalling or Adding Components

Any time you want to add or remove Outlook or Office components, click Start | Settings | Control Panel, and double-click Add/Remove Programs. Double-click Microsoft Office 2000 (or Microsoft Outlook 2000, if you installed it separately), and in the Maintenance Mode dialog box that appears, click the Add Or Remove Features button. In the Update Features page that appears, you can click the icon for each program or feature you want to change; select Not Available to uninstall the program or feature, and click Run From Computer or Run From CD to install a program or feature. Then, click the Install Now button to finish.

Microsoft Exchange Server

The Microsoft Exchange Server provides the maximum amount of network interactivity available in Outlook; it also requires that your computer be running the Windows NT 4 (or later) operating system, and that Outlook be set up in Corporate/Workgroup configuration. The nuts and bolts of Windows NT and the Microsoft Exchange Server are worth an entire book unto themselves, and if your company is using the Microsoft Exchange Server, you probably have a network administrator who can answer your network-related questions and set up your network connections.

To get Outlook set up to use the Microsoft Exchange Server, configure for Corporate/Workgroup and check with your system administrator to make sure you have a mailbox on the Exchange Server network. Then follow these steps:

1. Click Tools | Services. If you see Microsoft Exchange Server listed as a service, you can select it and click Properties to check or change your Microsoft Exchange Server properties.

2. If you don't see Microsoft Exchange Server listed, click the Add button. The Add Service To Profile dialog box appears.

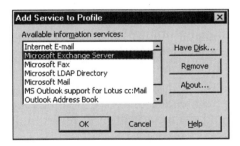

3. Click Microsoft Exchange Server and then click OK. The Exchange Server Properties dialog box appears.

4. Enter the name of the Exchange Server and your mailbox name, and any other information or options as directed by your network administrator.

5. Click the Check Name button, and Outlook will connect to the server to check your mailbox name. If it finds the name you entered, the name will be underlined. If Outlook doesn't underline the mailbox name, check that you spelled it correctly and that the mailbox was set up correctly on your network administrator's end.

6. When all the server properties are entered as directed by your network administrator, click OK twice to close the Properties dialog box and the Add Service To Profile dialog box.

Chapters 17 and 18 explain how to use the specific features available with the Microsoft Exchange Server.

Switching to a Different Configuration

You may find that, for any number of reasons, you need to switch your Outlook configuration. For example, if you installed in No E-Mail configuration because you already use another e-mail program, you'll discover that you can't use Outlook to send or receive e-mail. If you decide that you want to use Outlook to send e-mail, you'll need to add an Internet service so that Outlook has all the necessary Internet service account information it needs.

NOTE *If you installed in No E-Mail configuration because you've been using Outlook Express, Eudora, or Netscape for e-mail, you don't need to reconfigure Outlook. Instead, you can import your Internet account settings from any of those programs to Outlook (see Chapter 16 to learn how). On the other hand, if you have an AOL account, you won't be able to get your e-mail through Outlook (because AOL won't allow it), and you should install in No E-Mail configuration. If you decide to switch to a different ISP so you can use Outlook for e-mail, you'll need to switch your Outlook configuration.*

To add a mail service other than an existing Outlook Express, Eudora, or Netscape account, see the earlier section "Set Up an E-Mail Account."

Here's another reason to switch configurations: you have two computers, each with its own modem, connected in a peer-to-peer local area network, and you thought you needed to set up Outlook in the Corporate/Workgroup configuration. In the course of reading this book, you may decide that setting up both computers in an Internet Mail Only configuration is more practical, because it's simpler and faster, and the Corporate/Workgroup configuration doesn't offer you anything you can't live without.

On the other hand, you may decide to upgrade your small company network, and find it necessary to switch from your Internet Mail Only configuration to a Corporate/Workgroup configuration so that you can take advantage of the interactive capabilities of Outlook on multiple computers.

Switching configurations is easy, and you can switch back and forth between Internet Mail Only and Corporate/Workgroup whenever you need to. For example, suppose you normally use Outlook in an Internet Mail Only configuration, but you're leaving on a business trip with your laptop computer and you'll need to pick up e-mail from hotel rooms. To reduce the connection-time charges, you may want to use the Remote Mail feature that's available in Corporate/Workgroup configuration (Chapter 18 explains how to use Remote Mail). You can switch to Corporate/Workgroup configuration before you leave on your trip, and switch back to Internet Mail Only configuration when you return home.

To switch your Outlook configuration, follow these steps:

1. Click Tools | Options. If you're currently in Corporate/Workgroup configuration, click the Mail Services tab; if you're currently in Internet Mail Only configuration, click the Mail Delivery tab.

2. Click the Reconfigure Mail Support button.

3. Click the configuration option you want, and then click Next.

4. Follow the wizard steps to set up the new configuration.

   If you're switching to Corporate/Workgroup configuration for the first time, you'll need to set up a post office and mailbox to send and receive mail. See the earlier section "Corporate/Workgroup Configuration" to learn how.

   If you're switching to Internet Mail Only configuration for the first time, you'll need to import or set up an Internet account. See the earlier section "Set Up an E-Mail Account" to learn how.

5. To finish the configuration, close all of your open programs, and then restart Windows.

Now that you've got Outlook set up, you're ready to learn how to do everything in Outlook 2000!

A

Index

NOTE: Page numbers in *italics* refer to illustrations or charts.

A

Accept button
    Net Folders, 399–400
    tasks, 280
Access, importing contacts
    from, 437
access, remote. *See* remote access
activities, associating contacts
    with Journal, 295–296
Add Digital Signature To
    Outgoing Messages check box,
    161–162
Add Holidays to Calendar dialog
    box, 257–258
Add New Group command,
    Outlook bar, 440–441
Add Service to Profile dialog box,
    Microsoft Exchange Server,
    455–456
Add To Contacts dialog box,
    e-mail senders, 124
Add To Junk Senders List
    command, customizing
    toolbars, 361–364
adding fields to table views,
    reorganizing fields, 57–58
address books
    Corporate/Workgroup
        mode, 78
    making contact subfolders
        available as, 90
Address box
    creating contacts, 66–67
    Web toolbar, *334*
Address Cards view, contacts,
    63, 64

addresses
    choosing between for same
        person, 427
    contact, 69–70
    e-mail, 100–103
Adult Content filter, e-mail rules,
    142–144
advanced criteria, Filter dialog
    box, 47–50
Advanced Find dialog box
    message threads, 158–159
    searching for specific e-mail
        messages, 156–157
Advanced tab, Filter dialog
    box, 47
Advanced toolbar
    Current View List box, 86
    viewing files, 303–304
After Moving Or Deleting An
    Open Item list box, E-Mail
    Options dialog box, 154–155
Answer Wizard, help system, 31
AOL (America Online), e-mail
    and, 431–432
Appointment Recurrence dialog
    box, recurring appointments,
    253–254
appointments, 240, 246–255
    See also Calendars;
        scheduling Calendars
    Appointment dialog
        box, *248*
    changing, 251, *252*
    creating, 247–250
    dragging, 251, *252*
    notes and, 249
    overview, 246
    Private check box, 249
    recurring, 252–255
    Reminder check box, 249

Reminder Options dialog
    box, 250
responding to reminders,
    250–251
Show Time As list box, 249
turning into meetings via
    Meeting Planner, 264
archive.pst, switching from
    Outlook Express to Outlook
    2000, 391
archiving, 374–383
    Archive dialog box,
        378–380
    AutoArchive, 374–378
    Import and Export Wizard,
        381–390
    manually, 378–380
    overview, 374
    retrieving archived items,
        380–383
Assign Hyperlink dialog box,
    customizing toolbars, 364–365
Assign Task button, 280
assignments, task, 278–280
Assistants. *See* Office Assistant;
    Out Of Office Assistant; PDAs
    (personal data assistants)
associating
    Journal activities with
        contacts, 295–296
    notes with contacts, 236–237
attachments, 167, 170–172
    See also receiving files in
        e-mail messages; sending
        files in e-mail messages
    binary files, 170
    Insert File dialog box,
        171–172
    Letter Wizard and, 184–185